A World to Win

Paul Feldman is a journalist and editor of *Socialist Future Review*, the magazine of the Movement for a Socialist Future. Corinna Lotz is secretary of the MSF and an art critic. Gerry Gold is an ICT consultant and Phil Sharpe writes on contemporary philosophy.

A World to Win

A rough guide to a future without global capitalism

Paul Feldman and Corinna Lotz

with Gerry Gold and Phil Sharpe

LUPUS
BOOKS

LUPUS BOOKS

Published by Lupus Books
PO Box 942
London
SW1V 2AR

www.aworldtowin.net
info@aworldtowin.net

ISBN 0 9523454 1 2

Front cover by Nick Feldman
Photograph by Armelle Burke
Illustrations by Dybbuk
Design and typography by
Robbie Griffiths and Nick Feldman
Printed by Antony Rowe Ltd Chippenham Wiltshire SN14 6LH

Contents

Foreword

Peter McLaren

Americans are used to reading newspaper headlines about social chaos of world historical proportions. Such chaos has always been somewhere else, in some remote, foreign-sounding region, so it was natural to feel insulated, even protected. And while in relative terms, Americans enjoy comfortable lives, it is hard not to notice the rapidly degrading conditions throughout the country. The streets of major US cities teem with the poor, the homeless, and the insane. Nearly 700,000 people are homeless at any given night in the United States. Three million people experienced homelessness in 2002. One out of every four homeless persons is a child. Hospitals in poor neighbourhoods have shut down, and remaining social services are quickly disappearing as budget crises wreak havoc on state governments across the country.

The budget deficit is astronomical. The several million jobs lost by the Bush administration over the last four years will make "Bush the Lesser" the first president since the early days of the Great Depression to post a new loss of jobs. One out of every six children lives in poverty. One out of four Americans were making poverty-level wages in 2000, and while major health care providers such as Johns Hopkins Hospital in Baltimore are developing special health care coverage programs that offer "platinum service" to the rich (complimentary massage and sauna time with physical exams in state-of-the-art testing labs), nearly 40 million Americans lack health insurance.

Frequent terrorist alerts keep the population on edge, in a form of "ontological hysteria". People are fearful of being struck by a "dirty bomb" and report any suspicious behaviour in their neighbourhoods to police.

The more hardscrabble and fearful their lives become, the more they are likely to vote for the Republican Party, which for generations has mastered the means to deflect the anger and rage of mostly disaffected white working-class males from the root causes of their economic plight and to focus their rage on the weak-kneed liberals, immigrants, and multiculturalists who have let the country go to the dogs. Republican apparatchiks have camouflaged the socio-historical origins of the economic plight of this hard-bitten group and instead have emphasised their lived experiences in isolation from the socio-political order – the very order which helps to administer and enforce the reigning social relations of production.

Individual experience becomes the template from which all understanding and explanation proceeds, a belief which makes it all the easier for directing broad swathes of moral indignation at the multiculturalists who refuse to adhere to traditional conservative "family values" historically culled from the Anglosphere, for promoting a cultural nationalism tied to a romantic American exceptionalism, and manufacturing links between business élites and Christian evangelical groups in order to promote "faith-based initiatives" and direct political venom at environmentalists, anti-corporate and anti-globalisation groups, gay activists and feminists.

This creation of moral solidarity around rebuffing the "hate America" crowd who would call for more, and not less, socialist alternatives has proven to be an effective antidote to the breakdown of social cohesion and job security set in train by the transition from Keynesianism to neo-liberalism. Conservative hate radio shows have increased to 1,300 stations nationwide in tandem with steel-mill shutdowns and loss of manufacturing jobs. Former factory workers now try their hand at jobs in the no-benefits, low-wage service economy. The hands that wrap your new Levi's jeans at The Gap may have worked slag overflows in a smelting furnace. Hate radio hosts excoriate liberal critics of the economy and the war in Iraq as weaklings. The governor of California calls them "girlie men". The "liberal" John Kerry is derided for speaking more than one language and looking like a Frenchman. And once again a social group will vote against its own class interests, risking membership in Marx's reserve army of labour, for the chance to spit racist and homophobic invective against affirmative action programmes that supposedly pander to darker-skinned constituencies.

ᐟ As the war in Iraq wages on, corporations are considering pulling advertising dollars out of television programmes that cover the destruction there, preferring instead to shift their money to "safer" networks such as the Disney Channel, where their products will not be associated with suicide bombers, roadside explosions, and decapitations. Meanwhile, arms manufacturers and dealers celebrate as the Bush administration lets the assault weapons ban expire. Police departments brace for an upsurge in crime as people buy up previously banned weapons like AK-47s, Uzis and TEC-9s.

The country with the best government that money can buy is in a mess. Most people who seek answers to the chaos choose electronic over print media. Three of the major networks are owned by a defence contractor who is profiting from the war in Iraq (NBC, CNBC, MSNBC). CNN is outsourcing its technological workers to cheap-labour nations while Fox serves as little more than an auxiliary wing of the Republican Party and a cheerleader for its imperial overreach.

Three years after the September 11 terrorist crimes in New York, Washington, and Pennsylvania, the US is engaged in an illegal, immoral and unjustified occupation of Iraq, is still bombing Fallujah and other cities and trying to "pacify" with unmatchable high-tech weaponry vast areas of that country that still remain outside government control.

The "liberation" of Iraq has been such an unmitigated disaster that it has even provoked, on the day prior to the third anniversary of the September 11 attacks, an editorial comment in the *Financial Times* calling for the structured withdrawal of US and remaining allied troops.

The aftermath of a war won so quickly has been so utterly bungled, moreover, that the US is down to the last vestiges of its always exiguous allied support, at the time when Iraq needs every bit of help it can get. The occupation has lost control of big swathes of the country. Having decided that all those who lived and worked in Iraq under Saddam Hussein bore some degree of collective guilt, Washington's viceroys purged the country's armed forces, civil service and institutions to a degree that broke the back of the state, marginalised internal political forces, sidelined many with the skills to rebuild Iraq's services and utilities and, of course, fuelled an insurgency US forces have yet to identify accurately, let alone get to grips with.

Equally telling is the editorial in *The New York Times* on 12 September that sharply criticises the doctrine of preventive war. According to the *Times* editorial,

So far, the preventive war doctrine has had one real test: the invasion of Iraq. Mr. Bush terrified millions of Americans into believing that forcibly changing the regime in Baghdad was the only way to keep Iraq's supposed stockpiles of unconventional weapons out of the hands of al-Qaeda. Then it turned out that there were no stockpiles and no operational links between Saddam Hussein's regime and al-Qaeda's anti-American terrorism. Meanwhile, America's longstanding defensive alliances were weakened and the bulk of America's ground combat troops tied down in Iraq for what now appears to be many years to come. If that is making this country safer, it is hard to see how. The real lesson is that America dangerously erodes its military and diplomatic defences when it charges off unwisely after hypothetical enemies.

Despite a mounting media criticism of the war, the Bush administration shows no signs of budging on its position that the war was justified despite the fact that thousands of innocent civilians have been killed by US air strikes and tens of thousands more crippled and traumatised. Those who do not lie in their graves, or who refuse to go to their deaths without a fight, plan their revenge for lost loved ones, as a new generation of terrorists are being created from the bombed out cities of Iraq. Over a thousand US soldiers have died for the lies of a cowboy president. The worst fears of September 11th Families for Peaceful Tomorrows, an organisation born out of a criticism that America's military response to the 9/11 attacks would result in the deaths of countless innocent civilians and increase recruitment for terrorist causes, making the United States, and the world, less safe and less free for generations to come, have tragically been realised. As peaceful protestors continue to be labelled "traitors" by reactionary "patriots" and as the US Patriot Act overturns hard-won civil rights and sneers at those whose lives were lost fighting for them, the laws of the Geneva Convention are mocked in military concentration camps set up for detainees labelled as "enemy combatants".

A climate of US exceptionalism and a foreign policy of unilateralism fuelled by the knowledge that no nation or foreseeable group of nations can oppose the might of their war machine drives the Bush regime to conduct pre-emptive strikes against probable foes of US interests, or against countries who are sitting on or near large reserves of oil and gas and who can conveniently be demonised as evil rogue regimes. Countries who refuse to open up their markets to the corporations managed by the transnational capitalist class know only too well what the consequences will be.

The earth has opened up to a thousand maquiladoras between the US and Mexican borders, flooding the global south with toxic waste. Throughout the Third World chattel slavery and bonded labour is proliferating at an alarming rate. With no modern day Noah's Ark to save them from extinction, the toilers of the earth are making their presence heard. The cry of "another world is possible" that issues from the masses is expanding in waves to encompass not only new vistas of desperation but also the battlefield horizon of class struggle. But even as mouths crack open in protest, the fist of capital is thrust inside, force-feeding its false hope, coated with lies. The global crisis through which humanity is currently suffering – economically, socially, financially, ecologically, militarily and culturally – is inextricably linked to the quest for world domination by the US and the neo-

liberal global apparatus that conflates political freedom with
freedom of the market and equates social democracy with the
establishment of the rights of private property and the profit rate.

Since the successful revolution in fiscal and social policies that
occurred as a result of the election of Margaret Thatcher and her
monetarist solution to the crisis of capitalism – war against trade
unions and the welfare state, as well as the privatisation of public
services – neo-liberalism has continued to rudder the economic
and social policies of choice among the transnational capitalist
class. A similar "revolution" that included the violent repression
of trade unions as well as popular social movements and leftist
political organisations in the United States was carried out by
Ronald Reagan, who managed to deactivate social protest by
bullying and threats. His economic free-market orthodoxy –
often called "voodoo economics" – has not lost its leverage. The
social degradation that occurred during his time in office has yet
to be reversed and in fact is becoming worse under the Bush
administration. Neoliberalism is afoot, and doing well from the
standpoint of the ruling class. While profit-driven competition
has led to overproduction and ecological havoc, conditions for
capitalist class formation have been created in China, India,
Russia, and other countries, while the increase in inequality and
environmental destruction has been downplayed. The restoration
of class power in the United States and Britain owes a great debt
to neoliberalism.

Because in this historical juncture transnationalised fractions
of dominant groups have become the hegemonic fraction
globally, social groups and classes have been transformed into
central historical actors rather than "states" as power is
produced within the world capitalist class by transnationally
oriented state-managers and a cadre of supranational institutions
such as the World Bank, the World Trade Organisation, the
Trilateral Commission and the World Economic Forum. Of
course, there is still a struggle between descendant national
fractions of dominant groups and ascendant transnational
fractions.

The class practices of a new global ruling class are becoming
condensed in an emergent transnational state in which the

transnational capitalist class has an objective existence above any local territories and polities. The purpose of the transnational ruling class is the valorisation and accumulation of capital and the defence and advance of the emergent hegemony of a global bourgeoisie and a new global capitalist historical bloc. This historical bloc is composed of the transnational corporations and financial institutions, the élites that manage the supranational economic planning agencies, major forces in the dominant political parties, media conglomerates and technocratic élites. This does not mean that competition and conflict have come to an end or that there exists a real unity within the emergent transnational capitalist class.

Competition among rivals is still fierce and the US is playing a leadership role on behalf of the élite, defending the interests of the emergent global capitalist historical bloc. However, in a more integrated world economic system, development is no longer based primarily upon rival trading and political empires that aim at the protection of the interests of monopoly capital. As a result, the exploitation of the labour of those subordinated and dominated countries within the world economy dramatically intensifies. The content of this imperialism is no longer primarily based upon antagonistic and rival national monopoly capitals, but the forces of the transnational corporations supported by the nation state.

The labour aristocracy is expanding to other countries such that core and periphery no longer denote geography as much as social location. The material circumstances that gave rise to the nation state are being superceded by globalisation such that the state – conceived in Marxist terms as a congealment of a particular and historically determined constellation of class forces and relations (i.e., a historically specific social relation inserted into larger social structures) – can no longer simply be conceived solely in nation-state centric terms.

Paul Feldman and Corinna Lotz importantly maintain that this new phase in the imperialist stage of capitalism does not mean that the role of the nation state has become superfluous, or that inter-imperialist rivalries have been transcended.

Arundhati Roy strikingly captures the dynamic between the

state and capital in the following remarks:

> On the global stage, beyond the jurisdiction of sovereign
> governments, international instruments of trade and finance oversee
> a complex system of multilateral laws and agreements that have
> entrenched a system of appropriation that puts colonialism to
> shame. This system allows the unrestricted entry and exit of massive
> amounts of speculative capital – hot money – into and out of third
> world countries, which then effectively dictates their economic
> policy. Using the threat of capital flight as a lever, international
> capital insinuates itself deeper and deeper into these economies.
> Giant transnational corporations are taking control of their
> essential infrastructure and natural resources, their minerals, their
> water, their electricity. The World Trade Organisation, the World
> Bank, the International Monetary Fund, and other financial
> institutions like the Asian Development Bank, virtually write
> economic policy and parliamentary legislation. With a deadly
> combination of arrogance and ruthlessness, they take their
> sledgehammers to fragile, interdependent, historically complex
> societies, and devastate them. All this goes under the fluttering
> banner of "reform". As a consequence of this reform, in Africa,
> Asia, and Latin America, thousands of small enterprises and
> industries have closed down, millions of workers and farmers have
> lost their jobs and land. The *Spectator* newspaper in London
> assures us that "[w]e live in the happiest, healthiest and most
> peaceful era in human history." Billions wonder: who's "we"?
> Where does he live? What's his Christian name?

This dynamic works along the singular trajectory of capitalist
logic. Just as public capital is used to finance private investment
risk, whose profits are not returned to the public, but line the
pockets of the private investors, so too the nation state cannot
challenge the power of corporate finance, but is compelled to
defend it. Roy puts it this way:

> The thing to understand is that modern democracy is safely
> premised on an almost religious acceptance of the nation state. But
> corporate globalisation is not. Liquid capital is not. So, even though

capital needs the coercive powers of the nation state to put down revolts in the servants' quarters, this set up ensures that no individual nation can oppose corporate globalisation on its own.

The climate in the United States in this present moment is exacerbating forms of reactionary populism within regional communities. To cite one example, members of a Bainbridge Island community in Washington are upset with a social studies teacher at Sakai Intermediate School who developed and taught a sixth-grade social studies programme that criticised the internment of 110,000 to 120,000 Japanese Americans in the 1940s, hundreds of whom were forced to leave the island community six decades ago. Residents demanded that the school board change the programme so that it includes different opinions, including the view that the internment was justified. Arguing that the programme amounts to "propaganda", the group also wants to omit discussions that hint at parallels between the internment and the US Patriot Act and some members are threatening legal action – even though most scholars and the US government, which issued a formal apology and reparations to surviving internees, have officially criticised the internment. One resident called the programme "an example of an agenda-based curriculum that is designed to lead our 11-year-old Sakai students to hate America". It is clear what these same residents would say about the war in Iraq, and the endless wars that the United States have waged and sponsored for decades upon decades, often under the imperial nostrum of the White Man's Burden.

The problem is deep-rooted and can be traced, in part, to the notion that any criticism of the United States is equivalent to "hating America". Internalised in the minds and hearts of generation after generation, this notion carries the force of prevailing common sense among many Americans.

It is an example of an uncritical and largely unconscious way of thinking (ideologically deformed class consciousness) that forges an unseen ideological bond with capitalism and imperialism. Chalmers Johnson's comments are disturbingly apposite:

As distinct from other peoples on this earth, most Americans do not recognise – or do not choose to recognise – that the United States dominates the world through its military power. Due to government secrecy, they are often ignorant of the fact that their government garrisons the globe. They do not realise that a vast network of American military bases on every continent but Antarctica actually constitutes a new form of empire.

A World to Win was written with an eye to the dilemmas outlined above. It offers a lucid and much welcomed counterpoint to the alienated forms of socialisation that currently plague US society and culture. It provides an opportunity for overcoming the structuring effects of bourgeois ideology by offering a strikingly different form of self-identity. Readers are invited to see society as a coherent social totality, to discern the difference between subjective consciousness and the objective conditions of commodification under capitalism, and to exercise a critical consciousness on the path to becoming a self-active revolutionary agent of social change allied to substantive rather than formal citizenship. Critical pedagogy, as it has developed in North American and Latin American contexts shares with the writers of *A World to Win* the common philosophical architectonic that has grown out of Marxist humanism and the goal of economic reconstruction in favour of the popular majority. *A World to Win* is an important political and philosophical accomplishment, not least of which has to do with its focused inquiry on changing the world, and not merely understanding it.

In order to be effective in the fight against economic exploitation, terrorism, and ecological destruction, teachers and cultural workers need to move beyond solutions that legitimise or naturalise capitalist-driven globalisation and profit-driven competition as the only viable options available for humanity, and instead focus on the needs of the world's population. To this end, Feldman and Lotz have put forward a number of important socialist principles that are designed to extend the gains and advances that capitalism has given the few, to people in all countries, through the struggle toward and development of a global, socialist society and control over production by the direct producers. Such principles have arisen from an unbridled faith in humanity and its associated technologies in producing the possibility (but not always the reality) of a better life for the whole of humanity. Exercising these principles to the fullest mandates the struggle for a classless society that is not dominated by the narrow sectarian interests of capitalist accumulation and the valorisation of surplus value.

Teachers, cultural workers, administrators and researchers would do well to incorporate these principles in their struggle to reclaim democracy for a socialist future. The most important of these principles include the social ownership of land, banking and finance, transport and communications infrastructure; the social ownership of production facilities of the major corporations though a variety of forms of co-ownership; democratic control and self-management of economic and financial resources that include public services; steering the development of productive capacity towards satisfying need; ecologically sustainable production and distribution; encouraging and supporting small-scale enterprises, creative workers and farmers; favouring local production for local needs; and facilitating the development of the conscious market.

The central aims of the classless society for which these principles are put into practice encompass the following: ensuring that the majority have access to the benefits currently only available to the few; ensuring survival of the planet, ecosystems and humanity; the creation of a society based on co-operation, satisfying need and not profit; releasing the potential of automation, substantially reducing working hours; overcoming alienation of people from their work, what is produced and society as a whole; employing an abundance of products to alleviate poverty and need world-wide; allowing and enabling people to fulfil their potential and aspirations; and making health and well-being the single dominant social objective for the global population.

Feldman and Lotz have used these principles and aims in their development of specific strategies for addressing issues of the state, including communications and the media, the legal system, state administration, the political system, criminal law, and the police as well as cultural strategies aimed at the visual arts, the music industry, the Internet and the educational system. They are aware that existing modes of governance need to be replaced by socialist planning and self-management by means of elected workers' councils and the creation of local, regional and national Assemblies. While these efforts are context specific to Britain, they could be – and should be – productively adapted for the American scene.

The authors of this pathfinding volume have also worked out broad, ongoing strategies for transforming the global financial system and addressing the ecological crisis, all the while recognising that the seedbed for socialism is contained in the contradictions of capital, where new tools of revolutionary theory and party organisation, and new modes of politics and governance can be used for the benefit of human survival with dignity and the promise of a better future. Exposure to the inner workings of capitalism and imperialism is not enough; we need to be actively engaged in creating strategies and programmes for transcending the alienating imperatives of capital as a structure in order to bring us closer to the goal of constructing a socialist future. With the writing of this book, humanity is better equipped to face its future and is better prepared to realise the socialist alternative that the world so desperately needs.

Peter McLaren

Professor in the Division of Urban Schooling,
Graduate School of Education and Information Studies
University of California, Los Angeles

September 2004

Preface

A World to Win is published as a contribution to the discussion and debate about the present and the future of contemporary society. It is not a tirade against globalisation – which is a feature of the development of human history – but examines the way that the process is driven by capitalism. Our proposals seek to fulfil the potential that is already present through the creation of a new social, economic, political and cultural framework based on co-operation, co-ownership and self-management.

A World to Win arose out of the need to find answers. We had reached the view that a more profound understanding of globalised capitalism was urgently needed before it was possible to indicate a way forward. There was a self-evident political log-jam, with a general absence of a coherent theory about how to defeat capitalism in its modern form. On the one hand, there is a longing for a return to the pre-globalisation days and on the other a passive acceptance of the status quo on the basis that nothing could be done about it. In between are forms of nihilism that dispute capitalism and reject globalisation itself. Implied in this is that globalisation has not taken place at all or can be side-stepped.

We also became acutely aware of a gap between those of us who had witnessed revolutionary struggles in Vietnam, France, Britain, South Africa and later Eastern Europe – and a younger generation who find it difficult to visualise such upheavals. The challenge therefore, was not to tell ourselves what we already knew. We needed to look out there, into the changing world around us, to discover what was new.

So we set out to show the big picture about how the last three decades of globalisation have given rise to quite a different world and how people's lives have changed. We seek to demonstrate the changes as objective and independent processes, and their consequences in terms of social, economic and political life. At the same time it is vital not to lose sight of the way they are reflected in people's hearts and minds.

The book gives a unique picture of the whole of this process. Our approach is guided by a dialectical concept of the whole and its contradictory relation to the parts. This is important because all the aspects of globalisation are connected and in mutual development at the same time.

As the reader will see, we draw on existing research and knowledge to demonstrate these new relations in a concrete way. *A World to Win* shows, for example, how the emergence of the transnational corporation and a global economy have transformed many functions of the capitalist state. Our research reveals the deep penetration by corporations of culture, including science, art and forms of communication.

Altogether, the scale and depth of these processes show that commercialisation and commodification of human life cannot go further without actually destroying the planet and the life on it. Just as the planet's precarious position is clearer, we show that people's alienation from nature, from others and from themselves is far deeper than ever before. Many indicators revealed rapidly rising levels of depression and estrangement in the UK, for example.

From the present to the future

Capitalist globalisation is contradictory in the extreme. It is highly destructive on the one side. At the same time, it contains possibilities for a society based on co-operation and need. *A World to Win* does not reject everything that has been created under capitalism. Instead, we demonstrate how a world market, global information and financial systems and the socialisation of production and distribution can be made into the foundations of a new society. We do not claim to have a total blueprint for this, but, our proposals, hopefully, show that another world is not only possible but is a realistic proposition. We argue for a break with private ownership of capital through a struggle for political power. The book explains the need for a revolutionary theory and organisation to make this happen.

On a global scale, mass movements challenge the status quo, in both the advanced capitalist countries and developing nations. The countless millions who opposed the illegal invasion of Iraq surprised everyone by their determined opposition. Many more people continue to protest against ecological destruction, the imposition of GM food, World Bank-financed dams that destroy communities and the loss of welfare rights. Many are deeply alienated from state and political institutions. The prevailing scepticism about existing "democratic" structures and processes is a healthy sign that political abstractions and phrase mongering do not fool people. New generations are better informed and educated and more aware of what is going on locally and globally than ever before, through a host of information sources. Knowing that governments are lying was a key factor in the defeat of the right-wing Spanish government in the 2004 general election.

A World to Win asserts the ability and historic drive that human beings have socially to bring down and end unjust, dictatorial and regressive regimes of all kinds. We do not share the disenchanted view of those who reduce history to, as the 18th century historian Edward Gibbon called it, "the register of crimes, follies and mistakes of mankind". The last century saw two world wars and the rise of Fascist and Stalinist dictatorships. We undoubtedly have to learn the lessons of history. Yet we cannot use its ugly side to justify or rationalise passivity about the future. The challenge is to transform the rejection of the old into a positive force to bring into being a new society. That requires people and organisations who can see the real possibility of how such a world can be formed, and act on that knowledge in a collective way. This book is dedicated to that task.

Using this book

A World to Win is divided into three sections. Part One analyses the impact of profit-driven globalisation in a number of areas: alienation, economy, the state, culture, ecology and science. Part Two puts forward a series of proposals which would revolutionise the economy, the state and our attitude towards culture and the Earth's ecosystems. Part Three discusses human nature, looking at contemporary thinkers including John Gray and Francis Fukuyama. We then suggest a philosophy that can focus our efforts and finally put forward a new concept for a political party. We conclude that de-alienation is only possible through revolutionary social change carried out with the support and active participation of the mass of the population.

We studied the work of political opponents and defenders of the existing order. We went back to Marxist classics, especially *Capital*, *Grundrisse* and Lenin's writings on the state and philosophy. We were inspired by the dialectical outlook developed in psychology, philosophy and politics. The work done by Vladimir Lenin, Lev Vygotsky, Evald Ilyenkov, Roy Bhaskar and Gerry Healy proved particularly fruitful. The authors spent many months discussing with friends, colleagues and comrades. We were stimulated by a wide range of ideas and research carried out by economists, ecologists, social scientists, lawyers, media experts and artists.

The Movement for a Socialist Future, which produced *A World to Win*, hopes the book will stimulate discussion and lead to practical political steps to realise all our hopes.

Paul Feldman
Corinna Lotz

September 2004

Part 1
Globalisation and its consequences

Showing how the rule of the transnational corporations affects us

1 Alien nation

People throughout the world experience daily the impact of powerful economic and technological forces on their lives. The intensity and speed of change is unprecedented. Societies, communities and individuals are continuously buffeted by the globalisation whirlwind. Urban and rural areas have changed beyond recognition inside a generation while people's emotions and thoughts have been shaken to the core.

At a personal level, some groups in society have achieved better standards of living at the high price of a deepening sense of alienation, of powerlessness. This can take the form of drug and alcohol abuse, high levels of debt and stress. In richer nations, consumer capitalism is supported by the misery and low pay of desperately poor and super-exploited workers. Just surviving on means-tested state benefits and repaying debts dominates the lives of many, especially mothers, students, single parents, pensioners and young people.

At a social and international level, global market forces have transformed the lives of countless millions. Many toil for transnational corporations, often in appalling conditions. Some are driven to take desperate measures to escape poverty by trying to gain entry into the more affluent countries. Famine stalks Africa in the midst of over-production. Aids and other diseases kill vast numbers while the pharmaceuticals overprice life-saving medicines. In the world of nature, plants and animal life are enduring a thousand "silent springs" from global warming and ecological degradation. Further climatic disaster looms as the polar ice caps melt.

American writer William Greider, in *One World Ready or Not*, which described the manic logic of global capitalism, foresaw "a series of terrible events – wrenching calamities that are economic, social or environmental in nature". Abstracted from human reality, he remarked, the absolute rule of the global market had become an article of faith into which many people have put their trust.

The key words here are "human reality". Hidden behind the technical relations of production and exchange, even behind obscure financial terms like "junk bonds", "hedge funds" and "supermontage" are real living and breathing men, women and children and the bonds between them of social class, of nationality, ethnic group and family. But the vast global market place and the corporate interests that dominate it seem distant and impenetrable to most people and the lives of ordinary human beings seem to be on another planet.

Someone once compared the activities of speculators in the global money-markets to B52 bomber pilots, floating in the stratosphere oblivious to any "collateral damage". And yet, as even the metaphor indicates, there is a connection between the one and the other. In this epoch, it is the distance and complexity of the process that baffles people. It means that the way in which it affects people is unexpected and apparently random, contributing to a deepening sense of alienation.

Alienation demystified

Alienation describes a general condition which is not simply a result of today's society. Human beings arise out of and live within nature. We are part of the natural world, and yet we are forced to struggle with it in order to live at all. In doing this, humans distinguish themselves from other people and from the natural world. For example, building a house shields you from the elements. This is already an alienated relationship because we have to refashion the very forces that provide us with life. In this particular case, we have successfully realised our aim and established a closer relationship with the world around us.

The *Collins English Dictionary* defines alienation as: "1. a turning away; estrangement. 2. the state of being an outsider or the feeling of being isolated, as from society. 3. *Psychiatry*, a state in which a person's feelings are inhibited so that eventually both the self and the external world seem unreal. 4. *Law,* the transfer into the ownership of another."

The fourth, apparently legal, definition, provides the contemporary context for alienation. It is the transferring of ownership of our labour, the result and distribution of it, that is the material basis for powerful feelings of dislocation. It happens in everyone's lives, every day in the process of capitalist production. Every worker is forced to sell her or his labour power to an employer. In exchange she or he receives a wage or salary. But the product or service which the worker's labour creates or operates and the profit accruing from this, is "transferred into the ownership of another".

The *Encyclopaedia Britannica* says alienation is "the state of feeling estranged or separated from one's milieu, work, products of work, or self. The concept... is most famously associated with Karl Marx, who spoke of workers being alienated from their work and its products under capitalism. In other contexts the term alienation, like anomie, can suggest a sense of powerlessness, meaninglessness, normlessness, social isolation, or cultural- or self-estrangement brought on by the lack of fit between individual needs or expectations and the social order". Marx explained how our social connection with other people is turned into a social relation between things. "Our connection with other human beings now appears as something alien to us, autonomous, as a thing, an object with a price on it." The end result is that as workers we create an alien power over ourselves.

Gradually the pervasive human condition of alienation entered into art and literature as a major theme, especially in the haunting work of central-European poets and writers like Rainer Maria Rilke and Franz Kafka early in the 20th century. Later on, philosophers such as the Hungarian Gyorgy Lukacs and Spaniard Ortega y Gasset provided a new analysis of contemporary alienation. During the 1970s, sociologists analysed high levels of political alienation, especially in US society. In different ways, cultural and political alienation was shown to be a changing condition of society as the imperialist form of capitalism lurched through major economic crises and wars in the 20th century.

Science fiction TV series such as *Alien Nation* and its Internet spin-off have certainly shaped the popular conception of alienation. And the reason they are so gripping is because of their connections to real life. In *Alien Nation*, the incomers marooned on earth struggle to overcome racism and to make a new life for themselves, just like the millions of migrants who are on the move today.

In the *Alien* blockbuster film series, where a deadly parasitic creature threatens humanity, it is the greed of an interstellar corporation that unleashes the danger.

In *The Matrix,* alienation is portrayed in an even more sophisticated form. The humans have been reduced to an energy source, and are made docile by the provision of a dream "virtual" life. Alienated from themselves and their own real lives they have been unknowingly enslaved by the machine empire which is the "real world" – a powerful reflection on the effect of the continuous marketing of virtual "lifestyles", which will always remain unreal for the majority.

Alienation as a state of mind is not due to a "mistaken", "defective", or "overly emotional" reaction to the world. Rather it is the expression of the fact that people, both individually and socially, are deprived of the result of their own labour and the wealth produced by society as a whole, which also confronts them in a hostile way, especially through state institutions and bureaucracies. The contradiction is that work is what makes us human, and yet because we do not control the process as a whole, it dehumanises us. There is an ever-widening gulf: between things as they are and as people know or feel that they could be; between reality, and our individual and collective expectations and aspirations.

The true relations in our lives are turned upside down, so that the most entirely "human" or "social" aspects of what we do as producers and consumers are turned into "something alien and objective", as Marx wrote, "confronting the individuals, not as their relation to one another, but as their subordination to relations which subsist independently of them, and which arise out of collisions between mutually indifferent individuals". Thus in today's world we speak on the phone to a man in India. We ask him about the train times from Nottingham to London. He is paid less than a quarter of what we earn. We buy a pair of trainers made by a woman in the South China seas – she is not allowed to go to the toilet during her working day. We would never impose such conditions on them. But the connection between us is dehumanised and appropriated by powers that we do not control.

More than ever today this takes a highly personal form, destructive of the individual. We frequently feel "not ourselves". We experience problems communicating and relating to others, at work and in our personal lives. People wake up in the morning worried about whether they will make it through the day, and feel that what they are doing is pointless and they should be doing something else. They are unhappy with themselves and the people around them, but they can't find the person that will make them happy. They go through experiences at work and at home which are deeply frustrating and make them feel terrible.

People try to resolve this alienation in a variety of ways. Some work longer and longer hours, others may turn to heavy drinking or recreational drugs, over-eating or under-eating, in order to postpone or mask these feelings. The most acute effects are felt by young people. There is a yawning gap between the products and lifestyles marketed to them, not only in advertising but in the increasingly corporate education system, and the lives they and their families lead.

The transformation of the human into the inhuman dominates in a new and suffocating way. Globalisation has dissolved hundreds of social bonds which, for a significant part of the 20th century in the developed countries, softened the harshness of exploitation and alienation. The erosion has included:

‣ rights protected by trade union membership
‣ longer-term employment
‣ respect for skills, experience and knowledge

‣ working in a publicly-owned industry
‣ public funding of valued services
‣ healthcare that included older age
‣ a supply of decent council housing.

Late 20th century Britain saw the creation of a different kind of workforce and the decimation of the old. And it is not only skilled and unskilled manual labour that has been transformed as a result of the closure of older industries and the collapse of manufacturing. All workers, including white collar, nurses, civil servants and firefighters are subject to the same pressures.

Workers are constantly told by governments and employers that they should become more "flexible and dynamic". "Flexibility" means accepting lower pay, "dynamic" means travelling long distances to work. Getting rid of "rigidities" means allowing companies to become more competitive at the expense of the workers. "Facing new global challenges", means "if you don't like it, there are plenty of people in low-wage countries willing to take your job", according to Larry Elliott, the economics editor of *The Guardian* (22 March 2004).

These changes began in the Thatcher era with the deregulation of the economy and the mass closure of older industries. Under New Labour, the process has intensified with the blurring of the line between the commercial and non-commercial worlds in the shape of private-public partnerships, charging fees to university students and bringing private companies in to run or sponsor schools. Every single area of life has been made subject to the world of profit. As Madeleine Bunting noted:

> Rising mental illness seems an inescapable consequence of the kind of rapid, disruptive change driven by market capitalism. It's not that people have gone soft so much as that they are profoundly disorientated by the ceaseless discontinuity of change. Experience becomes utterly random and meaningless. You were doing really well in your job but you still got fired; you thought your relationship was strong but your partner has fallen out of love with you. Appalling images of suffering in the world are interrupted by advertisements for car insurance: barbarism and banality, cheek by

jowl. What lies behind the escalating weight of emotional distress is that awful struggle to make meaning, that instinct that our lives should have a narrative and a purpose and should make some sense. Whereas previous generations had a very strong grasp of the meaning of their lives (whatever the catastrophes which befell them), of their own identity and where they belonged, we are living out Marx's prediction that "all that is solid melts into air, all that is holy is profaned". Meaning inspires resilience: if you have some explanation for what happens, it gives strength. That's what past generations drew comfort from. It is the sheer meaninglessness of the chaotic instability of our experiences which exposes us to despair. We have no answer to "why me?" We have no account for the suffering which is the inevitable lot of human beings – death, disease, betrayal, frustration – other than to employ desperate strategies to avoid them. (*The Guardian*, 1 March 2004)

Alienation is deepened by the intense and continuous pressure from marketing, which contributes to people's sense of powerlessness. It shapes their aspirations and urges them not only to acquire a product, but along with it a so-called lifestyle – generally one that only a tiny minority can in reality enjoy.

Celebrities are used to sell products, many of them produced by super cheap labour on the other side of the planet, because people aspire to be like them. It is not the product people are buying but a share of the celebrity's charisma. Talented personalities, who are role models for millions – like David Beckham – turn themselves into brands. Individual personality, the thing that makes us different from objects that are bought and sold, is now the most marketable and saleable commodity of all. We are told that we create ourselves, our personality and worth through the acquisition of products. Perfumes, cars, ringtones are all now billed as "forms of self-expression" – "because you're worth it", you can "be yourself", you can "express yourself".

And it is impossible to escape from the constant stream of advertising pushing products at every "consumer". Every surface we see – from cinema screen to table top, billboard to T-shirt – is covered in product placement. This has a particularly powerful impact on young people who are in the course of shaping their lives and consciousness and looking to understand the world and to find role models. Their father's redundant out-dated job may offer them little to relate to – may indeed seem less stable and less real than the life of a rap star or footballer.

Feeling the pressure

There are those who dismiss symptoms of a deeply-divided and alienated society, saying that people have simply become too soft and pampered. All we need, they say, is some good old-fashioned discipline and the stiff upper lip that existed in the 1950s. Evidence of how people react to the intensified pressures they face from having to live and work under the conditions just outlined, tells its own story, however.

The fastest growing cause of absence from work according to the BBC's *Money Programme* is stress. More than 13 million working days were lost in 2003 as a result of stress-related illnesses. While employers' organisations like the Confederation of British Industry insist the problem was just whinging workers who "are now describing a normal day's period in the office as stressful", the reality is that psychological pressures at work do make people ill. The London *Evening Standard* (14 August 2003) reported that one insurance firm, Unum Provident, concluded that the last ten years had seen an explosion in employee claims for "mental and psychological problems", rare a generation ago. Every year around three in ten employees will have a mental health problem, according to the Royal College of Psychiatrists.

Towards the end of 2003, the Health and Safety Executive (HSE) estimated that the number of people suffering from anxiety, depression or bad nerves had risen to almost four million. This is an increase of 62% over the past decade, even though Britain as a whole has become healthier and wealthier. HSE commissioned research has indicated that:

▸ about half a million people in the UK experience work-related stress at a level they believe is making them ill
▸ up to 5 million people in the UK feel "very" or "extremely"

stressed by their work
▸ work-related stress costs society about £3.7 billion every year.

Workers, especially in the public sector, are destabilised by constant changes imposed by managers who are in turn under pressure to deliver "targets".

Not only workers' organisations like the Trades Union Congress (TUC), but also the HSE have pointed to how the way people are treated at work affects them. And, as one senior nurse put it, "the way an organisation is run", is what causes stress. In Europe's biggest employer, the National Health Service (NHS), stress levels run at extremely high levels. The West Dorset Hospital NHS Trust, for example, was one of the first to be put on notice by the HSE to reduce stress levels among its staff. A study into the impact of restructuring in the NHS in *Stress News*, reported:

> Hospitals, like many other organisations, are also being forced to cut back due to a shortage of funding. Thousands of hospital workers have lost their jobs and many others experience job insecurity. Since nurses are the largest group employed by hospitals, their jobs are very much affected by hospital downsizing and closures. As a result of seeing others lose their jobs, nurses experience job insecurity to various degrees. Restructuring and its changes can result not only in lower job satisfaction, but also in job insecurity. And not only common sense, but a great deal of research points to how job insecurity has been associated with psychological distress and poor health.

The *British Social Attitudes Survey* 2003 found that what it called the increasing "marketisation" of economic and social life had taken its toll. Three-quarters of managerial and professional employees found their jobs stressful (as compared to just under half of routine and manual workers. "The longer reported hours of work of professional and managerial respondents are an important factor contributing to their reported levels of work-life stress. These longer hours no doubt reflect the greater workplace pressures to be found in these kinds of jobs, but will also be a consequence of individual aspirations."

"Downsizing", management-speak for sacking workers, can actually cause death. The *British Medical Journal* reported that "employees who had experienced major downsizing were also twice as likely to die from cardiovascular disease, particularly during the first four years after the job cuts". Not only "restructuring" and "downsizing" but the way that new technologies are introduced and the lack of privacy rights at work seriously affect workers' health. The TUC-backed *Hazards* magazine, which monitors workplace health, drew on a US study showing that closely monitored staff suffered more work dissatisfaction, depression, extreme anxiety, exhaustion, strain injuries and neck problems than unmonitored workers. It also included research showing that a lack of autonomy at work is a major cause of work-related stress and strains, heart diseases and sickness.

Two case histories

The case of Doctor Stephen Farley, "loved by his patients and respected by his peers" but who committed suicide (3 February 2004, report in *The Independent*) showed in the sharpest way how individual despair was brought on by the conflict between the desire to do a job well and the demands made by the increasingly marketised health system. The secretary of the local medical committee in Leicestershire concluded that Dr Farley "was an old-style doctor who was operating in the new-style, Blairite system". Colleagues claimed that he killed himself "when depression set in after being hounded by NHS managers for referring too many patients to hospital".

A few months later, another family doctor working in Lancashire, Dawn Harris, described as an angel by her patients, hanged herself. The coroner described her as "a perfectionist in an inadequate and imperfect system". The inquest heard that Dr Harris loved caring for her NHS patients, "but was worried about the increasing governmental red tape and demands to meet an escalating number of targets". (*The Independent*, 14 May 2004)

In both cases, a simple commitment to patients and profession caused an intolerable stress.

Despite all the economic growth in Britain, the number of people of working age who are economically inactive is at its highest in history. In May 2004, according to the Department of Work and Pensions, it stood at 7.8 million, up a quarter of a million since New Labour came to power. The largest yearly increase for any age group was among 18-24 year olds. Due in part to stress, more than a million moved on to incapacity benefit as a result of mental and behavioural disorders between 1999 and 2004. In August 2004, it was reported that those who are paid incapacity benefit for at least five years account for more than 50% of the total. This took the total of long-term claims by those judged by doctors to be unfit for work to 2.7 million. Official figures indicate that many have dropped out of claiming Jobseekers' Allowance and become seriously depressed.

Drugs and alcohol

Not surprisingly, high levels of stress make people seek ways to relieve their anxieties in life. This is revealed in the patterns of drug-taking and the use of alcohol.

Drug use

▶ between 1991 and 2001 the number of prescription items for anti-depressant drugs dispensed in England more than doubled, from 9 million items in 1991 to 24 million in 2001

▶ between 1993 and 2000 the number of drug-related poisoning deaths in England and Wales increased by a third to 3,000

▶ in 1999, England and Wales and the Irish Republic had the highest proportions of young people using cannabis, amphetamines and cocaine in the EU.

Social Trends 34, ONS

Dependence on a large variety of mind and mood-altering drugs in recent years has led to forms of the type of mass-control described in *Brave New World*, Aldous Huxley's vision of the future written in 1932. Johann Hari, writing in *The Independent* (14 August 2003), went so far as to make the link between mass voluntary drug-taking and the effects of free market capitalism:

"If human beings cannot change harsh market processes, we will have to alter our brains chemically. If what exists today is the only possible way that society can be, it is easier and better to dull the painful sides through mind-changing chemicals."

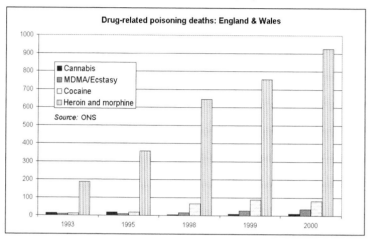

Drug-related poisoning deaths: England & Wales

- ■ Cannabis
- ▦ MDMA/Ecstasy
- □ Cocaine
- ▥ Heroin and morphine

Source: ONS

The Home Office's *British Crime Survey* for 2002/3 found there were around four million illicit drug users and around one million Class A (heroin, cocaine, ecstasy) drug users, with around three million 16-59 year-olds having used cannabis. The falling price of cocaine (which dropped to £40 a gram in 2004 compared to £70 a few years ago) has gone side-by-side with a tripling in the number of people using it since 1997.

The survey indicated that young people are more likely to use drugs than older people. The most commonly used drug in 2001/02 by 16 to 24 year olds was cannabis, which had been used by 33% of men and 21% of women in the previous year. Ecstasy was the most commonly used Class A drug, with higher

Drug taking rose from under 10% in the group born in 1946 to 60% for men and 40% of women in the 1970 group. In the five years running up to 2003, ecstasy use exploded in the UK, with double the number of people using the drug.

Changing Britain, Changing Lives, Institute of Education

use among the 16 to 24 year olds than those aged 25 to 59. In 2001/02, 9% of men and 4% of women aged 16 to 24 had used ecstasy in the previous year.

Deaths related to alcohol consumption have been rising in England and Wales for many years from just under 2,600 in 1980 to just over 5,500 in 2000, according to the Office for National Statistics. Between 1980 and 2000 deaths from alcohol-related diseases among males more than doubled from 6 to 13 per 100,000. Among males, there was an upward trend in alcohol-related death rates in all age groups above 15 to 24. The most marked increase occurred among those aged 25 to 44, with the rate increasing from 4 per 100,000 in 1980 to a peak of 10 per 100,000 in 1998.

Teenagers and young adults are particularly susceptible to problems of alcohol and drugs abuse as well as suicide. A World Health Organisation (WHO) study in 2004 found that the physical and mental health of UK teenagers was "more like that of poverty-stricken former communist nations than our western European neighbours". In the largest international study of adolescent attitudes it found that only Russian 11-year-olds and Czech 15-year-olds had a lower opinion of their generation than the same age groups in England. English and Welsh teenagers had the highest rates of drinking and got drunk at a younger age than children from most other countries. Going to school without breakfast was normal for a third of 11-year-old children in England, compared with 90% of Portuguese children who

---

Britain has one of the highest suicide rates in Europe. Each year in the UK over 5000 people take their lives. The suicide rate for young men has increased considerably since the mid-1970s. The suicide rate for 18-24-year-old males jumped from 58 deaths per million of population in 1974 to 170 deaths per million in 1997. In inner city areas, over 43% of children have considered suicide and one in six children under the age of 11 have attempted suicide. Common causes cited include bullying, abuse, poverty, homelessness, and alcohol abuse.

Bully OnLine

start the day with a morning meal. English children watched television for much greater periods of time than the average. The study found that British children in general were "the unhealthiest and unhappiest in the world". Another indication of the scale of social alienation amongst young people are findings by the Policy Exchange think tank, which estimates that 1.2 million people aged 18-24 are not in work, nor in full-time education, nor registered as unemployed. *Left Out, Left Behind* characterised these youth as "Generation X", saying "We know surprisingly little about what they are or what they are doing."

A 2003 Home Office report, *Hidden Harm*, calculated that as many as 300,000 children in England and Wales have at least one parent who is a drug addict. At the same time, nearly half of all social services departments have been found to be failing to adequately safeguard vulnerable children and in some inner city areas vacancy rates for social workers are running at 40-50%.

An indication of extreme levels of personal crisis was revealed by the drugs and treatment assessment body, the National Institute for Clinical Excellence (NICE). In July 2004, figures revealed that more than 170,000 people a year, most of them young, sought hospital treatment after "deliberately hurting themselves in apparent expressions of despair". It was the first time that such figures had been compiled. Mental health experts such as Dr Tim Kendall, co-director of the National Collaborating Centre for Mental Health, believe that the true picture is much worse since many more people do not seek treatment, and thus do not enter into the statistics. Marjorie Wallace, head of the mental health charity Sane, considered that self-harm has reached epidemic proportions and that "these people who are pushed to the bottom of the treatment queue are made to feel it is their own fault and denied any real understanding of their condition".

How do people deal with the extreme differences in social class and wealth which mean that the things they need and want are often beyond their means? The answer is simple – debt. While debt has haunted the poor and dispossessed for centuries, it has acquired new dimensions in the present economic order. Far from being sent to a debtor's prison as in the 18th century, people are encouraged to take on more and more debt.

People who are financially and/or psychologically vulnerable are easy meat for a myriad of lending institutions. This happens at many levels of the social scale. At the bottom are the doorstep lenders and loan sharks. At the level of mortgage lending, some of Britain's biggest estate agencies and financial advice groups, it emerged in 2004, encourage customers to break the law by lying about their earnings to secure higher mortgages than they could otherwise obtain. Banks, building societies, credit card companies and even supermarkets engage in aggressive tactics, bombarding homes with mail shots and emails. There are now 1,500 different credit card companies, as well as agencies ("debt management companies") who buy up debts from lenders who have been unable to recover them.

Over the past decade total consumer debt has risen steadily and dramatically. Mortgage lending was still rising at the fastest rate on record in the summer of 2004. Consumer borrowing reached £1 trillion (£1,000 billion) in the second half of 2004, despite four interest rate rises over nine months. Britain now has more debt as a proportion of its income than any other major country except Japan.

The level of indebtedness today is not simply due to indulging in "luxury" items. Mortgage borrowing made up £8.8 billion of the total £10.7 billion lent during September 2003. The basic need to have a roof over one's head continues to force millions of people to borrow at a time when property prices have risen beyond their means. When social housing is unavailable, there are few options other than buy. Citizens Advice Bureaux (CAB) found that one in every five people use credit cards to pay their household bills. This pushes them deeper and deeper into a spiral of debt.

In Too Deep – CAB clients' experience of debt, a report by Sue Edwards written in May 2003, makes chilling reading. Those suffering the most are the poor who resort to "doorstep lenders" charging the highest rates of interest – as high as 177%. Loan sharks can obtain a consumer credit licence with few questions asked. Research carried out by the National Consumer Council in September 2003 denounced government and regulators for failing to protect those on low incomes, the elderly, those with large personal debts and people in the countryside from rising prices and having energy supplies cut off. Over three million people found it difficult to pay energy bills, over a million had their telephones cut off and 4.7m were in debt to the water companies.

Women are particularly vulnerable to forms of stress. The Health and Safety Executive reported in August 2004 that severe stress could be a disproportionately female affliction, since most caring public sector jobs are filled by women. Women with little worktime control are not only much more likely to suffer from psychological distress, but have "a 50% higher risk of medically certified sickness absences than women with a high level of worktime control", according to *Occupation and Environmental Medicine Journal.*

A new illness has recently been identified by the medical profession – panic attacks. In the United States, studies have found that 35% of people had experienced at least one panic attack. There is a "new breed of sufferers" who are young, educated, successful and predominantly women, *The Independent* reported on 26 July 2004. A doctor who founded The Panic Disorders Institute in California, Stuart Shipko, has found that drugs are not the best treatment for this problem, which is more often than not the result of months and years of stress.

There is a gender-related twist to the drinking problem. Women in high-ranking jobs, for example, are far more likely to drink too much than men in the same position and more than women in more humble jobs. Dr Stephen Stansfield of the Institute of Community Health Sciences in London thought that women "may have to work harder and sustain more stress than men to attain a similar success". The Alliance for a Caring Economy founded by Riane Eisler in 1998, reporting to a corporate advice consultancy in California, notes:

Present economic models and rules fail to recognise the economic

value of the socially and environmentally essential work of caring
and caretaking. Marx wrote about the alienation of labour. I have
in the course of my research come to see that the alienation of
caring and caretaking labour is the hidden mass of the iceberg of
which many of our problems are only the tip. This alienation of
caring and caretaking labour has always had extremely negative
effects... Because caring work is often valued at zero by the
economy, with the growing emphasis on 'economic efficiency' we
are today getting less and less of it. Health care, child care, elder
care, even the sense of caring and community that we used to
associate with going to the corner store or coffee shop, are
systematically being squeezed out of our lives so they can be
provided in the most efficient, antiseptic, functional way possible –
at least until the social costs grow so high that they spill over and
force their way into the economy, in the form of delinquency, crime,
homelessness, mental illness, and social malaise.

A survey by the Trade Union Congress (March 2004) pointed out
that on average women's retirement income from all sources is
only 53% of men's. Only 30% of women receive a private
pension in their own right. "Women pensioners are particularly
affected – single women pensioners are half as likely again to be
poor as single male pensioners, and women pensioners in couples
have the least financial independence of any group in society,
with disposable individual incomes of just a third of those of a
male in a pensioner couple". In addition, a separate investigation
noted big differences among women in terms of ethnic origin and
social background. Only 3% of Pakistani women have an
occupational pension, it found.

Political alienation
Photo-journalist Nick Danziger provided a sobering picture of
Britain after living among the homeless and unemployed in many
of the ruined manufacturing and so-called "no-go" areas of
England, Scotland, Wales and Northern Ireland during the last
year of Tory rule before the election of New Labour. He
described inner city areas as well as towns throughout the
country, including Brixton, Leicester, Halifax, Newcastle,

Glasgow, Blackpool, Barrow-in-Furness, Liverpool, Salford, Brighton, Suffolk, Cornwall, South Wales and Belfast. He shows how globalisation has affected large parts of the country:

> In my rare spells in Britain during the past few years, I had noticed that the British are in flux, perhaps more than any other nation. They are trying to make sense of their identity... In the Midlands and North of Great Britain I found myself witnessing a destruction of the industrial and social fabric not experienced since the great crisis of the 1930s. Britain today might not be the class-ridden society it was then, but it is the working classes who still bear the brunt of unemployment.

Even while old industries were disappearing, he noticed that the class divide deepened rather than disappeared: "... Between my local council estate and the private housing 200 yards away there is an invisible Berlin Wall, separating the haves from the have nots... In Britain today I found a world of increased polarisation where both ends of the spectrum of material wealth lead to spiritual deprivation." He added:

> Real change could be effected by the political system, but instead there's a lot of shouting and screaming going on. The way I saw it, it wasn't just Nikes and crack that Britain had inherited from the United States; it had now also inherited its two-party political system, with neither side representing the downtrodden, the tens of thousands of impoverished residents of council estates and hardscrabble rural areas. They are potentially an explosive force, but an unpredictable one because they are as disorganised as they are poor.

One courageous journalist, Nick Ryan, spent six years as an undercover reporter investigating racist and neo-Nazi groups in Britain such as Combat 18 and the British National Party (BNP). Over the last few years, they evolved in response to the loss of credibility and legitimacy of traditional political parties, in Britain and elsewhere. He documented how BNP leader Nick Griffin poses as an anti-corporate campaigner, denouncing "the government, the agro-chemical industries… the big landowners who control the NFU, and the European Union".

Ryan shows how far-right organisations can cash in on the way in which large sections of the population have been abandoned by successive governments, especially New Labour.

2 The global corporate web

"Constant revolutionising of production, uninterrupted disturbance of all social conditions, everlasting uncertainty and agitation distinguish the bourgeois epoch from all earlier ones. All fixed, fast-frozen relations… are swept away, all new-formed ones become antiquated before they can ossify."
Communist Manifesto, Karl Marx and Frederick Engels, 1848

Corporate-driven, capitalist globalisation has in a relatively short time transformed the world we live in. In 30 years, this form of globalisation has had an immense impact on work, social and cultural life, the Earth's eco-systems, politics and the state. Alienation of individuals from themselves and each other is much deeper than before. What dominates our world is a globalised capitalist system whose actions carry far-reaching and increasingly unpredictable consequences.

Globalisation is not a new phenomenon. The formation of systems of interaction between the global and local has been a central driving force in world history. Seven centuries before Christ, the ancient Greeks built a civilisation that they extended to other parts of Europe and Asia. The Roman Empire was even more far flung and had a concept of citizenship that stretched over regions and continents. In the 1st century, Buddhism made its first appearance in China and cultural links were consolidated with India – alongside the foundation of the Silk Road trading route.

By 1350, networks of trade which involved frequent movements of people, animals, goods and money ran from England to China, through France and Italy and across the Mediterranean. A more intense period of economic and cultural globalisation began in the 15th century, with the discovery of new continents and the beginnings of a more extended international market. Technological progress within the old feudal order helped create an explosion of wealth, new industries, exploration and commercialisation during that period. The productivity of Italian weavers doubled and then tripled while the output of printers rose fourfold during the Renaissance. Between 1350 and 1550, English iron production rose seven or eightfold. Many of the advances came in shipping and trade.

Before Columbus discovered the New World in 1492, the crew-to-cargo ratio was one sailor for every five or six tons. The Dutch achieved a ratio of one man per ten tons by the end of the Renaissance. The Northern Italian city-states made dramatic improvements in shipbuilding technology. Using assembly lines and interchangeable parts, they could build large ships in a matter of days.

With the defeat of the Spanish Armada in 1588, England became the supreme maritime power and with the subsequent defeat of the Dutch, was in a position to protect her merchant trade. The resulting growth in international trade meant that in the 17th century the London-based East India Trading Company already operated on a transnational scale. Founded in 1600, with a charter from Queen Elizabeth I, the company created a base in Madras in 1640 and had expanded to Bombay by 1662. It was to become so powerful that in the mid-19th century the British state took the company over and, in doing so, acquired India as a colonial possession.

A contemporary process in England produced the first poor laws. Introduced in 1597, they were needed because a class of destitute, landless labourers had emerged in the countryside. Powerful landlords had discovered that the international wool trade was more profitable than small-scale arable farming. They ousted tenant farmers and began a process that would end with the enclosure of most common land and the eventual creation of a new social group – the property-less working class. Parliament's victory in the English Revolution of 1642-51, led by Oliver Cromwell, swept away the old feudal order based on the state power of the absolute monarch. The subsequent installation of what became a constitutional monarchy tailored the state to support the explosion in trade and commerce that followed. Parliament and a new state power now dominated politics.

The brutal exploitation of India and other colonies and the ill-gotten wealth from the slave trade all contributed to the accumulation by the British ruling class of the capital required to open a new chapter in history – capitalism. Marx, in *Capital*, describes in vivid words how this happened:

> In England at the end of the 17th century, they [moments of primitive accumulation] arrive at a systematical combination, embracing the colonies, the national debt, the modern mode of taxation, and the protectionist system. These methods depend in part on brute force, *e.g.*, the colonial system. But, they all employ the power of the state, the concentrated and organised force of society, to hasten, hot-house fashion, the process of transformation of the feudal mode of production into the capitalist mode, and to shorten the transition.

The invention of steam power and other revolutionary technology spurred on the rapid emergence of a new system of production and social relations. Factory production and the systematic extraction of minerals soon dominated an often rural landscape where none of these activities had existed before. A mass migration to the towns took place as a landless and hungry rural population sought work. Unregulated and free from state interference, the new capitalist class in Britain and elsewhere were, within decades, to change the face of the planet. It was truly an historic, revolutionary transformation.

The new working class struggled to find its identity. Trade unions were banned during the Napoleonic wars which began soon after the French Revolution of 1789. In 1834, six farm workers from Tolpuddle in Dorset were convicted under the 1797 Mutiny Act for taking an oath when they formed a union and were deported to Australia. Parliamentary democracy as a system of political representation did not yet exist. Despite the first Reform Act of 1832, only small sections of middle class men in Britain had the vote. In 1837, the Chartist movement published its six demands, including the right to universal suffrage. The following year, a petition with 1,250,000 names was rejected by a corrupt parliament, many of whose members literally bought their seats. One wing of the Chartists also believed that, once granted the vote, they would put an end to capitalism, using force if necessary. In 1848, as Marx and Engels drafted their famous manifesto, the Chartists obtained no fewer than five million signatures, while revolutions raged throughout Europe against remnants of the old feudal order.

Although the earliest stages of industrialisation were confined to products manufactured, finished and sold within national economies, the combined pressures to enlarge production, specialise activities and seek markets quickly outgrew local conditions. Larger domestic firms soon faced the choice of whether to compete internationally by extending production activities abroad or to export from their domestic base. International trade by nationally-based firms protected by powerful states soared throughout the 19th century.

Modern globalisation

The forces that shape our lives in the 21st century remain capitalist in their nature. Yet they are vastly different in their form and character. A rapid acceleration of the globalisation process that Marx first analysed has taken place. Out of it has come a group of powerful transnational corporations (TNCs) and a global financial system, endorsed by compliant states and the ideology of free market capital.

This new form of globalisation began to take shape following the break-down in 1971 of the post-war monetary and trade agreements reached at Bretton Woods in the United States in 1944. These agreements regulated and restricted movements of capital from one country to another. There were tight agreements on trade and tariffs, aimed at protecting domestic markets. All the major currencies were valued against the dollar – which itself was tied to gold – in a system of fixed exchange rates. But the system came under strain as international trade developed and separate markets in the dollar emerged in Europe. The strain of financing the war in Vietnam finally undermined the dollar and it was decoupled from gold, allowing currencies to float free.

The end of Bretton Woods precipitated economic chaos and resulted in major class conflicts in Europe and the United States. In Britain, these struggles culminated in the great miners' strike of 1984-85. The Tory governments of Thatcher and the Reagan administrations in the United States were the face of a new form of capitalism, which shunned compromise and consensus. They began the process of "liberalisation" and deregulation of capitalism from its Bretton Woods restrictions. The World Bank and the International Monetary Fund, set up at Bretton Woods, took on new roles and began to promote globalisation. Capital was given the freedom to move across borders and trade barriers were removed. Soon, globalisation was given a tremendous impetus by the revolution in micro-chip based information and communications technologies

Today, the forces unleashed 30 years ago have an unprecedented impact on the way we eat, think, and act. There are now few areas of public or private life that elude global capitalism. Corporations have even turned the very essence of life itself into areas for profit making. The human DNA map is subject to patents, as are seeds and basic products like rice. Public services are increasingly run along commercial lines or are privatised, while sport and culture is overrun by big business. While many parts of the world are without fresh drinking water, the World Bank insists that loans to poor countries are tied to privatisation of this natural resource.

The ideology of the free market – deregulation, privatisation, the dismantling of the welfare state and the withdrawal of the state from any significant public provision – has captivated and captured governments around the world. It is presented as the only way to organise society, as inevitable and natural. The Clinton and Bush governments in the US and the Blair governments in Britain all proved enthusiastic supporters of this manifesto of globalised capital. Their governments have acted as the senior management team on behalf of corporate interests, both national and international.

In *When Corporations Rule the World,* David Korten explains how the forces of modern globalisation are advanced by an alliance between the world's largest corporations and most powerful governments, writing:

> This alliance is backed by the power of money, and its defining project is to integrate the world's national economies into a single, borderless global economy in which the world's mega-corporations are free to move goods and money anywhere in the world that affords an opportunity for profit, without governmental interference. In the name of increased efficiency the alliance seeks to privatise public services and assets and strengthen safeguards for investors and private property.

In his ground-breaking book *The Transnational Capitalist Class,* Leslie Sklair notes:

> The truly fundamental change that capitalist globalisation has introduced... is that, for the first time in human history, there is indeed a material and ideological shift towards selling business as such as the only real business of the planet and its inhabitants. So, in the global capitalist system, agents and agencies of the state (among other institutions) fulfil the role of facilitators of the global capitalist project.

Today, 50 of the top 100 economies in the world are in fact TNCs. The revenues of Wal-Mart, the world's largest supermarket chain, are bigger than those of 161 countries. Mitsubishi, the Japan-based corporation, is larger in economic activity than the fourth most populous nation on earth, Indonesia. General Motors is bigger than Denmark. Ford's activity is larger in dollar terms than South Africa's. Toyota is greater than Norway. Cigarette manufacturer Philip Morris is larger than New Zealand, and it operates in 170 countries.

Today, the top 200 firms have sales that are the equivalent of

---

Key ingredients of capitalist globalisation
▸ trade and corporate deregulation
▸ the unrestricted movement of capital
▸ international, unregulated financial markets
▸ privatisation of public services
▸ commodification of new areas such as genetic resources and human DNA
▸ developed forms of property rights such as intellectual property
▸ integration of national economies into a global system
▸ promotion of hyper-growth and unrestricted consumption
▸ increased corporate concentration through global firms
▸ erosion of traditional powers and policies of nation states
▸ global cultural homogenisation.

---

almost 30% of the world's gross domestic product (GDP), which is a way of measuring income generated by economic activity. The vast majority (186) of the top 200 have headquarters in just seven countries: Japan, the United States, Germany, France, the United Kingdom, the Netherlands, and Switzerland. South Korea and Brazil are the only developing countries to break into the top group. Half of the total sales of the top 200 are in trading, cars, banking, retailing and electronics. Sklair explains:

> Globalisation... means transnational practices in which corporate agencies and actors (principally TNC executives and their local affiliates) strive to maximise private profits globally for those who own and control the corporations. TNCs seek profits without special reference to the interests (real or imagined) of their countries of citizenship. The transnational capitalist class mobilises the resources necessary to accomplish this objective, working through a variety of social institutions, including state and quasi-state agencies, the professions and the mass media. The culture-ideology of consumerism is the rationale of the system.

The concentrated economic power in these and other sectors is enormous. In cars, the top five firms account for almost 60% of global sales. In electronics, the top five firms have garnered over half of global sales. And the top five firms have over 30% of global sales in airlines, aerospace, steel, oil, personal computers, chemicals, and the media. The top ten drug corporations have an estimated 53% of the market while ten firms – including Dupont, Monsanto and Syngenta – control 80% of the global pesticide market.

As global corporations have developed, the nature of their ownership has evolved. At the dawn of capitalism, firms were owned by individuals or families. By the mid-19th century, the joint stock company was developed that allowed firms to raise capital by selling shares, which then traded on the stock market. Where once these shares were owned mainly by individuals, under corporate-led globalisation, their control has passed into the hands of "institutions", as figures from the Office for National Statistics reveal.

In 1963, individuals owned 54% of all the shares traded in London. But by the end of 2003, the total owned by individuals had plummeted to just 14.9%. During the same period, the proportion of shares in the hands of insurance companies and pension funds trebled – from just over 16% to more than 48%. These shares are, of course, purchased with the funds paid in the form of insurance premiums and pension contributions. In that sense, we together "own" almost a half of capitalist corporations operating in Britain, whose estimated total stock market value in 2003 was £1,368 billion.

Another significant development arising from globalisation is the overseas ownership of corporations. In Britain, during the 1980s, the proportion of shares owned by rest of the world investors increased substantially, from 3.6% in 1981 to around 13% during the period 1989 to 1992. By 1999, rest of the world holdings had reached 29.3% and more than 32% by 2003, of which 36% were held by European funds. This broadening of ownership is also reflected in the way that shares in the major corporations are traded on stock markets around the world, where before they were restricted to their country of origin.

Just in time... for some

Companies plan and organise the conception, production and

distribution of products and services not only regionally but globally. A relatively small number of TNCs contract with an estimated 850,000 associated firms to create global production systems. They co-ordinate supply chains which link firms across countries, including local sub-contractors who outsource to home workers. The TNCs are now estimated to account for two-thirds of world trade while intra-firm trade between the corporations and their affiliates accounts for about one-third of world exports. Many major TNCs, such as IBM, Microsoft, Mitsubishi, Samsung, Nestle, ICI, Unilever and Dow Chemicals, regularly earn more than half of their revenues outside their country of origin, according to the International Labour Organisation's (ILO) 2004 study of globalisation.

The growth of these global production systems is most pronounced in the high-tech industries (electronics and semi-conductors) and in labour intensive consumer goods (textiles, garments and footwear). It is also becoming significant in the service sector where technological advances have made it possible for services such as software development, financial services and call centres to be supplied from different countries around the globe. In the labour-intensive consumer industries the TNCs design the product, specify the product quality, and then outsource its production to local firms in developing countries. They also exercise control over the quality and timing of production, which is often subjected to changes in design and volume. The driving force is the flexible and timely adjustment to changes in consumer demand with minimal inventory costs. It is a global just-in-time production system. The corporations switch production and service industries around the globe in search of the cheapest labour, moving across borders without political interference. The dramatic fall in the cost of moving information, people, goods and capital across the globe has accelerated these changes.

New parts of the globe have fallen into the globalisation honey-trap, including China and countries of the former Soviet Union. The economic forces set in motion in the 1970s transcended borders and played a significant role in the demise of the Stalinist states of Eastern Europe, while in China a capitalist class has grown rapidly out of the industrialisation of the country. Whole areas of southern China, for example, have become industrialised and commercialised inside a decade. Today they have factories employing 100,000 workers, making everything from most of the world's fridges to the inevitable trainers for the sportswear firms.

This new international division of labour means that, throughout the world as a whole, there are millions more workers involved in production and administration, as well as retail and service industries. In China alone, the number of workers in factories has risen by 100 million in a decade, while an equal number are thought to be without work. The total world workforce has soared from 1.6 billion to 3.5 billion in 30 years. The migration from countryside to town seen in Britain at the beginning of the industrial revolution is repeating itself in Asia and South America. Millions of manufacturing jobs disappear in the United States and Europe, only to reappear in Mexico or in Asia. Dr Marten's work shoes were until recently produced in Northampton. The factory was shut and now they are being made in South China where the workers are paid 20 cents an hour. That is a lot cheaper than making the shoes in Northampton, even taking into account the additional transport costs.

A report by Oxfam showed how globalisation has drawn millions of women into paid employment across the developing world, producing goods for supermarkets and clothing stores in Britain and elsewhere, while working under appalling conditions. "Commonly hired on short-term contracts – or with no contract at all – women are working at high speed for low wages in unhealthy conditions. They are forced to put in long hours to earn enough to get by. Most have no sick leave or maternity leave, few are enrolled in health or unemployment schemes, and fewer still have savings for the future. Instead of supporting long-term development, trade is reinforcing insecurity and vulnerability for millions of women workers," says the report.

Oxfam's research revealed how retailers and clothing brands are using their power in supply chains systematically to push many costs and risks of business on to producers, who in turn pass them on to working women:

▸ in Chile, 75% of women in the agricultural sector are hired on temporary contracts picking fruit, and put in more than 60 hours a week during the season. But one in three still earns below the minimum wage
▸ fewer than half of the women employed in Bangladesh's textile and garment export sector have a contract, and the vast majority get no maternity or health coverage – but 80% fear dismissal if they complain
▸ in China's Guangdong province, one of the world's fastest growing industrial areas, young women face 150 hours of overtime each month in the garment factories – but 60% have no written contract and 90% have no access to social insurance.

"The impacts are felt by workers in both rich and poor countries. Women and migrants from poor communities in rich countries – such as US and Canadian agricultural workers and UK and Australian home-based workers – likewise face precarious terms of employment in trade-competing sectors. The pressure of

---

Lloyds under fire as jobs go to India
Friday 31 October 2003
The Guardian
Lloyds TSB was threatened with industrial action yesterday when it announced that almost 1,000 jobs in the UK would be outsourced to India. The bank said that it would close its call centre in Newcastle, which employs 986 people, and sub-contract the jobs to its new centre in Hyderabad.
Newcastle has one of the highest rates of unemployment in the country, but Lloyds TSB said it was difficult to recruit and retain staff in the city. The bank shut a call centre in Gateshead earlier this year. Financial services trade union UNIFI is considering industrial action. "The indication from members is that they want to take a stand. If that's still the feeling at the beginning of next week then we will put that in place for them," said a spokesperson.

competition from low-cost imports is clearly one reason, but so too is the pressure inherent in being employed at the end of a major company's global supply chain, whether it is sourcing overseas or domestically," Oxfam notes.

Call centres were supposed to be the new job opportunities of the 21st century in depressed areas of Britain like Glasgow and the North-East. Many of these are now being relocated to India, for example, where labour costs are much lower. Call centre staff in far away places watch *East Enders* and follow David Beckham's career so that they can appear to be local and chat with people. So when you get on the telephone to ask about your gas bill they know what the weather is like in London.

The scale of this transformation into a truly global economy can be charted through the movement of capital from one country to another. This process is known as foreign direct investment (FDI). As the graph shows, there was a sensational

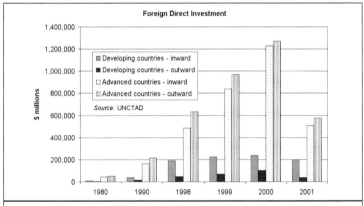

Foreign Direct Investment

- Developing countries - inward
- Developing countries - outward
- Advanced countries - inward
- Advanced countries - outward

Source: UNCTAD

$ millions

1980 1990 1998 1999 2000 2001

A new whole

These changes in trade, FDI (foreign direct investment), financial flows and technological diffusion are increasingly part of a new systemic whole. An underlying common factor is that all these elements necessarily evolved in the context of increasing influence of global market forces. This is a profound change, affecting the role of the state and the behaviour of economic agents.

A fairer globalisation: creating opportunities for all. ILO 2004

increase over the last 20 years of the 20th century, rising from $55 billion worldwide to $1,500 billion in 2000 until the financial crisis of 2001 took its toll. New economies emerged in Asia as a result of this large-scale investment in parts of the world where labour was bountiful and cheaper than in Europe and North America.

The WTO and its allies

The power of the corporations is expressed and delivered through three global organisations: the World Trade Organisation (WTO), the World Bank and the International Monetary Fund (IMF). Established in 1995, the WTO transformed the post-war General Agreement on Tariffs and Trade (GATT) into an enforceable global commerce code. The WTO is one of the main mechanisms of capitalist globalisation, using its status as a permanent institution with a huge secretariat. States have ceded enormous powers to the WTO. In fact, it is the only international body whose authority the United States accepts.

The WTO has functioned principally to open markets for the benefit of transnational corporations at the expense of national and local economies, workers, farmers, indigenous peoples, women and other social groups. It is responsible for administering dozens of international trade agreements and declarations on a range of issues from agriculture to intellectual property rights. The WTO also handles trade disputes, monitors national trade policies, and operates as the overarching forum for global trade negotiations, called "rounds". Operating out of Geneva, Switzerland, with an administrative staff of 500, the WTO enforces more than 20 separate international agreements, using international trade tribunals that adjudicate disputes. Although all countries appear equal under the WTO on paper, in reality, the major economies with economic and political power hold centre stage.

The WTO is constructed like no other international agency. Unlike the GATT, which was effectively a business contract between nations, the WTO has a legal personality and the power to enforce its rulings. The WTO has an international status equivalent to the United Nations, but unlike the UN, it carries the powers and tools to enforce its decisions. WTO rulings are so powerful, they take precedence over multilateral agreements such as the Convention on Biological Diversity, the UN's Universal Declaration of Human Rights, and international labour codes.

Under the WTO's dispute settlement mechanism, member countries, acting on behalf of their business sector, can challenge the laws, policies and programmes of any other country for being in violation of WTO rules. Panels of unelected experts have the power to adjudicate claims of alleged violations of these rules and to hand out punishments. The losing country has three choices: change its law to conform to the WTO ruling; face harsh, permanent economic sanctions; or pay permanent compensation to the winning country. The only task is to judge whether or not a country's policy is a "barrier to trade". The vast majority of WTO tribunal rulings have favoured the interests of corporations over objections by governments or social and environmental standards. Panel decisions can be appealed, but only a unanimous vote of all member nations can overturn a WTO ruling.

Although official WTO decisions are made by vote or by consensus of the 146-member General Council, real decision-making powers are now increasingly vested in what is known as "the QUAD" – the US, the European Union, Japan and Canada. The QUAD convenes several times a year, making key decisions on WTO priorities. These meetings take place behind closed doors without the participation of other countries, and although the QUAD is not formally structured as the WTO executive, it is by nature of its power, able to exercise executive powers.

Transnational corporations and their domestic and international associations have had a direct voice in shaping the entire structure of the WTO from the beginning. In the United States, more than 500 corporations and business representatives have official credentials as trade advisers. The US Trade Representative works closely with the Coalition of Service Industries. Their members include the major energy, insurance, and financial giants, as well as major pharmaceutical companies.

> **Your guide to what the WTO controls**
> ▸ the General Agreement on Trade in Services (GATS) is the first multilateral, legally enforceable agreement on trade in services
> ▸ Trade Related Intellectual Property Rights (TRIPS) sets enforceable global rules on patents, copyrights, and trademark
> ▸ Trade Related Investment Measures (TRIMS) dictate what governments can and cannot do in regulating foreign investment
> ▸ the Agreement on the Application of Sanitary and Phytosanitary Standards (SPS) covers food safety, animal and plant health
> ▸ the Financial Services Agreement (FSA) was established to remove obstacles to the free movement of financial services corporations
> ▸ the Agreement on Agriculture (AOA) sets rules on the international food trade and restricts domestic agriculture policy
> ▸ the Agreement on Subsidies and Countervailing Measures (ASCM) sets limits on what governments may and may not subsidise
> ▸ the Agreement on Technical Barriers to Trade (TBT) was set up to limit national regulations that interfere with trade
> ▸ the Agreement on Government Procurement (AGP) sets limits on government purchasing.

In Japan, it is the industry lobby group, the Keidanren that liaises with the WTO. In Europe, the Commissioner of the European Union on WTO Policies and Administration maintains direct links with the European Round Table of Industrialists (ERT), which is composed of representatives of the 50 largest European-based corporations. The European Services Forum has lobbied forcefully to remove exemptions for public services from the GATS.

In fact, in a May 2002 letter to the CEOs of Europe's three largest water corporations – Vivendi, Suez and RWE/Thames – EU Director General of Trade, Ulrike Hauer, thanked them for their contribution in negotiations to reduce trade barriers in water services. As a senior WTO official told the *Financial Times*, the WTO "is the place where governments collude in private against their domestic pressure groups".

The ultimate goal of the GATS is to "progressively liberalise" until all public services are fully commercialised. Behind this drive to bring new areas of life into the capitalist orbit is the increasing volatility of financial markets and the over-capacity in traditional manufacturing, both of which limit the possibilities for profit-making. But the pickings from the newly liberalised areas are potentially very rich indeed. Global annual expenditures on education now exceed $2 trillion and on health care $3.5 trillion. Predatory and powerful transnational corporations who want to use the WTO/GATS process to dismantle domestic public systems have targeted public education, health care, welfare, and water services. No one is really sure what is in or out, which is part of the strategy. Planning regulations affecting the expansion of large retail outlets could be ruled an "unnecessary barrier to trade" and overly "burdensome" on business, for example.

In Britain, the New Labour government is supporting the extension of GATS and has given WTO lawyers carte-blanche in negotiations. Since the UK signed up to GATS in 1994 it has not produced a single document fully explaining either what the UK is committed to or the implications of its commitments. Educationalist and anti-GATS campaigner Glenn Rikowski, in a paper prepared for a House of Lords inquiry, pointed out that in the long run, no area of social life was exempt from these developments. He told the committee:

> The political management of the process is made easier by the fact that the GATS is opaque regarding whether public services are exempt from the Agreement's trade rules and sanctions, or not. If it were the case that the GATS was inapplicable to public services, and that services like health, education and libraries were exempt from the GATS imperatives, then it would be clear that commercialisation, privatisation and capitalisation of public services was a governmental choice and strategy. Hence, objections to these processes could be made on that basis. On the other hand, if it were the case that public services such as education were clearly included in the GATS then the programme for subjecting the whole of social life to take-over by corporate capital would be obvious.

Thus, the complexity and unclarity of the GATS Agreement actually aids the translation of the GATS into national contexts. It allows governments to proceed under a cloak of obfuscation and uncertainty.

Behind the cloak of confusion the position is, however, well advanced in Britain. For example, the education business Nord Anglia is already exporting its services to Russia and the Ukraine as well as running schools and local education authority services in Britain. Many British universities have franchised operations and a whole raft of deals with other colleges and universities in other countries.

Speculating around the clock
The international financial system that has emerged over the last 30 years transcends the power of national banks and governments. Today's financial system is truly global in an unprecedented way and has a relative independence from, as well as dominance over, the real world of actual production and commodities. Where once locally-based commercial and national banks held sway, today a financial system operates as a series of inter-linked trading houses that operate electronically. They were first formed following the deregulation of finance, both domestically and internationally, that began in the 1970s and which was completed by the late 1980s. These markets now operate around the clock, as a result of the revolution in information technology. When London is sleeping, the markets in the Far East are open for business. The night shift in the City of London will be at their desks, on their phones and watching the screens.

The markets owe allegiance to no state. In London, the foreign exchange market is dominated by the Swiss-based UBS and Deutsche Bank, which have cornered 25% of the trading. Traders buy and sell currencies on screen, working on the narrowest of margins. They can make or break currencies in hours, as the financier George Soros proved during the sterling crisis of 1992 when he used his fund's resources to force the pound out of the European exchange rate mechanism.

Internationalisation of financial markets was also a strong feature of capitalism during the late 19th century, the system collapsing with the outbreak of World War I in 1914. Today the position is vastly changed, as Jan Annaert explains in an article on financial markets in *Globalisation and the Nation-State*:

> The present situation differs qualitatively from the one a century ago, in the sense that a larger part of the world and more independent countries are involved. Indeed, integration and globalisation is not only a characteristic of developed markets but also of emerging markets. Moreover, the *speed* with which capital flows can roam freely across the globe has increased spectacularly. [emphasis added]

National governments turn to the markets when they want to borrow money for a variety of reasons. The US government, for example, is the largest debtor nation in the world, running enormous trade deficits as well as a government budget where the gap between revenue and expenditure is colossal. So Washington has to go to the financial market to borrow the funds to cover these deficits. Corporations too borrow on the international financial market to finance their expansion plans. The sums involved are enormous. For example, the mobile phone operators in Britain borrowed £20 billion to buy the licences for a new generation of mobile communications. Similar sums were borrowed by corporations on the Continent. Repayment costs have, in turn, eaten into their profits and forced up prices for third generation mobile calls.

The quantity of funds available on these markets is astronomical. Between 1963 and 1995 total funds raised on international markets increased at an average annual growth rate of 24.3% compared to a 5.5% for world trade and 3.2% for world production. There is a huge market in cross-border transactions in bonds and shares, along with international share issues that result from large-scale privatisation as well as international mergers and acquisitions operations. The Bank for International Settlements (BIS) has reported that what it calls "notional amounts outstanding" in all categories of market risk (including equity, commodity, credit and "other" derivatives) stood at a staggering $100,000 billion, a 38% increase between 1998 and 2001. One estimate is that for every US dollar circulating in the real economy, $25 to $30 circulates in the world of pure finance.

This is entirely fictitious capital in the sense that it is the result of money/credit generating more paper money/credit through speculation or interest. There is no wealth creation involved where human labour has added value to help create something useful. These funds then accumulate and have a life of their own. Their need to earn a return gives the entire system its restlessness and inherent instability.

Speculation on foreign exchange

In 1986, the average daily turnover on the foreign exchange markets was around $188 billion. Today around $1,200 billion are exchanged daily, according to the BIS. Only 5% of the total are directly related to payments for traded goods and services. The remainder is devoted to sheer speculation, as traders work the thinnest of margins, with real-time pricing. As the *Financial Times* reported on 7 May 2004: "The global foreign exchange market represents capitalism red in tooth and claw. This largely self-regulated trading system never sleeps and routinely transfers staggeringly vast sums of money around the world in seconds at the click of a mouse."

Finance companies hired scientists and brilliant mathematicians in the 1990s to invent a bewildering array of devices intended to generate earnings. We entered the obscure world of derivatives, swaptions, junk bonds and other exotic forms. Entire banks and corporations live this way. Some like Enron have disappeared, engulfed in financial infernos. As Annaert notes: "Trading of complex financial instruments has increased the linkages between different market segments and participants without regard to national boundaries. Disruptions in one key market are therefore likely to be transmitted quickly to other markets, threatening the stability of the world financial system."

Unstable at the core, the financial system can and does disrupt whole sections of the global economy. In 1997 enormous sums were withdrawn overnight from East Asia, plunging local economies into disaster, destroying jobs and savings. More than 22 million people in Indonesia were driven below the poverty line within a few months. Russia also suffered a financial Armageddon in 1998 and its people are still paying the price. In 2001 Argentina had to separate its currency from the dollar after a precipitate flight of capital. The economy fell apart and a major political crisis erupted. The dot.com bubble – which was heralded as new form of wealth you could conjure up as if by magic by borrowing loads of money and not making a profit – burst, sending stock markets crashing.

The collapse in late 2001 of Enron Corp, the American energy trading company, and the shredding of documents by auditors Arthur Andersen, exposed a world of make-believe where debt was marked down as revenue. In less than a year, Enron went from what many regarded as an innovative corporation to a byword for corruption and mismanagement. At the heart of the crisis was debt.

In its first few years, Enron was simply a natural gas provider, but by 1989 it had begun trading natural gas commodities, and in 1994 it started trading electricity.

Enron tailored electricity and natural gas contracts to reflect the cost of delivery to a specific destination – creating for the first time, a nation-wide and ultimately global energy-trading network. The company claimed a 57% increase in sales between 1996 and 2000.

Much of Enron's balance sheet, however, did not make sense to analysts. By the late 1990s, Enron had begun shuffling its debt obligations into offshore partnerships. At the same time, the company was reporting inaccurate trading revenues. It was using its partnerships to sell contracts back and forth to itself and entering revenue each time. Enron put ordinary creative accounting in the shade!

As rumours abounded, the US Securities and Exchange Commission began an inquiry into Enron and the partnerships. Enron then revised its financial statements for the previous five years, acknowledging that instead of making profits, it had

> **Failure of foreign investment**
> In the wake of the debt and development crisis of the 1980s, a new policy approach looked to liberate enterprise from state intervention, deferring to the invisible touch of global market forces. The promise was for an end to macroeconomic chaos, stop-go development cycles and debilitating levels of debt, ushering in an era of sustained growth and poverty reduction. The collapse of the Berlin Wall gave this agenda global reach. The agenda was embraced with particular enthusiasm in Latin America... the floodgates opened to foreign capital in the 1990s. The green light from international capital markets encouraged a quickening pace of reform, attracting foreign investment and making international competition the engine of renewed growth. But after some initial signs of success, familiar structural constraints have resurfaced. Most countries have failed to accelerate capital formation and technological progress, and diversify into more dynamic sectors. As spending outpaced the expansion of productive capacity and imports boomed, the growing reliance on external capital left many countries exposed to external policy shocks. Over the past five years, as global economic imbalances have generated such shocks with increasing frequency, Latin America has endured a lost half decade, recalling the disappointing developments of the 1980s...The region received virtually no net inflows of private capital in 2002... it has had to combine a fall in output with a trade surplus and net transfers abroad, generated entirely by cuts in imports.
>
> *Trade and Development Review 2003,* UNCTAD

actually sustained $586 million in losses. Its stock value began melt down and fell below $1 per share by the end of November 2001. The corporation then collapsed, leaving its workforce without pensions as they had been persuaded to buy Enron shares with their contributions. In under a year, six of the 10 largest corporate bankruptcies in US history were recorded. Widespread accounting irregularities were reported, and Arthur Andersen, one of the Big Five accounting firms, went out of business after its criminal conviction on obstruction of justice charges regarding the Enron investigation.

The growth of inequality

A key feature of capitalist-driven globalisation is rising inequality between rich and poor countries, a polarisation within the major capitalist countries themselves and the ruthless exploitation of workers in poorer countries. Put simply, the richer have got richer and the poorer a lot poorer. In 1990, in Britain, the wealthiest 10% owned 64% of what is known as marketable wealth; by the turn of the century that had risen to 72%, according to Office for National Statistics (ONS). The ratio of the 10% highest paid over the 10% lowest paid rose by more than 35% between the mid-1980s and the mid-1990s. Even more striking has been the sharp increase in the share of the top 1% of income earners in the United States. The share of this group reached 17% of gross income in 2000, a level last seen in the 1920s.

Meanwhile, in the world's 30 richest countries the average level of corporate tax fell from 37.6% in 1996 to 30.8% in 2003. Tax incentives to attract investment contributed to this lowering of tax rates. A similar phenomenon can be seen in the taxation of high-income earners. Between 1986 and 1998, the top marginal tax rate on personal income declined in the vast majority of countries, both high and low-income, often substantially, according to the ILO.

At the same time, executive salaries have soared into the stratosphere. Citigroup, the US finance giant, disclosed that its top three executives earned a combined $102m (£56m) in 2003. Chairman Sanford Weill, who stepped down as chief executive of the world's largest financial services group, was paid $44.7m, almost five times as much as he took home in 2002. His compensation included a $29m bonus, $1m in salary and option grants worth $14m. Even when things go wrong, the money keeps rolling in. In Britain, Mytravel paid £4.5m compensation to five directors in 2003, despite racking up £911m losses and seeing its share price shrink to under 20p from a high of 544p. Departure is made much easier by big pay-offs, like the £10m BskyB chief executive Tony Ball received when he left the

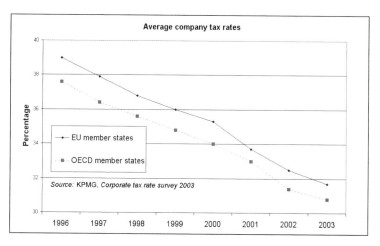

Average company tax rates

Source: KPMG, *Corporate tax rate survey 2003*

corporation. Jean-Pierre Garnier, the chief executive of GlaxoSmithKline was paid £7m in 2003, even though GSK shares had fallen, along with its profits, since he took over in 2000. Meanwhile, William F Aldinger III, the chief operating officer of Household International, a new US offshoot of HSBC, was enticed with a £37m pay package over three years, including a guaranteed annual bonus of £2.5m.

Meanwhile, migrant labour is smuggled into Britain to work in the most appalling conditions as firms try to compete on the world market by paying starvation wages. The drowning of 23 Chinese cockle pickers at Morecambe Bay in February 2004 was a tragic expression in Britain of what is happening throughout the capitalist world. The cockle pickers were paying most of their meagre wage to gangmasters and criminals and working round the clock to supply the kitchens of the rich. In Norfolk, it was reported that gang workers were paid just £3 to cut 1,000 daffodils. In Cambridgeshire, workers were forced to live in partitioned containers with no water supply and were deducted £80 a week rent for the privilege.

The World Bank and International Monetary Fund (IMF) were created at the Bretton Woods meetings in 1944. The Bank was set up to help rebuild war-torn Europe. As globalisation accelerated, it turned its focus to the "underdeveloped" world to bring poor countries into the international economy. The IMF

> ### Share bonanza for Sainsburys
> Richard Wachman and Sarah Ryle
> 28 March 2004
> *The Observer*
>
> Lord Sainsbury, the Science Minister, is to collect a special dividend worth £88 million from J Sainsbury, the embattled supermarket chain, following the sale of the company's US business for more than £1 billion.
>
> The company is returning cash from the deal to shareholders, which means a large payment to Lord Sainsbury, who has a 13% stake. Through various trusts, the family as a whole owns 38% of J Sainsbury, which means it collects £258m from the sale.
>
> The company shocked the City on Friday with a profits warning, which cast a shadow over news of the sale of the US operations.
>
> The shares slumped 7% to 260p despite renewed talk of a bid for J Sainsbury by Philip Green, the retail entrepreneur.
>
> The disclosure of the special dividend has raised eyebrows in the City, where there are suspicions that the family is keen to take money out of the business prior to a winding down of its holdings and a possible sale of the group. This, however, is denied by a source close to the Sainsbury family.

was to help stabilise currency exchange rates between nations. It too changed its role. By 1997 it had amended its constitution to ban borrowers from imposing capital controls and imposed restructuring, which meant opening up to foreign capital and free trade, as a condition of loans. These were euphemistically called Structural Adjustment Programmes (SAPs).

In 2002, the Structural Adjustment Participatory Review International Network (SAPRIN), published a report based on years of research and interviews with thousands of organisations. It concluded that:

▸ precipitate and indiscriminate trade and financial sector liberalisation, and the weakening of state support and the demand for local goods and services, have devastated local industries and created widespread unemployment

Rich world, poor world
▸ some 54 countries are poorer now than in 1990
▸ in 21 countries a larger proportion of people are going hungry
▸ in 14 countries more children are dying before age five
▸ in 12 countries primary school enrolment rates have fallen
▸ the richest 5% of the world's people receive 114 times the income of the poorest 5%
▸ the richest 1% receive as much as the poorest 57%
▸ the 25 million richest Americans have as much income as almost 2 billion of the world's poorest people.

Human Development Report 2003, United Nations

▸ structural changes in agricultural and mining sectors have undermined the viability of small firms, weakened food security and damaged the natural environment
▸ cheap food imports, the removal of subsidies from farm inputs, and the withdrawal of state financial and technical support, have further marginalised small farmers and forced them to overexploit natural resources
▸ "labour-market reforms" have worsened the position of workers. Employment levels have dropped, jobs have become more precarious, real wages have fallen and trade union rights eroded or weakened
▸ privatisation of public services and charges for health care and education, and cuts in social spending have reduced the poor's access to affordable services and resulted in rising school drop-out rates
▸ the increased impoverishment from SAPs has fallen hardest on women, who were most vulnerable to lay-offs
▸ many of the promised gains in efficiency, competitiveness, savings and revenues from SAPs have failed to materialise.

The IMF and World Bank have been empowered by the governments which control them (led by the US, Britain, Japan, Germany, France, Canada, and Italy – the Group of 7, which holds over 40% of the votes on their boards) to impose these free-market/austerity policies on developing countries. Once poorer countries build up large external debts, as most have, they cannot get credit or cash anywhere else and are forced to go to these international institutions and accept whatever conditions are demanded of them.

None of the countries has emerged from their debt problems. Indeed most countries now have much higher levels of debt than when they first accepted IMF/World Bank "assistance". The World Bank is best known for financing big projects like dams, roads, and power plants, supposedly designed to assist in economic development, but which have often been associated with monumental environmental devastation and social dislocation. Only big corporations who win the construction contracts benefit. In recent years, about half of its lending has gone to programmes indistinguishable from the IMF's.

Free-market globalisation is trumpeted as the best way poorer countries can share in wealth. This is the theme, for example, of New Labour's White Paper on international development 2000. In a foreword, prime minister Blair claims that: "Globalisation creates unprecedented new opportunities and risks. If the poorest countries can be drawn into the global economy and get increasing access to modern knowledge and technology, it could lead to a rapid reduction in global poverty – as well as bringing new trade and investment opportunities for all. But if this is not done, the poorest countries will become more marginalised, and suffering and division will grow. And we will all be affected by the consequences."

The fact is, however, that far from improving the lives of most people, globalisation led by the TNCs has made them poorer and more likely to die younger. Even the World Bank in its development report 2001-2002 has to acknowledge these trends. In 1960 per capita gross domestic product in the richest 20 countries was 18 times that in the poorest 20 countries. By 1995 this gap had widened to 37 times. Such figures indicate that income inequality between countries has increased sharply over the past 40 years. "More than 1 billion people in low and middle-income countries lack access to safe water, and 2 billion lack adequate sanitation, subjecting them to avoidable disease and premature death," the report admits.

Making profit out of water

The World Bank has offered an interest-free loan of $150m to re-equip the state-run Ghana Water Company and hire new management. Under the plans, new management would operate, maintain and sell the water under a 10-year contract in what would be an obscene form of so-called public-private partnerships.

Water supply in Ghana's cities and regional capitals has worsened over the past two decades. But campaigners say this is due to poor management and lack of investment in infrastructure. Most homes in urban cities have water tanks to store water because the taps run only for a few hours for two or three days a week.

And in parts of Accra, such as Teshie-Nungua, Madina and Adenta – sprawling residential areas in the south-east and north-east – residents pay anywhere between 500 cedis and 1,000 cedis (5-10 cents) per bucket of four gallons from private suppliers. The official Ghana Water rate is 64 cedis.

"You can't privatise something as close to air as water, and allow market forces and profit motives to determine who can and who cannot have some to drink," says Ameng Etego, spokesman for the Campaign Against Water Privatisation. The CAPW has mobilised the trade union movement and other organisations to halt the sell-off plans.

Meanwhile, in South Africa white farmers consume 60% of the country's water supplies through large-scale irrigation while 15 million black people are denied access to clean water. Privatisation has led to sharp increases in water rates and people in the poor townships have been cut off because they cannot pay the rates.

Today there is a global industry that specialises in the privatisation of water services. Two major French-based corporations – Vivendi and Suez – have control of 70% of the existing world water service market.

The major corporation Bechtel moved in on Bolivia when the World Bank refused to renew a $25 million loan unless water services were privatised. After water was privatised in Cochambamba, escalating protests led to a general strike and Bechtel packed its bags, only to sue the Bolivian government for $25 million.

www.socialistfuture.org.uk

In a world in which a few enjoy unimaginable wealth, 200 million children under age five are underweight because of a lack of food. Some 14 million children die each year from hunger-related disease. 100 million children are living or working on the streets. Three hundred thousand children were conscripted as soldiers during the 1990s, and six million were injured in armed conflicts. Eight hundred million people go to bed hungry each night, according to the United Nations.

The 1990s also saw declining development assistance from rich countries, increasing debt burdens in poor countries and falls in the prices of primary commodities – which many poor countries depend on for the bulk of their export revenues. Globalisation further plunged Africa into the prison of poverty. Africa has seen its share of the global wealth decline by more than 40% since the process of globalisation took hold.

The United Nations Conference on Trade and Development (UNCTAD) report for 2002 says that statistics showing a considerable expansion of technology-intensive, high value-added exports from developing countries are misleading. Such products indeed appear to be exported by developing countries, but in reality those countries are often involved in the low-skill assembly stages of international production chains organised by transnational corporations. The report adds: "Most of the technology and skills are embodied in imported parts and components, and much of the value added accrues to producers in more advanced countries where these parts and components are produced, and to the TNCs which organise such production networks."

Over the last 20 years, manufacturing has declined in the US and Europe. But they have actually increased their share in world manufacturing value added over this period. Developing countries, by contrast, have achieved a steeply rising ratio of manufactured exports to GDP, but without a significant upward trend in the ratio of manufacturing value added to GDP. The report concludes: "Certainly, few of the countries which pursued rapid liberalisation of trade and investment and experienced a rapid growth in manufacturing exports over the past two decades achieved a significant increase in their shares in world manufacturing income." Thus, most developing countries are still exporting resources – and labour-intensive products, effectively relying on their supplies of cheap, low-skilled, labour to compete.

While the United Nations can attack globalisation for failing to halt mass poverty in the world's poorest nations, the fact is that the UN is in bed with the same TNCs that drive the system on. In a 2002 report, the US-based Corporate Watch exposed the nature of the "global compact" that the UN has with big business. The brainchild of UN secretary-general Kofi Annan, the compact is the smuggling of a business agenda into the organisation, the report claims. In return for a loose commitment to a set of principles, corporations are allowed to use the UN logo and participate in compact activities to boost their claim to act as "socially responsible" organisations. CorpWatch says that what it calls "notorious violators" of the principles are allowed to participate in activities. It cites the opportunity for Nike's Phil Knight to be photographed with Annan in front of the UN flag, "without any substantial effort by the company to adhere to Global Compact principles".

In 2002, the Alliance for a Corporate-Free UN, a global network of human rights, environmental and development groups, wrote to Annan to ask him to reconsider the Global

---

Poverty kills

▸ every year more than 10 million children die of preventable illnesses – 30,000 a day

▸ more than 500,000 women a year die in pregnancy and childbirth, with such deaths 100 times more likely in Sub-Saharan Africa than in high-income OECD countries

▸ around the world 42 million people are living with HIV/AIDS, 39 million of them in developing countries

▸ tuberculosis remains (along with AIDS) the leading infectious killer of adults, causing up to 2 million deaths a year

▸ malaria deaths, now 1 million a year, could double in the next 20 years.

Human Development Report 2003, United Nations

Compact, telling him that the partnership and the guidelines for co-operation "allow business entities with poor records to 'bluewash' their image by wrapping themselves in the flag of the United Nations. They favour corporate-driven globalisation rather than the environment, human health, local communities, workers, farmers, women and the poor". The UN has dismissed these objections.

The world has deep poverty amid plenty. Of the world's 6 billion people, 2.8 billion—almost half—live on less than $2 a day, and 1.2 billion—a fifth—live on less than $1 a day, with 44% of those living in South Asia. In rich countries, fewer than 1 child in 100 does not reach its fifth birthday, while in the poorest countries as many as a 1 in 5 children do not. And while in rich countries fewer than 5% of all children under five are malnourished, in poor countries as many as 50% are. This destitution persists even though human conditions have improved more in the past century than in the rest of history.

What's new

The British economist John Atkins Hobson was one of the first to use the term imperialism to describe the nature of the international economy in his book of that title in 1902. The Russian revolutionary Vladimir Lenin used Hobson's work to develop this concept further. In 1917, on the eve of the Russian

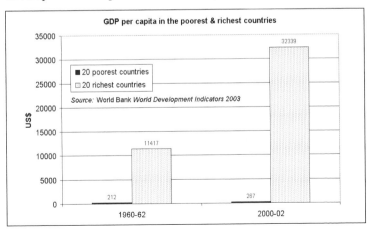

GDP per capita in the poorest & richest countries

■ 20 poorest countries
□ 20 richest countries

Source: World Bank *World Development Indicators 2003*

Africa suffers

▶ Zambia: 20% of the population is HIV positive, the government spends $17 per person on health and $30 per person on debt service to western financial institutions

▶ Niger: less than 20% of young women are enrolled in schools, more is spent on debt repayments than on education and health care

▶ failed development and economic programs such as structural adjustments programs (SAPs) continue to devastate the African continent and peoples

▶ African women are expected to meet needs no longer met by governments, such as medical care and food security while girls lose out on education when fees are imposed

▶ Tanzania: spends 9 times more on debt than health; 40% of population dies before age 35

▶ one out of 20 African mothers dies at childbirth

▶ 17% of Africa's children die before the age of five.

www.baobabconnections.org

Revolution, Lenin showed in his own work called *Imperialism* that the contemporary economy was based upon the joint roles of industrial and banking capital. Monopoly capital – which was increasingly organised into cartels – and finance capital tended to be nationally organised. This was crucial in explaining imperialism because the nation state became a protector of the interests of its own national monopoly capital, at home and in colonial possessions. Lenin described the system as capitalism in transition and detailed how imperialist nation states had been driven to world war ultimately by economic interests.

Recent globalisation of production and commerce, by contrast, has been structurally dependent upon the role of transnational corporations, which are no longer based upon a particular nation state. This does not mean that the role of the nation state has become superfluous, or that inter-imperialist rivalries have been transcended. But it does indicate that economic development is no longer based upon rival trading and political empires that aim at the protection of the interests of monopoly capital. Instead,

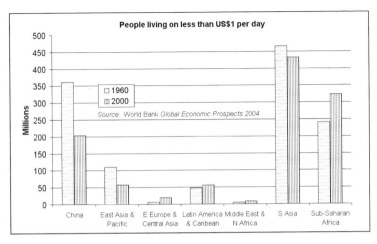

because of the growth of global corporations, capital has become a more integrated economic system. This is expressed by the development of worldwide institutions, such as the World Trade Organisation and the emergence of global financial markets.

Given the transformation of national monopoly capital into transnational capital, national political representatives of capital have found it possible to co-operate in unprecedented ways. This would have been inconceivable in the era of nationally-organised and competitive monopoly capital. For it is in the interests of the transnationals that political co-operation and unity is created between the advanced capitalist countries in order to enhance the possibilities for exploiting the labour of all countries.

The contrast between the period leading up to World War I and today is brought out by writers like David Held, in *Global Transformations*. In its early days, globalisation was about empire building. Today, he concludes, the process "reflects the varied and self-conscious political or economic projects of national élites and transnational social forces pursuing often conflicting views of world order". Controlling and managing globalisation is a "global politics" of "agenda-setting, coalition building and multilateral regulation". This challenges the territorial principle of the state as the primary basis for the organisation of political rule and the existence of political authority, he says. Summing up the changes, Held and his colleagues conclude:

> Of course... the appearance is one of catching up; a return to the status quo ante of the classic Gold Standard [pre-1914] era. But... in nearly all domains contemporary patterns of globalisation have not only quantitatively surpassed those of earlier epochs, but have also displayed unparalleled *qualitative* differences – that is in terms of how globalisation is organised and reproduced. ...The contemporary era represents a historically unique confluence or clustering of patterns of globalisation in the domains of politics, law and governance, military affairs, cultural linkages and human migrations, in all dimensions of economic activity and in shared environmental threats. Moreover, this era has experienced extraordinary innovations in the infrastructures of transport and communication, and an unparalleled density of institutions of global governance and regulation. Paradoxically, this explosion of global flows and networks has occurred at a time when the sovereign territorial state, with fixed and demarcated borders, has become the near universal form of political organisation and political rule. [emphasis added]

Others have described the "global shift" in the relationship between capital and labour since 1975. In *The Enigma of Globalisation* Robert Went maintains: "These changes have resulted in a substantial increase in capital's share of income in all parts of the world, and – more generally – in a political, social and economic agenda in which the interests of capital take pride of place." He believes that the United States has an overriding interest in establishing the free movement of capital world-wide. "There is probably no more important foreign economic policy issue for the US than this," he believes. This, as we shall see, is what the invasion and occupation of Iraq was essentially about. Most experts are agreed that the features of today's globalised capitalism are distinct in character from other periods. Went explains:

> Instead of the national cartels that competed for world markets at

the beginning of the last century, many types of international investors, alliances and multinationals are now competing and co-operating with each other on the basis of various different strategies in both developed and developing countries. At the same time, the number of international organisations and panels charged with co-ordinating and regulating economic policies has increased dramatically. In these organisations the big countries work together, particularly to open up developing countries to trade and capital. None of this means that there is no longer any competition among imperialist countries; but such rivalries are fought out economically rather than militarily...

A second difference linked to the previous one, concerns the role and structure of finance capital. The national bank-dominated financial systems [of the early 20th century]... have made way for a much more integrated world-wide financial system, where global norms are set for profitability. Because of the disappearance of capital controls, and immense expansion of financial markets, globalised financial markets, where a lot of speculation takes place, increasingly discipline investors and governments.

The development of global capital represents a new phase in the imperialist stage of capitalism. For what is occurring is the intensification of the exploitation of the labour of those subordinated and dominated countries within the world economy. In this sense, imperialism remains an expression of a relation of exploitation and oppression of oppressed nations, despite the important gain of political independence in the period of colonial liberation. But the content of this imperialism is no longer primarily based upon antagonistic and rival national monopoly capitals, but the forces of the TNCs. These new conditions are generally upheld by the role of the nation state.

Taken together, these developments amount to a qualitative change in the form of capitalism as a social system. The dictates of the global market economy drive the corporations, not the needs of any particular economy or country. The sheer concentration of economic power and its reach across national borders is unparalleled in the history of capitalism. The mega corporations and financial institutions now operate to an increasing extent independently of nation states and their governments. Governments do not have the power or the resources to prevent corporations moving their plants, offices, research facilities and call centres to other countries in search of lower labour costs. A financial system that owes no loyalties to central banks, even to the powerful Federal Reserve in America, can undermine currencies in a matter of hours. States are reduced to the role of enablers, promoting and implementing structures within their own borders that facilitate globalised capitalism.

The component parts of this economic and financial system operate in a self-related way, rather than as a result of some plan or strategy. They are justified by policies that have been labelled the Washington Consensus, or neo-liberalism, and have an agenda that includes trade liberalisation, competitive exchange rates, privatisation, deregulation and free movement of capital. But globalisation itself is not reducible to a policy of governments. Rather the policies are the reflection, ideologically, of a deeper reality – the imperatives of a corporate-led globalised economy. This reality of modern globalisation is greater than the sum of its parts and has a logic independent of the motives and actions of those who constitute its main actors.

This is not a secondary question. If modern globalisation were just a bad policy, a more rational approach based on better regulation, accountability and governance would do. In other words, it would be possible to alter this policy without the need for transforming revolutionary change. Instead, it is necessary to recognise that the forces of the globalised world economy are the basis for the actions of nation states. This does not mean that the state has become unimportant, without strategic or political significance. But it does establish the context and content of the

---

TNCs and the national interest

You cannot assume that all TNCs headquartered in the USA, or Japan, or any other country, somehow express a national interest. They do not: they primarily express the interests of those who own and control them.

Globalisation – Capitalism and its Alternatives, Leslie Sklair

nation state which is increasingly to facilitate the interests of global capital.

The crucial political question is to reject the illusory view that we can win over the existing nation state to act against global capital. As we show in the next chapter, any possibilities for using the existing state machine to extract reforms out of capitalism in practice no longer exist. This new situation reinforces the case for a strategic, revolutionary transformation of the state and property relations.

3 From welfare state to market state

"Perhaps the greatest threat to freedom and democracy in the world today comes from the formation of unholy alliances between government and business. This is not a new phenomenon. It used to be called fascism... The outward appearances of the democratic process are preserved, but the powers of the state are diverted to the benefit of private interests." George Soros, international financier

We are living through an ever-closer merging of the state, politics and economics into a sinister type of corporate rule, especially in Britain and the United States. This is one of the most significant qualitative outcomes of capitalist globalisation. Where once the state portrayed itself as an arbiter between classes and competing interests, it more and more speaks and acts for what it sees as the only game in town – the market economy and global corporations. A mounting authoritarianism, introduced under the cloak of the "war on terror", has swept away many democratic rights; representative government has been reduced to a sham. These developments have created an historic crisis of legitimacy of the current state system of rule in Britain and elsewhere. The state has, ironically, thereby made out a case for its own abolition and replacement.

The fact that the world economy is dominated by a decreasing number of transnational corporations (TNCs) is self-evident. Their brands and logos swamp every high street and they have an overwhelming impact on jobs and consumption. Less obvious are the means by which capitalism expresses itself politically. For capitalism not only has economic power – crucially it holds political power too through the state. Only this power is more disguised, is achieved indirectly and takes the form of an apparently democratic process open to all.

How we estimate the actual nature of the state is pivotal. How we act in future turns on whether we see the existing state as capitalist and an obstacle to a not-for-profit world or as a neutral body that will respond to pressure for change. Is the state an expression of popular will and support or a machine that enables capitalism to maintain its power and control over the working population? If it is the former, then reform is not only possible but preferable. If it is the latter, then revolutionary change is the only route to historical progress.

What the state does

The modern state evolved to carry out a number of functions that the emerging capitalist class could not by itself achieve. Although today the state has a relative autonomy and freedom of action, it nonetheless still performs this fundamental and historic role, as we shall show. Capitalists are a diverse class with competing interests which is one crucial reason why they cannot rule directly. So there is a division of labour within capitalism as a social system. The state first creates and then develops a framework without which the capitalist system of production cannot function.

In his preface to *A Contribution to the Critique of Political Economy*, Karl Marx explained the relationship between the "political superstructure" and the "economic structure" of society. He described how political relations arise on the base of economic foundations and ultimately reflected the interests of the dominant class in society:

> In the social production of their life, human beings enter into definite relations that are indispensable and independent of their will, relations of production which correspond to a definite stage of development of their material productive forces. The sum total of

these relations of production constitutes the economic structure of society, *the real foundation, on which rises a legal and political superstructure* [emphasis added] and to which correspond definite forms of social consciousness. The mode of production of material life conditions the social, political and intellectual life process in general. It is not the consciousness of human beings that determines their being, but, on the contrary, their social being that determines their consciousness.

The real foundations of the contemporary state are the relations of production between employers and their workers. Countless millions experience this most fundamental fact of social existence every day, in different working environments, in every country in the world. To live, we have to eat, clothe ourselves and find shelter. But the means for securing these basic needs are almost entirely within the power of those who own and control the forces and resources of production. So we sell our labour power in return for a wage in order to buy essential goods and services.

The state and its institutions – the "legal and political superstructure" – come into existence on the basis of and in response to these economic foundations and ultimately reflect in their operation the most powerful forces in society. The primary business of the contemporary state is to legitimise, justify, maintain and develop capitalism as a social system in whatever way it deems necessary. We are conditioned by our social existence under capitalism to think and act within a certain framework when it comes to economic and political questions. The state plays a key ideological role in conveying notions that, for example, capitalism is really all about "individual freedom" and "consumer choice", that the state governs in the "national interest", or that socialism "destroys initiative" while capitalism "promotes enterprise".

Established mainstream political parties, the mass media, employers, the education system and a multitude of civic organisations all lend support to the status quo. They help to obscure the real nature of political power. Appeals to the national interest and the like, are intended to mask the essence of the state and the fact that society is divided into classes with opposing interests. Other phrases you may have heard that perform the same role include: national unity, common interests, national interest, common good, in the interests of society, common goals, patriotic duty, freedom, consumer choice, social inclusion, enterprise society, competition, freedom of choice, public interest, British people, British public and the people.

Of course, there is a division of labour involved. Those who own and control the TNCs do not sit in parliament or directly command the armed forces, for example. Those tasks are left to professional politicians, civil servants, generals and others. Over time, specialists in ruling have come to dominate affairs and given the state a certain operational autonomy. In this way, the state, rather than serving society, stands above and aloof from the population and is insulated from popular pressures. This political alienation adds to the impression that the existing state system is independent, neutral, normal and, above all, irreplaceable. The overwhelming majority of the population have no direct control, access to or involvement in the running of the state. Occasionally we are consulted through a general or local election, or a referendum. We have the right to choose our rulers – but not the right to change the class that rules over us.

In Britain, the state is made up of governing bodies and institutions including the prime minister, the cabinet, the House of Commons, House of Lords, the civil service, government agencies, local government bodies, the monarchy and enforcing bodies such as the judiciary, police, intelligence agencies and the armed forces. The machinery of state rule exists independently of political parties and governments. Not for nothing are the heads of departments of state called "permanent secretaries". Governments come and go, but they remain in post, as do the generals, police chiefs and judges.

Members of MI5 and MI6, the secret spy agencies who form part of the Big Brother state, are not subject to redundancies like the rest of us and have official protection when they carry out their duties on behalf of the state, whether they are strictly legal or not. This is equally true of judges and soldiers. All these factors are designed to produce an automatic loyalty to the state, embodied in the government of the day. From time to time these relationships break down. Each branch of the state jealously guards its own territory and history and this can lead to conflict. Not all state employees show unflinching loyalty as strikes by civil servants and the occasional whistleblower show.

Only those civil servants who are essential to maintaining the status quo, plus the military, police and spy personnel, retain privileges of status, conditions of employment and pensions. This greater security and respect at work is the quid pro quo for their increasing co-option into the New Labour project and particularly into supporting repression. The mass of ordinary civil servants – those who deliver the services and benefits on which especially poor people rely – are now second class state employees. Many have been hived off into agencies and work in what are, in effect, call centres. They have as few rights as other workers and the government intends to cut 100,000 of their jobs.

One of the state's key functions is to maintain the degree of social and institutional stability necessary for production, commerce and trade. Thus the state is responsible for developing a legal framework that guarantees private property rights and contract law. Relations between social classes must not be allowed to get out of hand. After all, we must be persuaded to go to work day after day. In other words, the state regulates the terms and conditions of capital-labour relations and attempts to maintain the stability necessary for production.

The state also ensures the supply of new generations of trained and educated workers for the labour market.

The tendency to crisis inherent in the profit system also gives the state unavoidable tasks in dealing with the consequences of economic collapse. In addition, the state has the key role in maintaining a stable and recognised monetary system. This is absolutely indispensable for the production, circulation and exchange of goods and services that lies at the heart of the capitalist system of production. Another essential role that the state performs is the creation of mechanisms by which political support for the status quo of capitalism is reinforced. These include, for example, the parliamentary system of government based on universal franchise.

The capitalist state is certainly not synonymous with peace or democracy. Twice in the 20th century, inter-imperialist rivalry led to millions being sent to their deaths. At times, the system of parliamentary democracy has prevailed, within which there are conditional rights to organise, demonstrate, strike, and speak out. Sometimes the state is obliged to don its violent face, through the use of repressive para-military and state forces like the army and police. This was the case, for example, in Nazi Germany in the 1930s and Pinochet's Chile in the 1970s. In 1984, the Thatcher government deployed state forces on behalf of the publicly-owned National Coal Board and its plan to close pits. For a year, massed ranks of police were used to physically confront and attack striking miners, arresting hundreds of pickets and injuring many more. The union's assets were seized by the compliant courts as the Tory government made the struggle for jobs a defence of state political power. Behind the scenes, MI5, the internal spy agency, infiltrated the miners' union and staged provocations. Soldiers out of uniform were also used by the government.

The building of the modern state

The modern state, with its trappings of democracy and representation, is relatively new. In the last quarter of the 18th century, when capitalism in its industrial form began to emerge, the state in Britain was concerned mostly with collecting import duties and raising armies to fight wars against France and other rival nations. There were no departments of state in the modern sense with their huge bureaucracies and hundreds of thousands of civil servants. There was not even a semblance of parliamentary democracy. Few people had the vote and the land-owning aristocracy dominated the ranks of the MPs. Power and influence, including election to parliament, was gained more or less openly through bribery and corruption, as lampooned by the artist William Hogarth.

The French Revolution of 1789 inspired radical supporters in England to campaign for democratic reforms. In 1791, Tom Paine published *The Rights of Man*, which called for representative government. Part two of the book sold an estimated 200,000 copies in 1793 – the year Paine was driven into exile and his book banned. In the wake of the execution of the French king, Britain declared war on France and cracked down on opponents at home. Prime minister William Pitt suspended the ancient right of *habeas corpus*, which gave detained people the right to appear before a court; trade union activity was made illegal by the Combination Acts; new laws banned public gatherings and freedom of the press was restricted by the threat of seditious libel charges; national political organisations were made illegal. Many editors and writers went to prison.

Supporters of the French revolution became disillusioned that reform could proceed in a peaceful way in England. Organised around the London Corresponding Society, radicals won the support of artisan workers and talked of a revolutionary coup d'etat. They had support in the provinces and made links with leaders of the Irish rebellion. In 1794, perhaps as many as 150,000 demonstrated in Islington. In an appeal to King George III, the gathering declared: "Why, when we incessantly toil and labour, must we pine in misery and want?... Parliamentary Corruption... like a foaming whirlpool, swallows the fruit of all our labours." Three days later, a massive crowd jeered the King as he rode in procession to open parliament. Then in 1797, a large part of the British fleet mutinied and threatened to sail their ships to France. But the state eventually proved stronger than the fledgling movement and its leaders were arrested and jailed and some were later executed.

The wars against France lasted, with one interval, for 23 years. As soon as peace was declared, the radical movement gathered momentum. A rapid industrialisation had taken place during the war, leading to a growing working class in and around the towns of the north. Their demand for a reform of parliament was seen as the way to create fundamental social change and an end to their brutal exploitation by the new capitalist class. As E.P. Thompson writes in his epic *The Making of the English Working Class*: "Few reformers before 1839 [the Chartist movement's peak] engaged in serious preparations for insurrection; but fewer still were willing to disavow altogether the ultimate right of the people to resort to rebellion in the face of tyranny." The reformers demanded the right to vote, freedom of public meeting, freedom of the press and the right to political organisation.

Again the state struck back, this time with a vengeance that was to shock the whole country. *Habeas corpus* was suspended once more and radical leaders jailed. Demonstrations were banned. Then in August 1819, an estimated 100,000 workers assembled on St Peter's Fields, Manchester. They had drilled for weeks in preparation for the rally. They were cut down without warning by the local yeomanry and the cavalry. Eleven were killed and many hundreds wounded in the Peterloo Massacre.

It took until 1832 to achieve the first, limited reform of parliament. By then the radicals had taken fright of the growing working class movement. They made a deal with the government which enlarged the franchise – but only to include the middle-class property owners. In the end, the Tories were sufficiently frightened of a working class uprising – there had been one in France in 1831 – to pass the Bill proposed by the opposition. It was clear that workers wanted the vote for more reasons than just representation in parliament. John Doherty, a leader of Lancashire workers, and his supporters had argued that "universal suffrage means nothing more than a power given to every man to protect his own labour from being devoured by others". After the Bill was passed, the *Poor Man's Guardian*, recorded:

> The promoters of the Reform Bill projected it, not with a view to subvert, or even remodel our aristocratic institutions, but to consolidate them by a reinforcement of sub-aristocracy from the middle-classes... The only difference between the Whigs and the Tories is this – the Whigs would give the shadow to preserve the substance; the Tories would not give the shadow, because stupid as they are, the millions will not stop at shadows but proceed onwards to realities.

After this, workers built their own organisation, the Chartist movement, to fight for their right to vote. This produced petitions with millions of signatures and the largest demonstrations ever seen. Frustrated by their rejection, one wing of the movement advocated physical force and the overthrow of parliament. One of their leaders, George Harney, declared that in the event of the dissolution of parliament before the Charter could be presented, the people should "take their affairs into their own hands... let the people of each county, city and borough, wherever democracy hath reared its head" set about electing delegates "furnished with a bodyguard of sturdy sans-culottes" organised, varying "according to the strength of the democracy in the district". "What army", he asked, "could resist a million of armed men? ... Within a week not a despot's breath would pollute the air of England."

Although they did not achieve their immediate aims, the Chartists were a significant landmark in British social history as the first truly working class political movement. Workers in the towns had to wait until 1867 for the vote while rural workers only achieved it in 1884. Women were denied a voice until after World War I. So the modern state, with universal suffrage and democratic rights, is a relatively new phenomenon. Overall, these rights were conceded only grudgingly.

From the middle of the 19th century onwards, the state took on more and more activities and responsibilities designed to facilitate the capitalist system of production, which in a short period had swept all before it. Urbanisation was dramatic in its speed and size as the new working class rapidly filled the towns. Appalling living and working conditions that accompanied these changes eventually compelled the state to intervene. Cholera and other epidemics drove the development of a public health system. Rudimentary education, limits to the working day and factory regulations followed, under pressure both from progressive employers as well as workers. Income tax was reintroduced in 1853 to help finance these projects. These were still early days for the provision of services by the state, however. Public expenditure in 1853 was only £50 million a year and only double that amount by the end of the century.

Throughout the 19th century, the state increasingly assumed functions essential to the development of the system of private ownership, which capitalist firms on their own could not fulfil –

then or now. The state also responded to calls for a legal framework which reduced risks for investors. This led to the idea of share ownership and the concepts of the joint stock company and limited liability. The Companies Act 1862 transferred risk from a company's investors to its suppliers, creditors and customers. From now on, shareholders only had to worry about the value of their holdings in terms of stock market prices as their personal wealth was protected.

The creation of the British empire, which expanded rapidly between 1860 and 1880, was led by the state. India became a formal colony when the state took control of the crisis-ridden and corrupt East India Company. The state promoted the interests of its own national, capitalist class, providing them with markets in the shape of colonies. These were protected by the mightiest navy in the world and vast armies. A huge bureaucracy emerged to co-ordinate the military and civil aspects of empire.

Historically, these political and social changes were a great advance compared with feudal society, which had been based on despotic rule by an absolute monarch, landowners and the church. These major reforms also, importantly, helped to create and reinforce a definite view about the nature of the state which is still with us. The message was that capitalism offered democratic opportunities and that the state was the arena where reforms and changes could be made. Revolution was unnecessary because, it was later argued, parliamentary democracy could not only keep capitalism in check but was also a way to achieve socialism, or at least socialist-type policies. The state was presented not as an instrument for enforcing the rule of a particular class – which its history had showed it to be – but as an independent body that stood above classes. As Lenin said in 1919: "Without parliamentarism, without an electoral system this development of the working class [to identify its own interests] would have been impossible. That is why all these things have acquired such great importance in the eyes of broad masses of people. That is why a radical change seems so difficult."

When the trade unions and socialists formed the Labour Representation Committee (LRC) in 1900, as far as they were concerned the only way forward politically was working within and through the existing state. A circular issued by the LRC in 1903 called for support for trade union principles by "political methods". It added: "This new power of capital is already represented in parliament... It is fully alive to the fact that the great battles between capital and labour are to be fought out *on the floor and in the division lobbies of the House of Commons.*" [emphasis added]. Ramsay MacDonald, the first leader of what soon became known as the Labour Party, made clear from the start the strictly parliamentary character of the organisation's political aims. "Socialism marks the growth of society, not the uprising of a class," said MacDonald.

The state was depicted as a neutral body which could be bent to the wishes of the elected representatives of working people. MacDonald declared that "the modern state in the most civilised communities is democratic, and in spite of remaining anomalies and imperfections, if the mass of the ordinary people are agreed upon any policy neither electors, privileged peers nor reigning houses could stand in their way". Winning a Labour majority in parliament would, it was claimed, give workers through their representatives the only realistic opportunity of influencing capitalism in their favour. In a pamphlet published in 1905, MacDonald declared that there was no "profound gulf" between Liberalism and socialism, and that his party was the "hereditary heir of Liberalism", that is liberal forms of capitalism. This was a clear expression of the view that there were no irreconcilable differences in society and that compromise was not only necessary but desirable. The only real differences the left-wing of the party had were over the programme and policies. Few objected to working within the existing state. The "road to socialism", as set out, was parliamentary and evolutionary, and certainly not revolutionary.

Even as the Labour Party was growing, the real nature of state power was revealing itself in the Irish Home Rule crisis of 1914. The Liberal government's plans for limited Irish independence were thwarted by a revolt of the army in the province of Ulster, which was encouraged by the Tories. This proved that real power lay outside parliament.

A month before the revolt, the First World War had broken out. Seven years previously, in 1907, the Second International of socialist organisations, which included both Labour and the Independent Labour Party, had declared that, should imperialist war break out, members would fight to stop it. But, in the cold light of day, Labour MPs now endorsed a war waged for the division and redivision of the colonial spoils. The trade union leadership suspended all industrial action for the duration of the conflict. Their adherence to the state and its war machine helped send millions of workers to their needless deaths in the trenches of France and Belgium. The conflict sowed the seeds for a renewal of hostilities between capitalist states in 1939, which cost the lives of perhaps 40 million people.

From welfare state to market state

The crucial role of the Red Army in defeating Nazi Germany and the radicalised mood of the returning soldiers in Europe and the US, frightened international capital. After World War II, capitalism was desperate to find ways to avoid a return to the strife of the 1930s, with its civil unrest, mass unemployment, fascist/militaristic states in Germany, Italy, Spain and Japan and bloody imperialist war. In place of pre-war trade protectionism and deflation, the new world order was built on stable currencies tied to the dollar, strong levels of public spending, tight controls on capital flows and growth stimulated through international trade. These arrangements were made at a conference at Bretton Woods in the US in 1944. Different forms of what we know as the welfare state were created. In Britain, the state undertook to provide free health care and education, social security and affordable social housing.

The role of the state was central to the new strategy. It determined interest rates, controlled money supply, used taxation to increase or lower demand and attempted to maintain exchange rates with other currencies while maintaining high levels of public services. In Britain, many industries became state-owned, including steel, shipbuilding, mining, tele-communications, gas, water and electricity and transport. Most were nationalised in the immediate post-war period when British capitalism was bankrupt and could not sustain them.

For almost 30 years, the British state and others in the developed capitalist world sustained the role of mediator and moderator between competing class and economic interests. The state ensured that consensus and compromise prevailed and supported policies of full employment and welfare improvements under both Tory and Labour governments. Reforms were conceded while the essential basis of capitalism was preserved.

But by the early 1970s, the Bretton Woods arrangements were in a state of disintegration (see Chapter Two). In 1971, the United States broke the link between the dollar and gold because it could no longer honour the promise on the dollar bill to exchange paper for gold. As the international currency system collapsed, inflation became rampant and public spending was slashed. When oil-producing countries tripled their prices in 1973 to compensate for the falling value of the dollar in which the commodity was priced and traded, the post-war agreements finally collapsed. A three-day week in Britain was accompanied by strikes and industrial action by power station workers and miners. In the autumn of 1974, the Heath government fell after calling an election on the question: who rules Britain? The Tory government was not in control and had no answers to the crisis. The decade produced social conflict on a scale not seen since the 1920s, with both the Tory government led by Heath and the Labour government under Callaghan defeated by trade union actions. This marked the end of the period of post-war class compromise and culminated in a succession of deeply reactionary Thatcher governments in Britain and Reagan/Bush administrations in the United States.

The inability of the state at national level or international bodies like the International Monetary Fund (IMF) to crisis-manage the breakdown was evident and it stimulated a full-scale social revolt. Where the state once seemed all-powerful, it could no longer control interest or exchange rates, leading to higher imports and rapid inflation. As a result, stable public finances were undermined and the state proved it was no longer capable of maintaining social policies and public spending programmes needed to maintain consensus.

The collapse of the Bretton Woods system, together with the failure to answer the crisis by workers' unions and parties, helped trigger a process that has since come to be known as globalisation – the emergence of a global financial market and the rapid acceleration of internationalised production. Yet globalisation has not made the state as a machinery of rule irrelevant; capitalist globalisation is, in fact, encouraged and delivered through the state. What has taken place is a *transformation in the roles* played by the modern capitalist state. While the corporations have gained in power, influence and access, those who have looked to the state's institutions for representation have effectively been disenfranchised.

Politically, the corporations now act through governments such as New Labour and international bodies like the World Trade Organisation. Governments throughout the world have adapted and restructured the state apparatus, education and social policy to better fit the requirements of modern capitalism and particularly the knowledge-driven area of the economy. As a result, there has been a serious decline in the legitimacy and political authority of the state and its institutions, most notably in the US and Britain where globalisation is most advanced. Capitalist-led globalisation has, in effect, fatally weakened the very institution that was developed to take the political and social heat out of the system of private ownership for profit.

Governments now openly and enthusiastically advocate the free-market economy. As Simon Lee puts it in *The Political Economy of the Third Way*:

> The economic policies of the third way implemented by the Blair government have assumed that there are no insurmountable conflicts between New Labour's domestic modernisation agenda and the exigencies of globalisation. Indeed, New Labour has been almost messianic in the advocacy of the opportunities provided by liberalised markets and globalisation...

The international financier George Soros is, ironically, an opponent of free market capitalism because he believes it is destroying the social fabric of democracy. In *George Soros on*

Capitalism he says that the salient feature of globalisation is that it allows financial capital to move around freely: by contrast, the movement of people remains heavily regulated.

> Since capital is an essential ingredient of production, individual countries must compete to attract it; this inhibits their ability to tax and regulate it. Under the influence of globalisation the character of our economic and social arrangements has undergone a radical transformation. The ability of capital to go elsewhere undermines the ability of the state to exercise control over the economy. The globalisation of financial markets has rendered the welfare state that came into existence after World War II obsolete because the people who require a safety net cannot leave the country; but the capital the welfare state used to tax can.

According to the World Development Movement (WDM), ultimate control of significant parts of the UK services economy, including essential public services such as health and education, have been signed over to unelected trade lawyers at the World Trade Organisation (WTO) without any public or parliamentary debate. They came to this conclusion after studying the British government's commitments under the General Agreement on Trade in Services (GATS) – a far-reaching, but little understood free trade agreement.

The WDM reveals that the following sectors are partially or wholly already in the GATS net: health services, private education, rail maintenance, environmental (sewage and sanitation), retail, financial and banking services. Sectors currently being targeted in GATS negotiations for further opening to the free market include: postal services, broadcasting and communications, care homes, health care and education. Peter Hardstaff, Head of Policy at the WDM says:

> The extent of private provision and ability of the government to regulate the market in these areas is currently the subject of fierce public and parliamentary debate in the UK. GATS negotiations could bypass these debates by binding the UK to a set of effectively irreversible liberalisation rules at the WTO.

Hardstaff adds: "The government has made little attempt to inform the public or parliamentarians about the GATS agreement and has failed to produce research on the UK's existing commitments and the potential impact of future commitments. Since the UK signed up to GATS in 1994 it has not produced a single document fully explaining either what the UK is committed to or the implications of its commitments... Far from starting negotiations with a clean slate the UK has already made substantial commitments under GATS. The government is preparing to hand over much more without any real debate, by-passing MPs and without properly explaining the agreement or its effects to the public."

The WTO's powerful enforcement capacities effectively shift many decisions regarding public health and safety, and environmental and social concerns from democratically-elected domestic bodies to WTO tribunals. By creating a supranational court system that has the power to levy big fines on countries to force them to comply with its rulings, the WTO has essentially replaced national governments with an unaccountable, corporate-backed government. For many years, the European Union banned beef raised with artificial growth hormones. The WTO then ruled that this public health law is a barrier to trade and should be abolished. Since it was created, the WTO has ruled that every environmental policy it has reviewed is an illegal trade barrier that must be eliminated or changed. With one exception, the WTO also has ruled against every health or food safety law it has reviewed.

In his book *Globalisation and the Nation-State*, Philip Cerny points out that the provision of health and welfare benefits, education, employment policy and pensions "are under challenge everywhere in the face of international pressures for wage restraint and flexible working practices". He concludes that

> the distinction between "state" and "market" has not simply blurred; the goalposts have changed too. More than that, *both* state and economic institutions have been shown to consist of mixtures of hierarchical and market-like characteristics. In an era when markets, production structures and firms increasingly operate in the

context of a cross-border division of labour, can the state any longer remain a structure apart?

While the campaign group, the International Forum on Globalisation, notes in its proposals for an alternative to the present system:

> As social activists, we need to recognise that the world today is no longer effectively ruled by nation states, let alone democratically-elected governments. Instead, there has been a massive shift in power – out of the hands of nation states and governments and into the hands of transnational corporations during the final quarter of the 20th century... the prime role of governments is to reorganise their national economic, social, cultural, and political system for efficient transnational competition and profitable investment. In effect, we are living in a new age of globalisation that is characterised by forms of corporate rule.

New role of the state
- advancing interests of home-based TNCs
- creating conditions favourable for inward FDI
- technological intelligence gathering
- creates independent technology capacities
- promotes innovative capacities, technical competence and technical transfer
- creates institutions and structures that support an entrepreneurial climate
- promoting supranational national and regional innovation systems
- abandoning declining sectors
- promoting "sunrise" sectors.

The Future of the Capitalist State, Bob Jessop

Changing the face of the state

What is under construction now is a market state in place of the welfare state. The aim of the transformed state is to create the most favourable conditions for privatisation, deregulation, new trading blocks, the free movement of capital and flexibility of labour. Under the Thatcher and Major governments, great areas of state enterprise were denationalised and privatised. These included gas, water, electricity, telecommunications, steel, nuclear power, bus services, British Airways, coal and the national rail network.

New Labour picked up where the Tories left off by developing what are known as public private partnerships. First it was announced that the divide between public and private was dogma and no longer applied in the modern world. Then the state was reorganised to make private enterprise responsible for delivering public projects like schools and hospitals. By contrast with the welfare state period, the emphasis is on a partnership between the state and the corporate sector. In reality, this is a one-way relationship. The state hands out large sums to the private sector by way of contracts to the public sector.

The Blairites have given a gloss to this with a term borrowed from the lexicon of Thatcherism – the enabling state. The Tories used this concept to turn local authorities into milch-cows for the private sector. Councils enabled the private sector to make piles of money out of services formerly run by the local authority. The principle was established that councils "bought in" services from the private sector. In October 2002, Tony Blair in his speech to the party conference said: "Just as mass production has departed from industry, so the monolithic provision of services has to depart from the public sector. People want an individual service for them. They want government under them not over them. They want government to empower them, not control them... Out goes the Big State. In comes the Enabling State."

The big business beneficiaries of the enabling state cannot possibly lose. Returns on their investments are guaranteed by central government. When things go pear shaped, the state steps in and hands over buckets full of cash. The privatised railways are a prime example of this goodwill. Network Rail, which owns the track, has had an average of £5 billion a year in government guarantees and loans. The rail companies were getting about £1.5 billion a year from New Labour. That soared to £4 billion

---

Competing for patients

Private sector diagnostic and treatment centres are part of the introduction of a competitive commercial market into the NHS. The NHS will be obliged to compete for patients against a range of other providers.

UNISON believes that, far from leading to improvements, the marketisation of the NHS will have an adverse effect on NHS patients and will undermine core principles at the heart of the NHS. In particular, the new market will generate the following harmful effects:

▶ greater inequalities in patient care, as private providers cherry pick the most profitable patients and hospitals become winners or losers in the market

▶ reductions in the quality of NHS care, as private sector providers seek to drive down costs

▶ the erosion of the capacity of the NHS to continue providing certain services as work moves away to other providers

▶ higher costs, due to producer induced demand and private sector pressure for higher prices.

The NHS hospitals from which work is transferred will lose their routine cases, leaving them to deal with only more difficult and specialist cases. This will negatively affect these hospitals in a number of ways:

▶ there will be a reduction in overall volumes of work, leading to reduced funding and potentially causing staff redundancies

▶ the transfer of routine work will have a knock-on impact on hospitals' ability to undertake non-routine work and other activities such as research and training

▶ junior doctors in NHS hospitals from which work is transferred will no longer be able to develop their skills by undertaking routine cases

▶ the non-availability of routine cases will make it more difficult to maximise the use of operating time and resources.

UNISON www.unison.org.uk

---

in 2003-04. The sky's the limit when it comes to trying to prove that public ownership of the rail system is wrong and that partnership with the private sector is the only way.

By the end of 2003, there were more than 560 private finance initiative (PFI) deals worth more than £35 billion; over 500 were signed under the New Labour government. UNISON, the health union, reported that the private sector had penetrated around 35% of the total NHS market in "soft" contracts, covering such areas as catering, cleaning, security, reception and grounds maintenance, valued at £1.1 billion. Meanwhile, the cost of treating NHS patients in private hospitals was 40% more than it would have been in the health service, figures released by parliament's health select committee revealed. The NHS paid the private sector £100 million in 2002-03 for 60,000 operations that would have cost £70 million had they been performed in NHS hospitals. Private-sector financing is effectively a form of borrowing, not funding, that shifts the burden onto future generations. The public sector repays private companies which provide the infrastructure and services over 20 to 30 years. These payments include, of course, profit margins and dividends to shareholders. As repayments are spread over a long period, like mortgages, they cost much more than paying cash upfront.

Understating the cost

The Edinburgh Royal Infirmary sold the 70 acres of land released by concentrating facilities on a new greenfield site in Edinburgh for about £12m to a subsidiary of one of the PFI partners. The total capital cost of the hospital that has a 20-25% lower capacity is about £180m. A market price for the land would have paid one-third of the cost. But this in turn means that the real cost of the deal is about £240m. Most other deals involve similar arrangements that understate the total cost of PFI.

UNISON

Where there is no market, New Labour will create one as it is doing in higher education with variable top-up fees. This is done to make everything in society serve economic interests. Education is thus commercialised and turned into another commodity. As graduates start to earn, they have to pay back large parts of the cost of their education. This is effectively another blow struck at the post-war welfare state, replacing its emphasis on collective payment through taxation with "co-payment". Professor Allyson Pollock, head of health policy at University College, London, told *The Guardian* (11 February 2004):

> It is now government policy that it doesn't matter who provides the service as long as it is publicly funded. The result is that there is no area of the public sector, whether it be rail, postal services, healthcare, education or pensions, that has not been – or is being – broken up, commodified and privatised. Take long-term care as a prime example. In England and Wales this is no longer a right or a collective responsibility. Over the past 20 years the NHS has almost totally withdrawn from the provision of long-term care. It has closed beds and services, with the result that thousands of older people are paying for their healthcare needs where once they had been promised free care "from the cradle to the grave". The primary responsibility for the care of frail or sick older people and those with disabilities is largely left to the 5.7 million carers, of whom 800,000 provide unpaid care for 50 hours or more a week... it has turned the delivery of care over to private enterprise at an annual cost of more than £11.1 billion.

As the state has moved out of provision, it has increasingly attempted to co-opt the British penchant for charity to make alternative delivery of services for poor, older or disabled people, those who have turned to drugs or alcohol, been in jail or who are destitute asylum seekers. In 1991 there were around 98,000 general charities with a combined expenditure of £11.2 billion. By 2001-2, the number had soared to 153,000 with a total income of nearly £21 billion and a paid workforce of more almost 570,000. Bear in mind that these are backed up by more than three million volunteers. Most of the increase in financial resources came from government sources, which now accounts for 37% of their revenue.

Reinforcing poverty

When New Labour came to power in 1997, people were aware that previous decades had created growing inequalities. Blair's election success, after all, was a resounding rejection of 18 years

Housing – a case study

In the post-war period, the state was the main supplier of housing for those who could not afford to buy. Local authorities built millions of council homes and housing associations also produced low-rent accommodation. The new "market" state has wrecked all this. Under the Tories, tenants were encouraged to buy their council homes. Some 2,030,000 of the best homes were sold between 1980 and 2003, more than 220,000 under New Labour. Meanwhile, councils were banned from building new homes with responsibility passing to housing associations.

From 1988 they had to raise costly private finance to part fund new homes. As a result, rents soared to the point where only those on housing benefit could be accommodated. When New Labour came to power, they deepened what the Tories had started. Councils are still banned from building while grants to housing associations for new homes were cut. Just over 11,000 homes were built for rent by housing associations in England in 2003, a third of the level achieved by the Tories in 1993-04 and the lowest annual total of social homes constructed since the 1920s.

Shelter estimates that at least 89,000 new affordable homes for rent are needed each year to meet housing need. New Labour prefers instead to encourage people in need to buy, even if it is beyond their means. Rather than build new homes for nurses and teachers, for example, they handed out £600 million to help them raise a deposit on a mortgage. A shortage of new homes has helped fuel a boom in house prices. These tripled between 1997 and 2003, putting a first home out of the reach of all but the wealthiest.

The average price for a house in Britain in 2003 was £140,000, almost six times the average salary of nurses and firefighters. In London, the average price of a property stood at 8.8 times a nurse's average annual pay. Now New Labour is proposing to give public subsidy to private housebuilders in a further erosion of the welfare state. This was something the Tories thought about and dropped! Meanwhile, there were over 93,000 households in temporary accommodation in 2003. More than 130,000 households were accepted by councils to be in priority need, up 30,000 since 1997. In London and the South-East alone, there were in 2004 some 70,000 privately-owned homes that been empty for more than six months.

of Tory policies which had turned back many of the post-war gains of the working class, trade union movement and society as a whole. But New Labour's aim was to make Britain an attractive place to invest in. This meant keeping wages low, forcing people into work whatever the pay, and reducing access to benefits. People were told that the free-market economy would bring benefits for all. The brutal reality is that the poor remain poor and in many cases worse off, while the divide has become a yawning gap.

People at the bottom continue to rely almost entirely on state benefits in contrast to those on higher incomes. Disparity of incomes remains the order of the day. The welfare state has given way to mean-tested benefits. According to the British Social Attitudes Survey 2002, inequality fell in the 1970s, grew significantly between 1979 and 1992, fell during the recession of the early 1990s and then began to steadily climb from the mid-1990s. Official government statistics show that the gulf between the rich and the poor widened enormously. In 1986, 18% of Britain's wealth was owned by the top 1% of the population. By 2003, the richest 1% owned 23%. Excluding the value of property, they currently own 33% of the country's wealth.

Early in 2004 it was reported that the richest tenth of the population spends six times more in a week than the poorest. Those in the lowest income group spent £135 a week, £7,020 a year, while the wealthiest 10% spent £883 or almost £46,000 per year. The richest groups spent the same amount of money in a week as the worst-paid 10% of workers earned in a month. (*The Independent* 20 February 2004) The survey showed that the poorest devoted more than a third of their expenditure on the bare necessities: food, clothing, heating, light and rent, while the richest income bracket only need to use a quarter of their income for the basics.

One of the clearest indicators of poverty is the level of child poverty. In Britain the proportion of poor children increased from 14% to 31% from 1979 to 2001, only a little down from a peak of 33% in 1998-99. Six million children lived in poverty in the UK in the spring of 2003. This showed a fall of 200,000 over the previous year, mainly as a result of a tax credits and one-off payments. But, as *MediaLens*, which analyses TV and press, commented, "At best, government policy is akin to giving a sick child an inhaler to help her with her asthma, rather than tackling the root causes of the illness. At worst, it perpetuates a grievous and tragic system of social inequality." A coalition of charities, the End Child Poverty campaign, also accused the government of manipulating statistics to make it appear that child poverty had been reduced.

Children in poverty

▸ 54% of children in lone parent families are poor, compared with 22% of children in couple families

▸ 43% of children in families with a disabled adult are poor, compared with 27% of children in families with no disabled adults

▸ 27% of white children are poor, as are 36% of Indian children, 41% of Black Caribbean children, 47% of Black non-Caribbean children and 69% of Pakistani/Bangladeshi children.

TUC

The Office of National Statistics (ONS) reveals that well over half of pensioners are almost entirely reliant on the state pension, with couples sharing £300 or less per week. A report by the Trade Union Congress in March 2004 pointed out that "on average women's retirement income from all sources is only 53% of men's. Only 30% of women receive a private pension in their own right". The report added: "Women pensioners are particularly affected – single women pensioners are half as likely again to be poor as single male pensioners, and women pensioners in couples have the least financial independence of any group in society, with disposable individual incomes of just a third of those of a male in a pensioner couple". In addition, a separate investigation noted big differences among women in terms of ethnic origin and social background. Only 3% of Pakistani women had an occupational pension.

At the same time, the public is encouraged to make its own arrangements for retirement because the state either cannot or will not guarantee pensions. According to the government's own illustrations, workers on average earnings today can anticipate poverty in retirement. Their solution: postpone retirement! Or put another way, work until you drop. Meanwhile, hundreds of thousands of workers have suffered as company occupational pension schemes collapsed. Security in older age has become a significant victim of the market state.

Promoting the market

New Labour unashamedly promotes the alleged virtues of global capitalism. Patricia Hewitt, the Trade Secretary, told the CBI employers' organisation on 17 November 2003: "We are hearing siren voices in the US and Britain to pass laws against it [stop companies moving activities overseas] and who say: 'Don't put public contracts with companies that might decide to put some of their operations in India.' It is easy to see the benefit of jobs saved but more difficult to see the long-term cost to consumers and to business competitiveness."

At the same conference, Prime Minister Blair said: "We need to take the *partnership with business to new and deeper levels.* There are fundamental issues of public policy where we desperately need business to be engaged, telling us not just what the problems are, but the solutions as well." [emphasis added] He said he could not specifically support manufacturing. "What I can't do is shield you from the world economy." A TUC report published in July 2004 showed that government support for UK manufacturing was the lowest in Europe and that the UK had lost 750,000 manufacturing jobs since 1997, a quarter of these in high-tech industries.

Chancellor Gordon Brown is perhaps the most enthusiastic about the creation of an "enterprise" economy. In December 2003 he said in a speech: "And, mirroring America, that new consensus for enterprise should embrace not only commerce, finance and science, but all schools, all social groups and all local authorities. There should be no no-go areas and it should include even the poorest inner-city areas, where enterprise is the best solution to deprivation." He added: ""I want teachers able to communicate the virtues of entrepreneurship and wealth creation. And just as business tycoons have become the pop idols of the business world, I want our local business leaders to become role models for today's young."

An increasing proportion of state revenue comes from income tax paid by ordinary wage earners and value added tax, which is a tax on consumption. In 2003-04, total Inland Revenue income was projected at nearly £236 billion. Of this, £122 billion was income tax and only £31 billion corporation tax. Consumers paid another £66 billion in VAT.

Corporations are a law unto themselves when it comes to paying tax. They operate across borders and are able to disguise their profits by transactions within the firm. Of course, they also pay the smallest amounts of tax by registering in tiny countries that have few regulations. The average level of corporation tax in the world's 30 richest countries has been seen to plunge – from 37.5 per cent to 30.8 per cent between 1996 and 2003, according to a survey by accountants KPMG.

Nick Mathiason, writing in *The Observer* (29 June 2003) noted:

> Rupert Murdoch's main British holding firm, Newscorp Investments, paid no net corporation tax in the UK throughout the 1990s and it is highly likely, although unconfirmed, that it still does not. Sir Richard Branson's Virgin Group is based in the Caribbean, yet Virgin Rail has had £500m in public subsidy over the past year. A leading accountancy expert, Professor Prem Sikka, estimates that £25bn is lost to the Treasury each year through multinationals basing themselves in low-tax environments. "The precise figure is impossible to work out. Some say it could be as much as £80bn. We don't know because the Treasury refuses to undertake detailed research to get accurate estimates. It is dodging the issue."

Possibly the most serious tax avoidance technique is known as transfer pricing, a murky area where purchases and sales take place within the same company. Items are sold from high-tax environments to low ones, so the tax burden is dramatically reduced. A recent study estimated that the US Treasury lost $175 billion of tax revenues in this way between 1998 and 2001.

> **The untouchables**
>
> Money only goes where it is wanted, and only stays where it is well treated, and once you tie the world together with telecommunications and information, the ball game is over. For the first time in history the politicians of the world can't stop it.
>
> Walter Written, the former chairman of Citibank

Labour MP Austin Mitchell told Mathiason: "Around 60% of world trade takes place within multinationals, giving them enormous scope for fixing the prices of intra-company transfers. Armies of accountants are available to legitimise any phantasmagorical figure they can think of. Indeed, the big accountancy firms devise the schemes, audit them, then say the accounts are true and fair."

But with the New Labour government packed out with business advisers, there is no question of challenging the corporations. Instead, tax payers and consumers have to foot an increasing proportion of the tax bill. That is one reason why ministers are keen to keep consumers spending, even if it means ratcheting up enormous debts. Every sale brings in tax revenue in the shape of VAT.

We are all consumers now

The move towards a market state has brought with it an ideology that is unashamedly consumerist. In a speech to public sector workers in London in October 2001, Blair set out his four principles for public services: high standards; local diversity; flexible employment; choice of providers. "All four principles have one goal," he said, "to put the consumer first." In a pamphlet published in September 2002, he stressed that public services needed to change "to deliver in a modern, consumer-focused fashion". In public services, he wrote, "customer satisfaction has to become a culture, a way of life, not an 'added extra'." The Office of Public Services Reform (OPSR) was later created to concentrate explicitly on us as customers.

The language of New Labour mimics the principles of the consumer movement that were established more than 30 years ago. These stressed that consumers had to have equal access to goods and services. For New Labour, however, the emphasis is on *choice* and consumer *values*. The new ideology reduces society itself to competing "associations of consumers", with their different spending powers. So we are no longer passengers but *customers*. People who depend on care or welfare services are more often than not *clients*. There will soon be no patients in the National Health Service – just users. State officials become little more than purchasers in competing corporations, "buying in" services or creating public-private partnerships based on "best value". In all this, consumers replace producers as the "key interest group".

A study by Catherine Needham for the Catalyst Forum analyses how, first the Tories and then New Labour, introduced the notion of citizens as consumers in a bid to imitate the market and the private sector. In *Citizen-consumers: New Labour's marketplace democracy*, she writes that

> recent governments in the UK have been consumerising citizenship. Rather than exporting the political dimension of citizenship into consumer behaviour, they have sought to import consumer values into the government-citizen relationship. The effect has been to turn democracy into a marketplace, downgrading those elements of citizenship that presume a more collectivist and political linkage between individual and state.

Needham explains how New Labour has intensified trends developed under the Tories. "It has been evident in a style of communications which utilises marketing techniques borrowed from advertising to promote its messages, and an approach to consultation which emphasises market research and quantitative measures of customer satisfaction over more discursive and participatory methods. Presently it is most apparent in the area of public service reform, where, particularly since the 2001 election, New Labour has explicitly focussed on consumer choice and the responsiveness of services to their 'customers'."

She believes that this has "profound implications" for the relationship between government and citizen. It restricts citizens

---

On message with New Labour

Under New Labour, advertising and promotional techniques dominate government communications. The language of branding, key messages and targeting is commonplace. Soon after the 1997 election, Alastair Campbell, the prime minister's communications chief, sent a memo to the heads of information in all government departments requiring that the government's "four key messages" be "built into all areas of our activity". The ostensibly politically neutral Government Information Service (GIS) was reorganised to "improve co-ordination with and from the centre, so as to get across consistently the Government's key policy themes and messages". It was renamed the Government Information and Communication Service (GICS) to reinforce the change in attitude. In a few years, all the departmental heads of information had quit under pressure from New Labour. Commercial market research techniques like opinion polls, feedback forms and satisfaction surveys, are rife. Government spending on market research increased by 43% between 1998 and 2001, according to figures from the British Market Research Association.

---

to a "passive consumption of politics" and results in a situation where the "relationship between government and citizen is individualised and transactional". This, of course, is precisely what New Labour wants and is only a modern form of Thatcher's infamous statement that there is no such thing as society. Needham herself is not surprised that more and more people decline to vote and do not trust the government. "Citizens are given no reason to support and participate in public life beyond the desire to attain a package of benefits and services. They are being treated not as citizens, but as consumers."

Needham warns that New Labour's emphasis on consumer values presents government and the state "as a realm utterly detached from the individual, rather than a realm that the individual is a part of and an active participant in". What she then summarises is a useful description of what the "market state" aspires to, saying:

There is no room for ideology in a consumerised vision of

citizenship. There is no sense of a shared project on which consent for government depends. The consumerisation of citizenship damages not only the interests of service users and the community, but the very presumption of a political basis to democratic governance.

Singing from the same hymn sheet

The market state has to integrate all systems and processes within its structure so that they all sing from the same hymn sheet. This includes the civil service, government departments, regulators, quangos, local authorities, the police and secret intelligence services. They must all be imbued with advanced business techniques and see themselves as part of a new whole – the world of global capital. New Labour has devoted two governments to this project, not always with success, as a series of political crises over Iraq and other issues have demonstrated. Yet the logic is inescapable. The state and its agencies will subordinate themselves to the unifying force of global capitalism. There is no alternative, a phrase attributed to Thatcher, is the rallying cry of New Labour. Even areas formally outside of its control, like the voluntary sector, are subjected to the same imperatives.

For example, much of the work of the Department for Trade and Industry (DTI) is now turned over to promoting the virtues of the "knowledge economy". The modern globalised economy is largely knowledge-driven, in terms of the information in computer programs and databases used to develop products. A

Education an 'extractive' industry

Higher education is no longer simply an adornment to our national life – of immense value and prestige, but only to a small privileged minority. It is now a sector as important to our society and economy as the big 'extractive' industries of the past – and just as important to our nation's future in providing the raw material, in terms of skills and innovation, that individuals and whole industries will require to succeed.

Tony Blair, 14 January 2004

significant new role for the state is to create the conditions for the development of "knowledge workers" in the economy. Much of this is done through government funding of science and technology projects with the aim of promoting enterprise (see Chapter 6).

In a strategy document published in 2003, the DTI declared: "We will promote more effective transfer of knowledge by stimulating the push of ideas from universities and research institutions, the pull through of ideas by business and the sharing of ideas between businesses. We will increase our funding of science through the Research Councils by 10% each year – from £2 billion in 2002 to £3 billion in 2006 – to maintain the world-class performance of UK science. We will foster stronger links between scientific research and business innovation, doing more to encourage our academic community to help UK business."

The DTI said its "new business-focused technology strategy" would help business by providing some of the funding and "sharing some of the risk in taking new technologies to the market". In the area of raising workplace skills, the DTI will help firms to recruit and bring on people with the skills they need. "This in turn will help develop high performance workplaces. DTI will encourage business to make better use of innovative working practices, modern management techniques and good leadership, working in partnership with employees and their representatives." New Labour has created regional development agencies to speed up the work on the knowledge-driven economy and supported the extension of intellectual property rights to protect their private ownership.

In a paper called *The state and the contradictions of the knowledge-driven economy*, Professor Bob Jessop of Lancaster University, commented that in pursuing these kinds of policies

> states thereby get locked into the pursuit of technological rents on behalf of capital and this leads to the subordination of the totality of socio-economic fields to the accumulation process so that economic functions come to occupy the *dominant* place within the state. Other functions thereby tend to gain direct economic significance for economic growth and competitiveness and this

> tends in turn to politicise those formerly (or still formally) extra-economic domains that are now direct objects of state intervention.

Over the last 25 years, as the state moved away from direct economic activities – shifting from government intervention to governance, it created a series of regulators in various industries. Their role is to ensure that industries remain competitive in the world market. These range from the Office of Fair Trading, to the Financial Services Authority as well as regulatory bodies for energy and communications. While much of their propaganda is directed at how they work for consumers, in reality business interests come first. For example, the Competition Commission established in 1998 miraculously failed to find anything wrong with the way supermarkets operate. This is despite the fact that they regularly mark up prices way above what they pay to farmers.

There have been corresponding changes in the role of the central state apparatus, as well as parliament and Downing Street, particularly since New Labour came to office. Parliament's role has diminished still further towards vanishing point, while a presidential-style apparatus has developed around the prime minister. New Labour has politicised the civil service and introduced business-style techniques into the state machine itself. They have achieved this through a combination of special advisers who stand above the civil service; the widespread use of consultants; specially-appointed task forces; tight control of information flow and the creation of a number of special policy units based in the Cabinet Office and reporting directly to the prime minister. Between 1997 and 2000 there were more than 200 task forces, most of whose members were drawn from business.

In February 2004, Blair made a major speech on changing the civil service, where he stressed once more his belief in an "enabling government" to "help people to help themselves". He told his audience that despite its wealth, Britain faced insecurity because of the speed of change which made industries obsolete and tore communities apart. "Above all, the premium is on a country's ability to adapt. Adapt quickly and you prosper. Fail to do so and you decline."

So his message to the civil service was that it had to be transformed into one that was "capable of serving governments of any colour in the era of globalisation". Blair said: "We need a civil service which aims to amplify the implementation of successful change rather than, as sometimes in the past, act as a shock absorber in order to maintain the status quo... Government has to become an instrument of empowerment, quick to adapt to new times, working in partnership with others, to deliver clear outcomes so that the public sees a return on its investment through taxation. It has to go through exactly the same process of change as virtually every other functioning institution in Britain."

The civil service had to become "more entrepreneurial, to be more adventurous like their private sector counterparts". Prefiguring the massive job cuts announced later in the year, Blair explained how in the business sector the centre had become smaller and more strategic in order to "exploit the opportunities of the rapidly changing world". He added: "There are clear implications here for government. Many government departments have a function similar to those of a headquarters of a major business operation."

The politicisation of the civil service found its expression in an astonishing intervention in March 2004 by the Cabinet secretary Sir Anthony Turnbull, who is also head of the civil service. He took it upon himself to send former minister Clare Short a warning letter after she had revealed what everyone knows – that British spies bug the United Nations. Turnbull said he was "extremely disappointed" with Short's behaviour. One constitutional expert said he was surprised at Turnbull's action because he was merely the adviser on the ministerial code of behaviour. He told *The Guardian*: "The point of the code is that it is for the prime minister to decide whether it has been broken. Does this letter now mean that the Cabinet secretary has now become its enforcer?"

Meanwhile, the Joint Intelligence Committee – made up of civil servants under the chairman at the time, John Scarlett – duly delivered an embellished account of Iraq's alleged weapons of mass destruction (WMD). The infamous September 2002 dossier was enough to swing parliament to vote for the pre-emptive and illegal invasion. The Butler inquiry that reported in July 2004 found that the intelligence on which the government based its case for war was "deeply flawed". The notorious 45-minute claim about Iraq's alleged ability to launch WMD should never have gone into the dossier, said Butler. In language that only a former senior civil servant could deploy, Butler said that "more weight was placed on the intelligence than it could actually bear". No-one resigned of course and Scarlett was promoted to become head of MI6 – which was responsible for the intelligence in the first place.

When defence ministry scientist Dr David Kelly questioned the claims in the dossier in briefings with journalists, he was witch-hunted and driven to his death. Blair told the Hutton inquiry that Kelly had put the government in a quandary. Meetings were held involving the highest ministers and officials in the land without a

---

Politicising the civil service

But what many do not realise is that official reports are routinely politicised as far as is defensible. The extreme nature of the politicisation of the WMD dossier was a one-off, carried out because exposure was never contemplated – David Kelly's actions and the Hutton inquiry were inconceivable at the time. Most official reports, however, are based on evidence that is challengeable, and the degrees of defensible politicisation are much lower.

It has not always been thus. Before the 1980s, civil servants owed an immediate duty to the government of the day, but, as servants of the crown, they could retain some independence by advising in the national interest – a conveniently undefined concept. If ministers strayed too far from the national or public interest, they were admonished by a 'permanent secretary's letter'. Such a letter might have questioned why an attack on Iraq was being justified by the questionable WMD argument when many thought the real motivation was oil and a strong military presence.

John Chapman, former senior civil servant
The Guardian 1 March 2004

note being taken. The Cabinet secretary was absent from all crucial meetings. Key phone calls went unrecorded, which is against civil service rules. Over a two-week period, there were only three written records for up to 17 meetings a day as the state machine rolled into action against Kelly and the BBC. Hutton, of course, whitewashed the state cleaner than white and New Labour exacted its revenge by removing the chairman, the director-general and reporter Andrew Gilligan in the space of three days. Greg Dyke, the ex-director general, then revealed what pressure the BBC had been put under by the government. He revealed that Alastair Campbell had demanded the withdrawal from Baghdad of BBC reporters such as Rageh Omaar, claiming they were "compromised".

Campbell had sent letters to Richard Sambrook, the BBC's director of news, attacking the BBC's coverage of Iraq "week in and week out for a period last year", said Dyke. "It was a classic case of the Downing Street press office trying to intimidate the BBC," he told the *Sunday Times* (1 February 2004). In a letter to Blair on 21 March 2003, he displayed open defiance. Dyke wrote: "I do not mean to be rude, but having faced the biggest ever public demonstration in this country and the biggest ever backbench rebellion against a sitting government by its own supporters, would you not agree that your communications advisers are not best placed to advise whether or not the BBC has got the balance right between support and dissent?" Dyke went on to make a stout defence of what he saw as the BBC's duty to be impartial: "You have been engaged in a difficult battle fighting for your particular view of the world to be accepted and, quite understandably, you want that to be reported. We, however, have a different role in society. Our role in these circumstances is to try to give a balanced picture." What Dyke had missed, however, was the changed nature of the state, of which the BBC is a part.

The authoritarian state

The growth of the power of the prime minister has evolved into an effective presidency. This has made it much more difficult to present Britain as a functioning parliamentary democracy. In his

book *The Last Prime Minister*, the moderate Labour MP
Graham Allen, commented that the office was in effect an
unelected, unacknowledged presidency.

Blair is also seen by his colleagues in this way. "The Prime
Minister is operating as chief executive of various subsidiary
companies and you are called to account for yourself", Jack
Straw, told *The Times*. (25 September 2000) Allen described
concepts such as the "supremacy of parliament", "parliamentary
sovereignty" and "democratic accountability" as "comforting
myths which allow the executive to maintain its apparatus of
power without anyone noticing". The British parliament has "an
impotence" and an "irrelevance", he added for good measure.
The MP said that for

> almost 200 years the British Prime Ministership evolved and
> adapted in a way that no other political institution was able to, or
> allowed to… By the early part of the 20th century, this asymmetry
> was such that the executive, selected from the House of Commons,
> had become dominant, and was checked by nothing more
> substantial than its own self-control.

During this time, the legislature, which is the Commons and the
Lords, has evolved into a rubber stamp. This is seen in the way
that after an election, it is a royal summons that creates the prime
minister. The House of Commons is effectively the House of
Government. Out of 412 Labour MPs elected in 2001, 142 were
in the government and 113 on select committees because
Downing Street has allowed them to be. Allen says sorrowfully:
"The presidential quango has developed – without being directly
elected in a way which has effectively privatised political power

---

The death of Cabinet

Cabinet died years ago … It is now a matter of strong leadership at
the centre and creating structures and having people to do it. I
suppose we want to replace the Departmental Barons with a
Bonapartist system.

No.10 aide. *The Guardian*, 24 September 1999

Decisions made elsewhere

There is no glib solution to this trend [non-voting]... And the inevitable tendency of decision-making in the modern world to recede to European and even global forums makes political power appear even more remote to individual electors and even further beyond the practical influence of their votes… The problem is not that the British people have no opinion on the issues of the day but that more and more of them no longer feel ownership of their parliamentary democracy or believe that its political culture can solve the problems in their lives.

The Point of Departure, Robin Cook MP

---

beyond our publicly owned and representative institutions." As for the Cabinet, Allen describes it as "a relic of pre-presidential government".

A similar process has overtaken the Labour Party itself, with a decline of representative democracy that parallels the changes in the state. New Labour created national policy forums, where discussions grind on and no criticism ever gets through. It is not possible to refer back the forum reports when they come to the conference. The national executive committee, once a powerful body inside the party, now has little influence, while the role of the constituency parties has declined. The party conference, where policy decisions would be taken – and then ignored – no longer goes through the motions. Any unexpected defeat is shrugged off and ignored. New Labour's conference is now heavily sponsored by global corporations and directed towards impressing the media, particularly the Murdoch press. "Preferred speakers" are drawn up by the delegate support office and constituencies which had 10% of votes now have 50%. Membership has fallen sharply. Figures published in August 2004 showed that membership had halved since Blair became prime minister. Discounting lapsed members, the total stood at 190,000 – the lowest since Ramsay MacDonald split the party in 1931. This is a reflection of the fact that New Labour is not so much a political party as a managerial organisation in charge of the state.

While the state has given up economic and political powers to a variety of non-elected national, regional, international and global bodies, it has strengthened its power to oppress people at home and abroad. Although this was well under way before the September 11 attacks on the United States, the process has accelerated with the "war on terror". Philip Bobbitt, a noted academic and adviser on security questions to the Clinton administration, has written an analysis of the modern state, its origins and the question of war. What he calls the market state lacks the legitimacy and authority that the post-World War II nation states established. For him this means war, prolonged war at that, before humanity can create a new "society of market states". Gloomily he contends:

> The pattern of epochal wars and state formations, of peace congresses and international constitutions, has played out for five centuries to the end of the millennium just past. A new constitutional order – the market-state – is about to emerge. But if the pattern of earlier eras is to be repeated, then we await a new epochal war with state-shattering consequences.

Among those cited as architects of the new constitutional order are Clinton, Bush and Blair. Bobbitt adds: "The nation state is dying, but this only means that, as in the past, a new form is being born. This new form, the market state, will ultimately be defined by strategic threats that have made the nation state no longer viable. Different models of this form will contend. It is our task to devise means by which this competition can be maintained without its becoming fatal to the competitors."

Bobbitt acknowledges that as a consequence of global economic developments the state seems "less and less credible" as a means by which a "continuous improvement of its people can be achieved". The inability of the nation state to protect its own culture from globalisation is another key weakness. The result of all this, according to Bobbitt, is the "disintegration of the legitimacy of the nation state".

In perhaps his most sinister sentences, Bobbitt insists: "There is a widespread view that war is simply a pathology of the state, that healthy states will not fight wars… War, like law, sustains the state by giving it the means to carry out its purpose of protection, preservation and defence." He concludes: "If we wish to ensure the new states that emerge are market states rather than chronically violent nation states it may be that only war on a *very great scale* [emphasis added] could produce the necessary consensus. We should not exclude the democracies from idealistic ambitions that could lead to conflicts on such a scale." Bobbitt urges the use of the tactics of relentless air strikes, special forces teams and indigenous allies to deal with the threat posed by opponents of the market state. "Out of this epochal conflict can come, some day, the consensus that will provide the basis for a constitution for the society of the new form of the state."

This is what the invasion and occupation of Iraq was essentially all about. Iraq was outside of the new market state arrangements, while it possessed a large slice of the world's oil reserves without being able to finance their development. The regime change carried out by force of arms is intended to pave the way for the wholesale privatisation of the formerly state-run Iraqi economy. Global corporations have formed a US-approved queue to carry out major infrastructure work. The degeneration of the capitalist state at nation level is the impulse, therefore, for a relentless drive to war against the opponents of the market economy.

Meanwhile, in Britain, the state has taken powers to detain people without trial, while the police are able to intercept emails and mobile phone calls without warrants. New legislation allows the state to assume dictatorial powers under the guise of a terror alert. Jury trials have been curtailed and mass imprisonment introduced to deal with an increasing range of offences. CCTV surveillance is becoming ubiquitous and ID cards are on their way. Richard Thomas, the Information Commissioner who is responsible for data protection, expressed his concern at ID cards and two other Home Office population registration schemes. He told *The Times* (16 August 2004): "My anxiety is that we don't sleepwalk into a surveillance society where much information is collected about people, accessible to far more people shared across many more boundaries than British society would feel comfortable with."

New Labour has supported the illegal detention of its citizens without charge or trial in Guantanamo, with Straw declaring: "As a result [of their detention] valuable information has been gained which has helped to protect the international community from further al-Qaeda and terrorist attacks." Britain has its own Guantanamo at Belmarsh, south-east London. Here non-British nationals are held indefinitely, without charge or trial, on the say-so of the Home Secretary. The state has ridden roughshod over the rule of law and democratic rights (see Chapter 8). In 2003, there were 30,000 raids under terror laws, resulting in only 100 people being charged with terrorism offences.

As we have seen, the capitalist state is less and less democratic, more and more autocratic and authoritarian. The market economic forces unleashed by globalisation have transformed the way we live – from what we eat to how we are governed. We are living through a pronounced and irreversible shift away from parliamentary-based democratic forms of rule. The new market state is by its nature incompatible with previous forms of rule based on representative parliamentary democracy. An historic, qualitative change is taking place in the way that the state functions.

The loss of legitimacy that has resulted is clearly seen in the turn-out for general elections in all the major countries. In Britain, it has fallen from 82% in 1950 to 59% in 2001. The fall between the 1997 and 2001 elections was a remarkable 12%. Meanwhile, the proportion of people who "just about always" or "most of the time" trusted British governments fell from 39% in 1974 to 16% in 2000, according to the British Social Attitudes survey. That figure has undoubtedly fallen even further in the wake of the Hutton whitewash and the Iraq WMD fabrications. The proportion saying there was "not much" difference between Labour and the Tories rose from 24% in 1997 to 44% in 2001. Of the 18-24 age group, 61% voted in 1997 – falling to 43% in 2001. Figures for 25-34 were 68% and 55%. In a further report, the survey cautioned against assuming any revival in voting. "After all, many an analyst has suggested that globalisation has reduced the freedom of policy manoeuvre available to governments, and thus the ability of political parties to offer divergent political programmes."

In February 2002, the MORI opinion research organisation found that 73% of those questioned believed that politicians generally did not tell the truth. An in-depth survey in June 2003, found that half the public believe that the government distorts facts in its favour on issues like genetic testing, GM food and climate change. Only about one person in nine had confidence they do not. Only one in four believe the government acts in the "public interest". As to listening to public opinion, only 15% believe the government listened to opinion about radiation danger from mobile phones. Only one person in 10 thought the government provided them with all the information available on these issues, while two-thirds were laughing at the idea, MORI reported.

It is interesting to note that the Blair government has given people even more opportunities to vote, with the formation of the Scottish Parliament, Welsh Assembly, the Greater London Authority and planned regional assemblies in the north of England. This extension of the right to vote has, however, done nothing to inspire a belief in people that they are more represented, nor that they have more control of their affairs. The point today is not so much to have the opportunity to vote, but the opportunity to vote for something that will really change things.

In the formative days of industrial capitalism there were no democratic institutions to speak of. These were created in the 19th and 20th centuries under great pressure from the mass of the people. Now, in the 21st century, we have democracy as a shell, with parliaments that are of more significance to tourists than working people. The principle of representation that the Levellers fought for during the English Revolution of the mid-17th century and which reached its climax in the late 19th and early 20th centuries in Britain, has been eroded and undermined. This is the dialectic of the parliamentary democratic state, whose form has represented a political compromise between the employers and working people. Globalisation means that this arrangement can no longer work. The long period of parliamentary politics is giving way to a new, authoritarian state rule.

What we have can perhaps be termed an "unfinished democracy". In Britain, the dialectic of the struggle for the vote produced enfranchisement for the masses, many of whom saw the vote as a route to transforming society; today they are effectively disenfranchised. The Labour Party was formed to represent workers' interests in parliament, with the long-term hope of introducing socialist-type policies to mitigate and control the worst effects of capitalism through reforms.

The aim was the avoidance of open conflict with the ruling class. But globalised capital is not in the business of making concessions or promoting reforms. The forces of production and finance transcend borders and this is sufficient to undermine nationally-based reformist policies and programmes. This process has produced New Labour as the unashamed champion of the free-market economy and trade unions whose supine leadership has resulted in the loss of half of the TUC's membership inside a decade.

The state, even if it wanted to, cannot constrain or dictate to the corporations. It is also patently incapable of getting to grips with the growing ecological crisis (see Chapter 5). The state cannot defend its citizens against terrorism. Instead, Britain and the United States promote policies which intensify the very grievances that give rise to blind acts of terror in the first place. Shorn of legitimacy, the state resorts to the "war on terror" to bolster its rule, knowing that this kind of conflict against an abstract phenomenon can never be said to have ended.

The right to vote allowed for representation without power. Power with representation should be our new goal. How this can work is examined in Chapter 8.

4 All consuming culture

The content and meaning of culture is human life, its sustenance and reproduction and how humans relate to each other in complex social ways. Culture primarily embraces all the shared and inherited knowledge of human beings, as well as the practical forms of social interaction. But today, culture is cornered, more and more under the dominance of giant media corporations. We have seen a merging of communications and the media with culture itself. The same conglomerates own and control the media, plus the marketing and sale of cultural products. It is increasingly hard to distinguish between the medium and the message. These media empires are indifferent to the content of their products. What counts is how many customers they attract.

The scale of the penetration by profit-seeking companies into the most intimate and deepest human needs and aspirations is a phenomenon of globalisation. London School of Economics globalisation theorist David Held has noted:

> In the past, imperial states, networks of intellectuals and theocracies were the key agents of cultural diffusion. In the contemporary world, their role has been displaced by large media industries as well as by greater flows of individuals and groups. Multinational corporations are at the heart of these interconnected processes... Their cultural reach and power is historically unprecedented.

The corporate giants' drive to capture people's buying power, continually destroys the notion that any area of life is immune to, or safe from the reach of the global market. In their frenzy, they even ride roughshod over long established dogmas of moral and political control. Record companies, for example, promote ghetto culture such as gangsta rap.

David Bollier, an independent policy strategist, shocked by the loss of what he sees as America's most ancient heritage, describes today's transformation of socially-owned physical and intellectual property as "the enclosure of the commons". He likens it to the enclosure of the common lands in Britain during the rise of capitalism.

Bollier lists various types of "common wealth" which are being captured or given away to "market interests". Some of these areas, such as property, and natural ecosystems, are dealt with elsewhere in this book. But those created by human beings, individually and socially are the stuff of culture itself. They include, as he writes, "shared, inherited knowledge such as scientific research, historical knowledge and folk wisdom, all of which contribute to the public domain and cultural traditions and norms... These resources have no officially recognised value, let alone the legal definition and protection enjoyed by private property".

The fact is that the conversion of "human" values into "exchange values" has been going on ever since capitalism became the dominant economic and social system. What is new is the destruction of even those secular domains that were considered as special and private sides of life and society. They include notions of a natural childhood, collective and personal experiences, unspoilt nature, art, education and knowledge. These have had a relatively independent non-commercial life, as part of humanity's collective culture which was until now mostly free from commerce and industry. Today they are being swamped and overwhelmed by corporate ownership and control. In *The Big Picture: Understanding Media through Political Economy*, Robert McChesney and John Bellamy Foster comment:

All human needs, relationships and fears, the deepest recesses of the human psyche, become mere means for the expansion of the commodity universe under the force of modern marketing... the translation of human relations into commodity relations... has expanded exponentially.

The rise of the media conglomerates is bound up with and driven by the communications revolution of the last few decades, which has transformed culture globally. New technologies, like the Internet, mobile phones and downloadable music tap into basic needs and instincts in personal ways unthinkable only a few years ago. They enhance and extend the most basic qualities of human beings – our requirement to communicate socially.

The huge expansion of the sector has given a mass nature to a host of cultural products, many of which would have been available only to the few in the past. The number of people with access to the Internet grew by 365 million in 2003-04 An additional six percent of the world's population pushed the total who are connected to around 800 million.

Getting connected

Clickz.com, a web-tracking company, estimates that users will reach 1.1 billion by the year 2005. Britain, with over 35 million, had the fourth highest number of Internet users in the world in April 2004. Parallel to the Internet is the vast growth of mobile telephones. Worldwide unit sales reached over half a billion in 2003 and there were more than one billion subscribers by early 2004. Forecasters expect another 560 million units to be sold by the end of 2005. Chinese users sent some 15.6 billion short messages through their mobile phones during January 2004 alone, a rise of 91% over the same period last year.

The impact of being connected is changing social life irrevocably – affecting work, leisure, research, shopping, creativity and crime. Not only do people view websites and send emails, but three quarters of Internet users send digital pictures and videos, a quarter watch TV or video streams, while online banking grew 26% in 2003. This is just a glimpse of the speed of change affecting the relations between people which form the basis of all culture. The scale of the technical-information revolution was summarised by a UN Human Development Report: "In 2001, more information could be sent over a single cable in a second than was sent over the entire Internet for a month in 1997." But the same report also noted the drive behind the new technology: "Technology is created in response to market pressures, not the needs of poor people, who have little purchasing power."

The big few

Who controls, owns and determines the content which flows through the diverse high-speed channels? In the global music industry, for example, there are presently five major record label conglomerates, who control over 80% of all the titles produced in the United States and comparable percentages in the rest of the world. Warner Music, EMI Group, Universal Music Group (UMG), Bertelsmann Music Group (BMG) and Sony. These also own distribution companies that control over 80% of the wholesale market as well as having stakes in virtually all the other significant forms of media and cultural products. At the time of writing, Sony and Bertelsmann were awaiting the final EU clearance on a merger that would leave just four music industry giants. The EU initially charged the deal could lead to higher CD prices and less choice for music lovers, and could stifle the development of legal on-line music downloading. But it concluded after internal review that it did not have "sufficient evidence" of collusion or future harm to consumers.

The global film and television market in 2003 was worth around one trillion dollars, of which $63 billion was spent on filmed entertainment. But in the last decade, corporate globalisation has all but destroyed the diversity in world cinema:

‣ between 1992-98 US film distributors destroyed the popular film industry in Turkey where 200-300 films were made annually prior to 1992
‣ by the end of the 1980s, the thriving and innovative Brazilian cinema was destroyed
‣ Mexico dropped from producing 100 films per year to fewer than 10 by 1998

‣ Japan's internal market share shrunk to 37%
‣ in Europe, Hollywood films account for 80-90% of cinema, apart from France
‣ Indonesia dropped from 119 films in 1990 to 12 in 1992
‣ in Canada 95% of movie time is devoted to foreign (overwhelmingly US) films
‣ in 1986 there were 400 cinemas in Algeria. By the end of 2000 only ten were left
‣ African films are not distributed in Africa
‣ in the UK 90% of the market is dominated by five US companies and one UK distributor – with only 5 out of 20 films distributed by the UK company.

Arts Under Pressure, Joost Smiers

In Britain a Parliamentary inquiry into the film industry in 2003 heard submissions from all sectors in the film and television industry, including BECTU, the broadcasting workers' union, Phoenix Arts Centre in Leicester, the Animation Network, actor Tilda Swinton and UK film makers. What became clear was how globalisation had hit the British film industry over past years. BECTU's submission said:

> We face a continuing structural problem of a fragmented, production-led industry seeking to compete in a world market dominated by the distribution-led, integrated US film industry. The distribution process is overwhelmingly led by the US majors, with a strong interest in the production and marketing of Hollywood productions. The results are well documented. US films predominate in British cinemas and many British productions fail to achieve distribution even in the UK. Distributors, with a spread of risks and great control of rights simply do not face the crippling financial uncertainties that bedevil our indigenous, production-led industry.

The crisis in regional film theatres linked to the closure of the British Film Industry's regional programme unit was clearly acute, as a memorandum from the Phoenix Arts Centre made clear:

The regional Programme Unit and its tiny sister department, the Exhibition Development Unit (collectively known as *bfi* Cinema Services, employing a total of nine persons) is currently under a threat of closure determined by *bfi* senior management as part of a cost-cutting exercise. If this action is carried out the consequences are likely to be extremely grave for many specialised cinemas throughout the UK.

▸ access to certain titles will be extremely limited
▸ booking terms for smaller, independent cinemas are likely to rise
▸ the range of cultural product will narrow
▸ education about the moving image, past and present, will become increasingly problematic
▸ purely commercial programming will become the norm
▸ a truly national cinema culture operating outside London will be seriously damaged.

In her evidence to the Inquiry, Tilda Swinton pointed to the failure of the UK Film Council to promote cultural film making. She noted that £18m of the budget allocated to the English Arts Council – supposedly devoted to cultural funding – was used to equip Warner and UCI multiplexes with digital equipment! She said that smaller regional arts cinemas devoted to independent film making urgently needed government support as they were "perilously threatened by the development of multiplexes dominated by Hollywood studio product".

The destruction of independent film making over the past decades finds a parallel in the world of publishing:

▸ in the UK the top nine publishing groups control 60% of the market
▸ Latin American writers are now published by global conglomerates only
▸ in Mexico 400 publishing houses went bankrupt between 1989 and 2003. Fewer than 10 have survived
▸ in the UK independent bookshops are disappearing in the face of competition from giants like Waterstones (which belongs to the media part of HMV)

▸ Heinemann's *African Writers Series* is promoted with glossy catalogues while African publishers have only poor quality paper and flimsy covers

▸ only 17% of books and magazines in Canada are of Canadian origin.

Arts Under Pressure, Joost Smiers

Monopoly control of the world market is leading to fewer and fewer titles being published. The industry's trade journal *The Bookseller* reported that HarperCollins, Britain's fourth biggest publisher, planned to cut the number of its new titles each year by about 20% by 2006. Time Warner nearly halved its list between 2000-2004 and Pan Macmillan cut new titles by seven per cent in 2004.

Media ownership

Britain and the United States are undergoing a major consolidation of media ownership. Present corporate strategies could mean that there will be only three global media corporations by 2007. One of the three will be News Corporation, owned by Rupert Murdoch. The new Communications Act in Britain will allow Murdoch to buy up ITN news, which could leave Murdoch's Sky News as the only bidder for Channel 4 news. This would leave UK broadcast news as well as important sections of the print media, dominated by Murdoch's right-wing political influence. His support for Margaret Thatcher's union-busting regime was notorious and his stable of UK tabloids (including *The Sun*) supported New Labour's election campaign.

The Communications Act was intended to "to see market principles spread to all areas of public life" in the words of media-tracking specialist, Des Freedman. Freedman points to how Ofcom, the new super-regulator, has already signalled its intent to smooth the way for further liberalisation. One of its first decisions was to appoint Luke Johnson as the new chairman of Channel 4. He is a businessman with no experience of broadcasting apart from the fact that he made his money from owning the restaurants in which TV stars eat. What are his real qualifications? According to Freedman, quoting someone who knows Johnson: "'Luke's completely money-mad. There is not a scintilla of understanding of public service broadcasting in him. He does have a sort of glamour that comes from being rich and comparatively young' (*The Guardian*, 2 February 2004). Just the sort of man to deliver public service principles in a liberalised climate. Ofcom's light touch regulation is accompanied by the highly interventionist and politicised role of government in influencing both long-term policy and everyday media content."

The Communications Act 2003 runs to a total of 825 pages. Its sponsors, Media Secretary Tessa Jowell and Trade and Industry Secretary Patricia Hewitt, have said that its purpose is to make regulation "light-touch and unobtrusive". What this means is that the big companies will be much freer to own the different areas of mass media. In summary:

- no limitation on non-European Union companies owning ITV or Channel Five
- less control on cross-media ownership and cross-platform promotion
- less control on local radio broadcasting.

New Labour succeeded in getting parliament to pass the new legislation, despite some opposition from rebels led by Lord Puttnam. A much-vaunted public interest test was introduced, which will be totally under the control of the Secretary of State for Trade and Industry!

A parallel process is going on in the United States. One month before the British legislation was enacted, the US Federal Communications Commission (FCC) revised its limits for broadcast ownership. The FCC voted on 2 June 2003, to relax the rules governing media ownership. These changes, which affect everything from television to radio to newspapers, allow for a fundamental reshaping of US media structure at the local and the national level. The loosening of ownership restrictions brought a host of court cases from consumer and media activists and opposition on Capitol Hill itself during the latter half of 2003. In March 2004, the US Senate voted to bar the FCC from implementing its controversial media merger for a whole year.

Highly respected TV journalist Bill Moyers in a webcast discussion explained on the Public Broadcasting Service website (www.pbs.org) how the FCC is changing the rules for media ownership. "That revolution", he said referring to the changes in broadcasting, "has brought new technologies, like the Internet, cable and satellite television. But it has also brought on the greatest concentration of media ownership in American history. Now the FCC is considering dismantling the last rules that would prevent even more consolidation. That's exactly what the media giants have been lobbying for... In the name of economic efficiency." This extract from the discussion said it all:

Michael Copps, FCC Commissioner: If you take this to its logical conclusion, you could end up with a situation where one company owns the newspaper, the television station, the radio station and the cable system.

Moyers: Michael Copps is the lone Democrat on the FCC.

Copps: That may have some economic efficiencies attached to it, but I daresay it also has some profound democratic and social and political considerations that we ignore only at our own tremendous peril.

Moyers: But consolidation is the trend. In 1975 there were some 1500 owners of full-power TV stations and daily newspapers. By 2000, that number had dropped to about 625...

And remember the Telecommunications Act of 1996? It led to a wave of mergers. There are now 1,700 fewer owners of commercial radio stations – a one-third decline. Today, just a few players dominate. One conglomerate alone – Clear Channel – owns more than 1,200 stations and controls 11 percent of the market...

Yes, it's true: the typical cable consumer today receives about 60 channels. But those so-called "choices" are determined by a handful of corporate giants... companies like Viacom, AOL-Time Warner, Disney, and News Corp.

The World Trade Organisation (WTO) was instrumental in pushing through the new legislation. In 1996, a Regulatory Reference Paper signed by 55 countries was the signal for corporations and governments to steamroller through a global information technology structure. Lievrouw and Livingstone, in their *Handbook of New Media,* note: "High level government officials seized the opportunity to rely on its negotiations to dismantle domestic political opposition and to move forward with new market strategies that would otherwise be impossible to implement." As a result of the next agreement in 1997, the Basic Telecommunications Agreement, there was a rush to "wire up cities and the globe on an unprecedented scale". The global telecoms system grew from half a billion telephone subscribers in 1989 to an estimated 2 billion by 2000.

But, although the gap between the richer and less developed countries' access to telecommunications services narrowed, in some instances the difference between those who had access to information and those who did not grew even wider. Argentina, Brazil, China, Columbia, Korea, Singapore and South Africa were the chief countries accounting for the rise in telephone and Internet subscribers, but the rest of the developing world hardly got a look in, until China's Internet usage started to soar after 2001.

The fibre-optic cables laid across the Atlantic and Pacific oceans by the year 2002 terminated in networks concentrated in 150-200 cities worldwide. As major cities, corporate offices and residential suburbs in Europe and North America are wired up, entire swathes of the globe are being virtually eliminated from cyberspace. This is most observable with respect to Africa, where many countries have fewer than 0.5 telephone lines per 100 people. In those developing countries that have seen rapid growth in telephone and Internet use, such as Latin America, services are confined to 10% of the élite residing in only three cities – Sao Paulo, Rio de Janeiro and Belo Horizonte.

When the brand becomes the star

Looking at these sides of life, in Britain and elsewhere, we find that they are subject to a process of "McDonaldisation". No opportunity is lost to market global brands under the guise of culture. Children's films such as Disney's *Monsters, Inc* and AOL Time Warner's *Harry Potter and the Sorcerer's Stone* are seen as a competition between Pepsi and Coca Cola. Children's books have been full of branded objects and licensed characters for years, but from just being placed, products now take starring roles. One example is Simon and Schuster's *The Oreo* [US biscuit brand] *Cookie Counting Book*, which teaches children to count down from 10 cookies while, of course, reminding them and their hard-pressed parents of something nice to eat.

Ever-sensitive to future trends and concerns, companies like McDonald's are constantly looking for new areas to extend the reach of their brand. Its fast food has come under fire from anti-obesity campaigners. Fearing that some customers may switch their allegiance, the company has launched a range of children's clothing. McDonald's brand diversification is another example of "dark marketing" to bypass restrictive marketing legislation such as that which affected the tobacco industry. It is also another example of firms exploiting pester power – parents feeling under pressure from their children.

Product placement is becoming more and more prominent as people find ways of ignoring or switching off when commercial breaks take place on television. Coca Cola paid $25 million to have characters in a TV series "down Cokes in each episode" as well as paying another $25m to be a sponsor of a reality show. The producer of one reality TV show, *Survivor*, said that he saw it as much as a marketing vehicle as a television show.

The race is on to find ever new forms of advertising to overcome resistance to it. McChesney and Bellamy Foster reported one US advertising executive who reportedly said that "consumers are like roaches – you spray them and spray them and they get immune after a while". So advertisers are also turning to "indirect" marketing. Seinfield's advert for American Express included the line: "This isn't going to be interrupted with advertising because it *is* advertising." The distinction between commercials and editorial content vanishes – the advert is the story and the story is the advert.

Virtual advertising is now possible. Products may be placed a long time after shows are actually made. Advertising can be digitally inserted in televised football matches which are not seen by the spectators at the event. Product placement is now assessed at ten levels. The ultimate achievement is when a whole episode or even a book is written around the product. British author Fay Weldon's recent book *The Bulgari Connection* was named after the famous jewellery company. A top advertising magazine praised Steven Spielberg's film *Minority Report* for "starring Lexus and Nokia... while Pepsi's Aquafina and Reebok had supporting roles".

McChesney and Foster describe what they call "a massive and qualitative leap in a pre-existing commercialism" and say that

> advertising itself is far too narrow a concept to encompass the effects of the rampant commercialism that now confronts us. Much attention is devoted today to how marketing and public relations are effectively merging, as both swallow up and direct the entire culture. In this sense the commercial tidal wave is interchangeable with a broader media torrent, or blizzard, that overwhelms our senses. The culture it generates tends to be more de-politicised, garish, and vulgar than what it has replaced.

Few arts bodies can survive without the ubiquitous sponsorship. The withdrawal of state subsidies over the last 20 years has forced theatres, orchestras, museums and others to go cap in hand to business and wealthy individuals in order to survive.

Targeting children

▶ children are bombarded with advertisements for junk food at the rate of 1,150 TV commercials a day

▶ the average child watches 20,000 adverts a year on children's television

▶ among food commercials, 95 per cent are for products high in fat, sugar and salt

▶ 48 per cent of schools now have vending machines, largely selling crisps and sweets

▶ in 2003 McDonald's spent £32.5 million on television advertisements, while Coca Cola spent £13 million and Pringles £7 million.

Daily Telegraph, 1 June 2004

Business sponsorship in 2002-03 rose to £120m, compared with £600,000 in 1976, according to a report by *Arts & Business*. Some 1,160 organisations received money from the private sector. The Royal Bank of Scotland, for example, sponsors arts projects and the bank's website explains the motives: "Sponsorship is a commercial, rather than a philanthropic activity, and must achieve goals which benefit the Bank. Corporate objectives aimed at raising our profile to target audiences form the basis of the decision-making process in considering what to sponsor."

Chin-Tao Wu, in her excellent book, *Privatising culture: Corporate Art Intervention since the 1980s*, describes the enormous pressure put on recipients by sponsors. Press officers are reduced to begging journalists to mention sponsors when they review an exhibition, for example. She believes:

> When government 'cosies up' to big business in the name of the people, or when multinationals dress up their commercial self-interest in the name of culture, it is ultimately left to the people to show how far they are willing to tolerate the unchecked power of big business. When other democratic means are ineffective, it is the people who alone have the collective power to resist.

Sport is big business

The commercialisation of sport over the last 25 years has known no bounds. Fuelled by TV money, football and the Olympics in particular have become big business. Clubs like Manchester United, Chelsea and Arsenal are now publicly-quoted companies on the stock market. Transfer deals have to be reported to the market first because it will affect share prices. Financial services group Deloitte & Touche estimate that European clubs and federations now generate more than £7 billion of income each season. Commercial activities like the sale of replica shirts is as big a part of the business as actually playing matches.

A handful of the richest clubs have cornered the transfer market, enabling them to buy any player they want and dominate the national leagues. Clubs themselves are bought and sold like any other company. Ramon Abramovich, who ripped

off the assets of the former Soviet Union, was able to buy Chelsea
and then spend £200m on players in under two years. Since
1992, when the top clubs were allowed to break away and
negotiate TV rights on their own, admission charges have gone
up 300%. Football attendance, previously the domain of
ordinary working people, is now dominated by the reasonably
well-off because of the expense involved. Those without work or
on low pay find it difficult to pay for a Premier League match.
Meanwhile, the game in the lower divisions lurches from crisis to
crisis. The playing fields where Premier League clubs find their
talent and on which the vast majority play the game, are often in
a state of disrepair. Many grounds have been sold to become out-
of-town shopping centres.

With the game literally awash with money, many star players
have succumbed to the pressures associated with huge wages and
celebrity status. In demand they certainly are. Television
audiences figures for the Euro 2004 tournament were so huge
that 30 seconds of airtime on a commercial break were being
sold for around £200,000. David Beckham is thought to have
received £16m from his endorsements in 2003-4, twice as much
as Real Madrid actually paid him. As for the tournament, most
of the top players seemed either too tired or disinterested to
make a telling contribution. It could have been the ball that was
to blame, of course. Adidas came up with a new match ball. The
silver and blue sphere was likened to a "beach ball" by Spanish
star Ivan Helguera.

The biggest money-spinner of them all, of course, is the
Olympic Games. From their humble beginnings at the end of the
19th century, the modern Games have become very big business
indeed. Television rights for the 2010 winter and 2012 summer
events are being negotiated by the International Olympic
Committee, who said they were confident of getting more than
$3 billion from TV companies world wide. The IOC works
closely with transnational corporations in sponsorship deals and
sells the famous five ring Olympic symbol to the highest bidders.
As for the IOC, its members enjoy a lavish lifestyle and have been
known to take bribes in order to vote for a bidding city. As
athletics and other sport has become highly commercialised, so

too have the pressures on the participants. Drug taking is rife in athletics, and many stars had to pull out of Athens when they were caught taking banned substances. There is no doubt that for many, rampant commercialism has devalued the meaning of sport.

The blurring of distinctions

Decisions by TV executives has led to a coarsening and dumbing down of programmes. Viewers are categorised into cultural élites and a popular mass. Audience size is the sole goal, both for the state-owned BBC and its commercial rivals. Telephone voting linked to reality TV has made fortunes for production companies. *Big Brother* votes brought in £3m in the 2002 series and the makers could charge premium rates for advertising during the show. In addition, live webcast of the *Big Brother* house made the show's website a runaway success throughout Europe. In the summer of 2004 there were an estimated 70 reality and lifestyle programmes a week on TV. In the opinion of the *Daily Telegraph's* Alice Thomson (6 August 2004): "Most are couched as real-life learning experiences, professing to help turn their subjects into happier people, when all they are really doing is exploiting their misery – shaming, chastening and humbling them in front of an audience of millions."

Some *Big Brother* "housemates" exposed how they were strictly controlled during the making of the 2002 series. One participant, Josh Rafter, said even after he was voted off the programme, his movements were still monitored by security guards. He and others were made to fit into character slots which were quite alien to their real personalities. He said that participation had wreaked havoc with his emotions, warning other celebrity hopefuls that they could suffer psychological damage.

Speaking for the British Association for Counselling and Psychotherapy (BACP), Philip Hodson accused TV companies of "playing God" with the lives of people: "It's a huge responsibility to subject people to enormous expectations and then suddenly to huge disappointment." One BBC programme, *The Experiment*, had to be stopped after six days when the students drafted in to be "guards" in a "prison" experiment started behaving sadistically towards their wards. In the US, complaints were made against a money-spinning programme in which homeless people and tramps were filmed punching each other.

BBC Radio 4 presenter John Humphrys has denounced the damaging effects of reality TV, saying "it turns human beings into freaks for us to gawp at". At the 2004 Edinburgh media festival he spoke of "a battle between people who are concerned about society and those whose interest is simply to make programmes that make money. Those who fought for the word fuck in Lady Chatterley didn't do it to make money. Now the cash registers go ker-ching every time there's a fumble beneath the bed sheets".

The blurring of distinctions which we've seen in the world of broadcasting is affecting what has been known as fine art. Ever since the Pop Art of the 1960s, the cross-over between product marketing and art has become a big area for artists to explore. Andy Warhol was a pioneer in this field, with his glamorisation of Campbell's baked bean cans, along with Jasper Johns and many others. There was of course an ironic, deconstructionist streak in Pop Art, which both celebrated and parodied the American consumerist dream.

In Britain during the late 1990s, there was a new, extreme phase, with the unashamed marketing and hyping of artists by dealers and critics. Creative productions of any kind do need to be discussed and interpreted, and exchanged in a free, uncensored market. But what has become predominant, is the purely commercial aspect and the rise of art-media empires and super stars artists who thrive on shock-techniques, kitsch, commercialism and fakery.

Just as the distinction between advertising and reporting is now blurred in newspapers and magazines, the difference between "art" and "commerce" is increasingly impossible to define. British artists of the 1990s such as Damien Hirst and Glenn Brown have unashamedly copied the work of other designers and artists without giving them recognition. Only litigation, or the threat of it, brought the original creators to wider recognition. In one case, Hirst was forced to compensate a medical model constructor. In another, Brown used an exact reproduction from a paper-back cover by Anthony Roberts.

The Saatchi phenomenon in Britain is indicative of the seamless fusion of commercialism and art. Millionaire collector Charles Saatchi's buying up of a budding artist's work immediately endows it with a huge market value. The endorsement by big money seemed almost fetishistically to endow objects with artistic or cultural merit. Saatchi, ably assisted by dealers like Jay Jopling, became the arbiter of (supposed) artistic value and success for a whole generation of artists.

The mechanism by which Saatchi's patronage produces grossly inflated prices was exposed in an investigation by Anthony Barnes in the *Independent on Sunday* (21 March 2004), who wrote: "Patronage from the former advertising guru [who orchestrated the Tory party media campaign which brought Prime Minister Margaret Thatcher to power] can boost the value of an artist's work. The figures show the sums Mr Saatchi first paid for a number of then fledgling artists – and what their work goes for now. It shows as much as an 80-fold rise in value."

The 2004 Turner Prize winner, ceramicist Grayson Perry, sold a range of pots to Saatchi in 2000 for £4,000 to £6,000 each. They are now worth around £38,000 each. Ron Mueck, whose crouching boy figure was in the Millennium Dome, famously made a wax effigy of his dead father for the Sensation exhibition at the Royal Academy in 1997. Mueck sold his first work to Saatchi for £3,000. His new works now go for as much as £250,000.

Unravelling the purely commercial from the artistic seems to be more and more difficult.

At a recent "Becks Futures" show at the Institute of Contemporary Art, for example, a young artist decided to make censorship of her own work into her submission. She exhibited a framed agreement that she was banned from showing her artwork by the sponsors, Becks beer, who demonstrated their open-mindedness by allowing her to do this. She was happy to accept prize money at the same time, saying she needed it to survive.

But blaming artists for all this is like holding the messenger responsible for the message. The gross commercialisation of the art world is simply a true reflection of what is going on in society at large. In fact, some of the most successful British artists have themselves made criticisms of the commercialisation of the Saatchi and Tate Modern galleries. Jake Chapman has spoken of the "de-skilling" of serious, discursive art.

As design critic David Thompson put it in *The Guardian* (5 April 2004): "Fine art is faced with a very real problem presented by a rapidly evolving technological world, which means, in effect, a rapidly changing commercial world. What actually distinguishes 'fine' art from the advertising techniques that it parodies and appropriates?"

5 Simply not natural

We are part of nature ourselves and ought to have a respectful, mutual relationship with the world around us. After all, we could not survive without food, water and sunlight, or build shelter and clothe ourselves without a continuing dialogue between human beings and nature. In reality, however, our existence within nature is grossly distorted and one-sided. The way in which production is carried out erects barriers to a mutually beneficial relationship.

Alienation from our own nature has taken place over a lengthy period. Britain is a classic example of this experience. From the 17th century onwards, common land was enclosed by big land owners. Small farmers, who lost their grazing rights, had to join the swelling numbers of landless labourers in the towns. They were to become the first free workers – freed from the land, that is, to sell their labour power to the owners of the new factories. They were then further alienated by losing all control over what they produced, and over the process of production – the creative activity that defines what it means to be human. This social estrangement remains the condition of our social being and social consciousness today.

During the same period, the Earth's natural resources, raw materials and minerals, were declared privately owned and ripe for exploitation. In the 19th century this took the form of colonial expropriation of entire countries and continents. At home, coal deposits were declared private. Money had deprived the world of humanity and nature of real value. From then on, nature, including humanity, was viewed primarily as a collection of potential commodities from which profit could be made.

After the Russian Revolution of 1917, a holistic view of nature and society was encouraged by the government. But as the country's economic and political isolation grew, this approach was gradually abandoned. The Stalinist bureaucracy which seized power and ended democratic discussion, imposed arbitrary planning targets. These were delivered – but at a great cost to people's lives, to scientific inquiry and to the ecosystems of vast areas of the Soviet Union. The current, rapid industrialisation of China is having a similarly devastating impact.

The last quarter of a century has marked a dramatic extension and deepening of capitalism's penetration of nature for the purpose of profit making and taking. The technique of genetic modification, first achieved in 1973, is the basis for an entirely new area of exploitation of nature. This knowledge is being privatised through patents on genes and the processes used in their discovery, re-engineering and production. The mapping of the human genome paves the way, potentially, for the wholesale alteration of the human species by corporations. As Jeremy Rifkin says in *Biotech Century*:

> Imagine the wholesale transfer of genes between totally unrelated species and across all biological boundaries – plant, animal and human – creating thousands of novel life forms in a brief moment of evolutionary time. Then, with clonal propagation, mass-producing countless replicas of these new creations, releasing them into the biosphere to propagate, mutate, proliferate, and migrate, colonising the land, water, and air. This is, in fact, the great scientific and commercial experiment underway…

The unbridled abuse of nature, viewed crudely as an economic resource, has had dire consequences in the period of capitalist globalisation. Millions of poor people have been driven off their land, whole areas of agricultural land are damaged, rain forests are destroyed by global logging companies, and ecological ruination is visited on areas like the oil region of Nigeria. Climate change, reinforced by the most intensive period of production in the history of the planet, poses many dangers. Nature's once common resources are exploited to destruction, for one short-term purpose: profit.

Climate change is here

The "greenhouse effect" refers to the natural phenomenon that keeps the Earth in a temperature range that allows life to flourish. The sun's enormous energy warms the Earth's surface and its atmosphere. As this energy radiates back toward space as heat, a portion is absorbed by a delicate balance of heat-trapping gases in the atmosphere – among them carbon dioxide and methane – which creates an insulating layer. With the temperature control of the greenhouse effect, the Earth has an average surface temperature of 59°F (15°C). Without it, the average surface temperature would be 0°F (-18°C), a temperature so low that the Earth would be frozen and could not sustain life. Global warming is the result of the rise in the Earth's temperature resulting from an increase in heat-trapping gases in the atmosphere. The more carbon dioxide, methane and other greenhouse gases produced by agriculture, industry and transport, the greater the risk of the Earth heating up.

The evidence that human-induced global warming is real is increasingly clear and compelling:

▶ since the beginning of the 20th century, the mean surface temperature of the earth has increased by about 0.6°C
▶ warming in the 20th century is greater than at any time during the past 400-600 years
▶ seven of the ten warmest years in the 20th century occurred in the 1990s, with 1998 the hottest year on record.

In addition, changes in the natural environment support the evidence from temperature records:

▶ mountain glaciers the world over are receding
▶ the Arctic ice pack has lost about 40% of its thickness over

the past four decades
▸ the global sea level is rising about three times faster over the past 100 years compared to the previous 3,000 years
▸ there are a growing number of studies that show plants and animals changing their range and behaviour in response to shifts in climate.

In 1988, the United Nations Environment Programme and the World Meteorological Organisation set up the Inter-governmental Panel on Climate Change (IPCC) to examine the most current scientific information on global warming and climate change. More than 2,500 of the world's leading climate scientists, economists, and risk experts contributed to the panel's most recent report, *Climate Change 2001: The Third Assessment Report.* The IPCC concluded that "an increasing body of observations gives a collective picture of a warming world and other changes in the climate system".

In this century, it says, we can expect temperatures to increase by as much as 6°C. Warming oceans will expand, raising sea levels round the world. Some 50 million people a year already have to deal with flooding caused by storm surges. If the sea rises by half a metre, this number could double. A metre rise would inundate 1% of Egypt's land, 6% of the Netherlands and 17.5% of Bangladesh. Only 20% of the Marshall Islands would be left above water.

Scientists agree that cuts of at least 60% in carbon dioxide emissions, and in some areas up to 90%, are needed to halt climate change. Yet the Kyoto Protocol, which the US – the world's largest polluter – has refused to ratify, aimed only to reduce industrialised countries' emissions by just over 5% below 1990s' levels by between 2008 and 2012. Realistic new assessments suggest it will achieve cuts of only between 1% and 2%.

More than 150 nations signed Kyoto back in December 1997. But they left much of the detail about how it would be implemented to future talks, which have floundered. The Kyoto talks agreed that countries could meet some targets by encouraging the natural environment to soak up more CO_2

rather than by cutting emissions. Eventually, a carbon trading market emerged where emissions can be bought and sold. The madness of capitalism! Meanwhile, official figures show that CO_2 emissions in Britain actually rose between 1-2% in 2003, leading Sir David King, the government's chief scientific adviser, to warn in the journal *Science* (January 2004) that climate change was more serious than terrorism. "The Bush administration's strategy relies largely on market-based incentives and voluntary action... But the market cannot decide that mitigation is necessary, nor can it establish the basic international framework in which all actors can take their place."

Climate changes take their heaviest toll on poor nations, which have contributed relatively little to the problem in the past century. "African countries are expected to be the hardest hit by climate change because they have the least resources to adapt,"

Carbon trading takes off

In June 2004, a peculiar type of trade fair was held in Cologne. Urging attendance, the organisers said: "This emerging carbon market is potentially very substantial and provides business development opportunities for market intermediaries and service providers such as brokers, traders, auditing and certification entities, consultants, and law firms." Following the failure to implement Kyoto, a market developed whereby companies could buy and sell carbon credits, which are rights to emit greenhouse gases. This bizarre market mechanism has, of course, failed to tackle global warming but has made a lot of people a great deal of money. The Cologne conference was sponsored by the World Bank and the International Emissions Trading Association, which has 80 members around the world. Admission for the three-day conference was □980 + VAT. Carbon trading rose to 70 million tonnes in 2003, up from 30 million in 2002 and 13 million in 2001, according to the World Bank's *State of the Carbon Market 2003* report. Jorund Buen of Point Carbon projects an even bigger market. "The market is still in an early phase, and Point Carbon's best estimate would be that the value of contracts will increase towards 10 billion dollars in 2007."

says Brett Orlando, a climate expert at the World Conservation Union (IUCN). "The difference between impacts on developing and industrialised countries is categorical. In industrialised countries one speaks of loss of property and income, whereas in developing countries one speaks of loss of life and livelihood."

A report from scientists at the University of East Anglia concluded that current trends of droughts in Southern Africa are most likely linked to climate change. While occasional droughts are common in the region, the scientists found that the last 20 years "have seen a trend towards reduced rainfall", as well as an increase in the number of serious droughts – two or three during the early 1990s alone. "The decade 1986-95, as well as being the warmest this century, has also been the driest," according to *Climate Change and Southern Africa*.

The World Health Organisation (WHO) says that climate change is responsible for 2.4% of all cases of diarrhoea

---

Ice cover retreats

A NASA satellite survey of the Arctic has revealed just how rapidly the region is warming. The overall trend of rising temperature over the past 20 years is eight times higher than that recorded by ground measurements over the past century. The data also shows that summer sea ice cover is continuing its retreat. "Climate is changing, the Arctic is changing rapidly, and it has significant effects on lower latitudes," says Mark Serreze, of the University of Colorado in Boulder. The analysis of Arctic surface temperatures was conducted by Josefino Comiso, of the NASA Goddard Space Flight Centre in Maryland and reported in the *Journal of Climate*. His data show that sea-ice temperatures during the summer – the most critical season for ice cover – increased 1.22°C per decade. Although winters have cooled, that effect was more than offset by rising spring, summer and autumn temperatures, which combined to stretch the melt season by between 10 and 17 days. The retreating summer sea ice has knock-on effects. The exposure of more open water, which absorbs more solar energy than ice, means further warming is likely. More open ocean also means winds can build up stronger waves that are eroding Arctic coasts. Communities in Alaska are already having to move their villages to escape erosion of low-lying coasts.

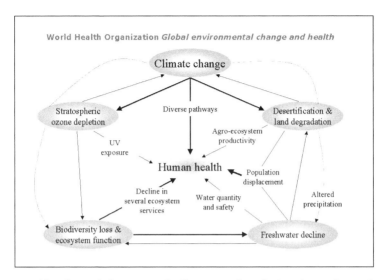

World Health Organization *Global environmental change and health*

worldwide and for 2% of all cases of malaria. An estimated 150,000 deaths and 5.5 million disability-adjusted life years in 2000 were due to climate change. "There is growing evidence that changes in the global climate will have profound effects on the health and well-being of citizens in countries throughout the world. We must better understand the potential health effects particularly for those who are most vulnerable, so that we can better manage the risks," said Dr Kerstin Leitner, WHO assistant director-general, in launching a new study in December 2003.

A report published in the journal *Nature* (January 2004) concluded that climate shifts could soon surpass habitat loss and other threats to wildlife and plants. The study, which examined six biodiversity-rich regions around the world representing 20% of the Earth's land area, projects that the consequences could be significant for Africa. Important African conservation areas, such as Kruger National Park, could risk losing up to 60% of their species. More than one-third of the 300 plant species studied in South Africa are expected to die out, including the country's national flower, the King Protea. Researchers found that 15% to 37% of species sampled could be threatened with extinction by 2050 as a result of their inability to adapt to changes in climate. "If the projections can be extrapolated globally, and to other groups of land animals and plants, our analyses suggest that well over a million species could be threatened with extinction as a result of climate change," said lead author Chris Thomas of the University of Leeds.

Destroying resources

The intimate and deadly connection between profit margins and the impact on ecosystems is illustrated in a report published by the Worldwatch Institute, an environmental think tank. "As investors search the world for the highest return, they are often drawn to countries with bountiful resources and weak environmental laws, a potentially disastrous combination for the environment and economy," says the report. Hilary French, author of the report and vice president of Worldwatch Institute, says: "Though the booming economies of the developing world raised national incomes, they left ecological devastation in their wake. Urban air pollution levels in many Asian and Latin American cities are among the worst in the world, and natural resources such as forests and fisheries are badly depleted on both continents."

Most of the money now flowing into developing countries is underwriting projects that are potentially damaging to the earth's ecology, according to the report. International investment in

---

Global warming is a WMD

As a climate scientist who has worked on this issue for several decades, first as head of the Met Office, and then as co-chair of scientific assessment for the UN intergovernmental panel on climate change, the impacts of global warming are such that I have no hesitation in describing it as a 'weapon of mass destruction'. Like terrorism, this weapon knows no boundaries. It can strike anywhere, in any form – a heat wave in one place, a drought or a flood or a storm surge in another. Nor is this just a problem for the future. The 1990s were probably the warmest decade in the last 1,000 years, and 1998 the warmest year. Global warming is already upon us.

John Houghton *The Guardian*, 28 July 2003

resource extraction, such as mining, for example, is flowing rapidly into many countries with valuable natural assets such as primary forests, mineral and petroleum reserves, and biological diversity. From 1991 to 1997, international spending on exploration for non-iron metals grew six times in Latin America, almost quadrupled in the Pacific region, and doubled in Africa, notes the report. The major oil and gas companies are also increasingly striking deals – and oil – in new regions such as the Central Asian republics and the South American rainforests.

Mining to destruction

▸ more than one quarter of active mines and exploration sites overlap with or are within a 10-kilometre radius of a strictly protected area

▸ more than one-third of all active mines and exploration sites are located within intact areas of high conservation areas

▸ nearly one-third of all active mines are located in stressed watersheds

▸ nearly three-quarters of active mines and exploration sites are in areas deemed to be of high ecological value.

World Resources Institute

With their own forests badly depleted, Asian companies are now vying for the vast timber concessions in Africa, Asia, and Latin America, threatening some of the world's last remaining untouched forests, says the Worldwatch Institute report.

Brazil, Cambodia, Congo, the Democratic Republic of Congo, Guyana, Nicaragua, Papua New Guinea, the Solomon Islands, and Surinam are among the countries that have granted, or are on the brink of granting, rights to log large tracts of primary forests.

"International investment can facilitate access to new technologies that minimise energy use and waste generation, helping developing countries leapfrog over the most damaging phases of industrialisation," she says. "But these funds can also bring highly polluting industries that jeopardise human and ecological health." Hazardous industries, such as battery manufacturers, chemical companies, and computer manufacturing and assembly facilities, are becoming increasingly concentrated in developing countries as a result, where safety practices and environmental enforcement and monitoring are basic at best, says the report. It cites a review of 22 computer-related companies based in industrial countries, which found that more than half of their collective manufacturing and assembly operations – processes intensive in the use of acids, solvents, and toxic gases – are now located in developing countries.

Major global car companies are also expanding into the emerging markets of Asia, Eastern Europe, and Latin America. If current projections hold, some three-quarters of the auto factories to be built over the next three years will go up in these regions, says the report. "If developing countries acquire auto based transportation systems along the lines of the US model, there will be grave consequences for local air pollution and food security as well as global climate change," French warned.

At the turn of the century, the United Nations Environment Program (UNEP), the World Bank, and the World Resources Institute assessed five ecosystem types – agricultural, coastal, forest, freshwater, and grassland – in relation to five ecosystem services – food and fibre production, water quantity, air quality, biodiversity, and carbon storage. It found that of these 25 ecosystem-service combinations, 16 had declining trends. The only positive trend was in food and fibre production by forest ecosystems, which has been achieved by an expansion of industrial forest monocropping at the expense of species diversity.

In 2001, some 60 million transistors – the tiny components used to build semiconductor chips – were manufactured for each person in the world. But because of the rapid pace at which electronic products become obsolete and are being replaced, production is expected to skyrocket in coming years, to perhaps as many as 1 billion transistors per person in 2010, according to the Worldwatch Institute. Yet the industry requires huge amounts of chemicals and leaves behind large quantities of dangerous wastes. Production of a single six-inch silicon wafer

> **Endangered rainforests**
>
> Indonesia's rainforests are some of richest in the world and are home to countless species of endangered wildlife, including the Asian elephant, Sumatran tiger, Sumatran rhino and orang-utan. Over 72% of Indonesia's forests have now been destroyed and according to a recent study by the World Bank, the Indonesian deforestation rate has reached 2 million hectares a year. This is equivalent to an area of forest the size of Belgium being lost each year. Asia Pulp & Paper (APP), one of the world's biggest paper companies, through its main subsidiary, Indah Kiat, has destroyed at least 287,000 hectares of rainforest and in 2000 sourced 75% of its logs by clear cutting forests. APP is also at the centre of a number of conflicts with indigenous communities. APP is reported to have cleared over 3000 hectares of forest belonging to the Sakai indigenous people in Sumatra. It is reported that on 3 February 2001, employees of APP's main logging company were involved in serious clashes with Sakai villagers. According to those reports, at least five villagers were injured, two seriously and 52 people were detained by the company before being temporarily handed over to the local police.
>
> *Paper Tiger, Hidden Dragons,* Friends of the Earth

results in 14 kilograms of solid waste and 11,000 litres of waste water. Workers in the industry are on the frontline of exposure and at risk of developing cancer or seeing birth defects in their children. More than 80% of the world's hazardous waste is produced in the United States. One half to three quarters of annual resource inputs to industrial economies are returned to the environment as wastes within a year.

Unhealthy food

The intensive farming of the last 60 years and the turn to industrialised agriculture under globalisation, have produced an ecological catastrophe in many parts of the world. An estimated 10-20% of the world's 1.5 billion hectares of cropland are degraded to some degree. This is the result of excessive tillage and fertiliser use, the removal of vegetation and over-grazing. In the developing world, according to the Worldwatch Institute, the pace of decline has accelerated to the point where a quarter of farmland suffers from degradation. Worldwide, farmland degradation has reduced cumulative food production by about 13% over the last 50 years. Urban expansion is also responsible for the loss of farmland. In the United States, more than one million hectares of arable land are paved over each year, while in China the figure is 200,000 hectares. About 20% of the world's irrigated land is damaged by salinisation – a build-up of salt that occurs when excess irrigation water evaporates. By 2015, it is estimated that 40% of humanity will live in water-stressed countries. Finally, two-thirds of all fisheries are exploited at or beyond their sustainable limits.

Pesticide poison

Pesticide use (two thirds of it in agriculture) has grown 15-fold since 1950 but imposes a terrible toll, poisoning 3 million people severely and killing 220,000 each year. Meanwhile, farmers confront increasing pesticide resistance. For consumers, food quality ranks among the most widespread health concerns. Food borne diseases strike 30% of the population in industrial countries each year, but people living in developing countries bear a more frightful burden due to a wide range of hazards and inadequate prevention and treatment.

Vital Signs 2002, Worldwatch Institute

While food is plentiful in the rich capitalist countries, what we eat is more harmful than ever before. Our own internal ecosystems are under attack from antibiotics in factory farming and processed food containing high levels of salt, sugar, fats and preservatives. Pesticides in food contain carcinogenics or hormone disrupting properties. The results include Creuzfeldt-Jacob "Mad Cow" Disease in humans, obesity and deep concerns about genetically-modified food. The Health Development Agency says that obesity – often the product of a poor diet and lack of physical exercise – kills about 34,000 people a year. It also says obesity costs the NHS an estimated

£2.6 billion a year in treating conditions such as diabetes and heart disease. This figure is expected to rise to £3.6 billion by 2010.

Meanwhile, the supermarkets (see Chapter 10) and government bodies engage in a dance of confusion about labelling and what can or cannot be added to food. It is estimated that 70% of the £20 billion global annual food advertising budget is used to promote soft drinks, sweets and snacks. Good food is priced higher so that poorer people end up buying the cheapest, but least healthy products.

In her book *Not on The Label,* Felicity Lawrence describes what really goes into the food on your plate. She worked anonymously in a chicken processing factory and found that the doctoring of processed foods was commonplace as well as being legal. She explained: "Water is routinely added to catering chicken, together with additives to hold it in. If you've ever eaten a takeaway, a ready meal, or a sandwich containing chicken, the chances are that you will have consumed chicken adulterated like this." Lawrence says:

> Chickens, like other animals, have become industrialised and globalised. We no longer know where they are produced or how they are processed. By the time we buy them in aseptic little packages, or processed into convenience meals, we have lost any sense of their origin."

She decided to reconstruct the contents of a 99p bag of washed and ready-to-eat salad, and was shocked by what she discovered. Modified-atmosphere packaging (MAP) was used to increase shelf-life, and to keep the salad looking fresh for up to 10 days. This allowed the supermarkets to get food from around the world, where it was often produced by migrant labour living in appalling conditions and earning a pittance. She writes:

> The salad is cut or separated out into individual leaves by gangs of workers, then washed in chlorine, dried and sorted before being packaged in pillows of plastic in which the normal levels of oxygen and carbon dioxide have been altered. Typically in MAP, the oxygen

is reduced from 21% to 3% and the CO_2 levels correspondingly raised. This slows any visible deterioration or discolouring.

This process, however, is thought to destroy many of the nutrients in the original salad. In addition, chlorine washes leave surface residues of chlorinated compounds on lettuce and some compounds used are known to cause cancer.

The genetic gap

In March 2004, the New Labour government announced that genetically engineered/modified (GE/GM) maize can be grown in the UK – provided it gets national seed list and pesticide approval. This is despite the fact that the field tests that preceded the announcement were carried out using a pesticide that was about to be banned! This crop will be fed to cows to make milk that will not be labelled as GM. Not at all bad for a day's work for a government committed to promoting biotech corporations, whatever the doubts and public hostility.

Sue Mayer, GeneWatch UK's director, commented: "They've betrayed the public's trust, no wonder people are cynical about our political system." She added: "The [government's] Science Review concluded that the public were not anti-science and that there are gaps in our knowledge about the issues worrying people. Clearly, the government is more interested in the profits of the biotech industry than good science. Giving the go-ahead before any rules are in place to deal with contamination or if other things go wrong, shows how little regard the government has for the public, non-GM farmers or the environment."

In the hands of a small group of biotech corporations, this new science has potentially deadly outcomes. Genetic engineering is not, as the biotech companies claim, a precise science that simply extends traditional breeding techniques practised over thousands of a years. It involves taking a gene from one species and inserting it into another distinct species, a process known as recombination. When crops are engineered, the gene is inserted randomly into another sequence that may have taken hundreds of millions of years to evolve. Bringing them into mutual action is therefore certain to have unpredictable results.

These uncertainties have been acknowledged by some of the leading UK institutions. The Royal Society said in a 2002 report that the potential health effects of GM foods should be rigorously investigated before allowing them into baby food, or to be marketed to pregnant or breast-feeding women, elderly people, and those with chronic disease. This was because GM "could lead to unpredicted harmful changes in the nutritional state of foods".

In March 2004, in an update of its 1999 statement on the health implications of GM food crops, the British Medical Association warned against complacency, saying: "Public health surveillance should be so complete that we can be certain that adverse effects from any dietary change would be recognised. We also need a commitment to research in key areas to minimise the potential risks to human health and the environment posed by genetically modified food." The BMA said work was still needed on the potential for GM foods to cause food allergies. A statement added: "The transfer of genetic material (DNA) between species has been observed but its significance is uncertain. While we daily consume large amounts of non-GM DNA with no identifiable problems, we need to know whether the risk of DNA transfer is in any way enhanced by genetic modification of food. It is important that individual crops are assessed on a case-by-case basis using extensive field trials of the type undertaken recently in the UK and that crops which are more harmful to the environment than conventional varieties are not licensed for commercial use."

In its submission to the Scottish Parliament's health and community care committee in November 2002, the BMA stated that "there has not yet been a robust and thorough search into the potentially harmful effects of GM foodstuffs on human health... In the UK not enough is known to enable us to give an accurate risk of assessment of the health impact of GM crops on the health of local communities".

None of the independent tests carried out so far have examined the issue of the health effects of GM technology. When the scientist Dr Arpad Pusztai examined the health impact of GM organisms on rats and potatoes, he found negative effects. His

The Sainsbury web

The leading centre in biotechnology research in this country is the Sainsbury Laboratory. It's a joint venture between Lord Sainsbury's Gatsby Foundation, the University of East Anglia, the BBSRC and the John Innes Foundation. Funding is primarily through grants from the Gatsby Foundation but also via the public funding body for the bio-sciences, the BBSRC, whose grant is determined by Lord Sainsbury's department. As Science Minister, he had overseen a massive 300% increase in funding for the Sainsbury Laboratory.

He is also a member of the cabinet biotechnology committee, Sci-Bio, responsible for national policy on biotechnology including GM crops and foods. Although a key adviser to Blair on biotech, he apparently absents himself from decisions impacting directly on GM foods because, it is said, of his connection to the Sainsbury supermarket chain. When he was made Science Minister, Lord Sainsbury resigned as chairman of the Sainsbury's supermarket chain and put into a blind trust major investments in two plant genetics-related investment companies (Diatech and Innotech Ltd). Innotech is known to have a substantial stake in a firm called Paradigm Genetics involved in a joint GM-related venture with Monsanto.

Lord Sainsbury's GM investment company Diatech has funded research at the Sainsbury Laboratory. Dr Roger Freedman, the Director of Diatech approved the work. Dr. Freedman is also on the board of the Sainsbury Laboratory Council, which oversees the Sainsbury Laboratory. In short, Sainsbury heads a government department that gives money to the Laboratory (via the BBSRC) that he supports and which bears his name, and on whose board is the man who runs his company, currently held in a blind trust. But the story doesn't end there. In 1987 the scientist Mike Wilson was named as the inventor of a UK patent that could generate millions from GM commercialisation.

Diatech was listed as the patent applicant. The patent is seen as being crucial to the future of genetic engineering. Sainsbury gave Labour its biggest ever single donation in 1997. On October 3 1997 he was made a life peer by Blair and a year later Minister for Science. By 2003 he had given over £11 million to the Labour Party.

What's Wrong with Supermarkets? Corporate Watch

research was rubbished in government circles and the scientist was driven from his post by the extraordinary pressure piled on him by his employer and the biotech industry. So, at this point, no one knows whether GM crops are safe for humans and farm animals to eat, or about the damage that they can inflict on neighbouring, non-GM fields.

What is clear, however, is that GE has enabled capitalism to extend its reach deeper into nature through control of food production. When you think of this technology, there is only one corporation that really counts. Monsanto products accounted for over 90% of the total area planted with GE crops in the world in 2001. This is a company that exerts considerable political influence, particularly in the US, and is experienced in manipulating governments, the media and scientific opinion in order to gain approval for its products. Monsanto made large contributions towards Clinton's election campaigns. Monsanto bought its way into a key position in the seed market by spending billions of dollars buying up plant-cultivating firms, including the market leaders in maize, soybeans and cotton. At the same time the company acquired important GE-related patents and access to valuable germplasm.

The power and influence of the biotech corporations in the World Trade Organisation was undoubtedly behind its six-year battle with the European Union over the sale of a brand of American GE corn, known as Bt-11, for human consumption. The European Commission decided in May 2004 to lift its ban. In a predictable response, David Bowe, a New Labour minister, declared: "This is good news for consumers because it will increase choice and competition. It is also good news because it will increase choice and competition for producers, too."

Most of the GE seeds marketed by Monsanto are resistant to the company's own "broad-spectrum" herbicide, Roundup/Glyphosate. So the more GE seeds Monsanto sells, the more profit it makes on its herbicide. In 2001, herbicide tolerant crops accounted for 77% of the acreage sown to GE crops, and Roundup is now the world's biggest selling herbicide and Monsanto's main source of profit. When US and Canadian farmers buy GE seeds they are – more often than not – tying themselves to a contract which bars them from saving seed for use the following year and obliges them to buy Monsanto's chemicals. These contracts, and the patents on GE seeds, deny farmers the right to save, exchange and replant seeds, and forces them to buy new patented seed each season. Monsanto is currently suing hundreds of US and Canadian farmers for saving seed or otherwise breaching the patent. At the same time, Monsanto itself is being sued by farming, scientific and civil society organisations for the contamination of conventional and

Monsanto comes calling

Percy Schmeiser is a farmer from Saskatchewan Canada whose Canola fields were contaminated with Monsanto's genetically engineered Round-Up Ready canola by pollen from a nearby farm. Monsanto says it doesn't matter how the contamination took place, and is therefore demanding Schmeiser pay their Technology Fee (the fee farmers must pay to grow Monsanto's genetically engineered products). According to Schmeiser, "I never had anything to do with Monsanto, outside of buying chemicals. I never signed a contract. If I would go to St. Louis (Monsanto Headquarters) and contaminate their plots – destroy what they have worked on for 40 years – I think I would be put in jail and the key thrown away."

GM doesn't help poor farmers

Today, 21% of the food grown in the developing world is destined for animal consumption. In many developing countries, more than a third of the grain is now being grown for livestock. The animals, in turn, will be eaten by the world's wealthiest consumers in the northern industrial countries. The result is that the world's richest consumers eat a diet high in animal protein, while the poorest people on earth are left with little land to grow food grain for their own families. And, even the land that is available is often owned by global agribusiness interests, further aggravating the plight of the rural poor. The introduction of GM food crops does nothing to change this fundamental reality.

Jeremy Rifkin, president of the Foundation on Economic Trends
Guardian 2 June 2003

organic agriculture.

Far from solving world hunger, as the corporations and governments tell us, genetic engineering is used to exploit the farmers of poorer countries. By exercising intellectual property control over the genetic traits of the world's major food crops, companies such as Monsanto stand to make huge profits while the world's poorest farmers become increasingly marginalised. It is estimated that OECD countries hold 97% of all patents, and global corporations 90% of all technology and product patents. The concept of intellectual property rights was developed by a committee made up of the leading biotech corporations.

Monsanto's James Enyart explained how it happened: "Our trilateral group was able to distil from the laws of the more advanced countries the fundamental principles for protecting all forms of intellectual property... Besides selling our concepts at home, we went to Geneva where [we] presented [our] document to the staff of the GATT secretariat. We also took the opportunity to present it to the Geneva-based representatives of a large number of countries... Industry identified a major problem for international trade. It crafted a solution, reduced it to a concrete proposal, and sold it to our own and other governments. The industries and traders of the world have played simultaneously the role of patients, the diagnosticians, and the prescribing physicians."

And there is nanotechnology – the manipulation of material at the scale of the nanometre (one billionth of a metre), which is the scale of atoms and molecules. Precise manipulations of nanoscale materials became possible towards the end of the 20th century. Already hundreds of tons of nanoscale particles are showing up in consumer products as diverse as sunscreens, car parts, tennis balls, eyeglasses, and paint. Particles that had been approved for consumer products at the micro- or macro-scale were not tested again when introduced into the same products at the nanoscale, so their effects on health are unknown. Nanotechnology is not limited to the development of new materials with new characteristics. Scientists are also hoping to someday master new forms of molecular scale manufacture that could transform how everything in the world is made, including the raw materials we start with. Because quantum mechanics takes over at the nanoscale, there may be unpredictable changes to a substance's conductivity, elasticity, reactivity, strength, colour, and tolerance to temperature and pressure. Some nanoparticles can slip past immune systems and even cross through the blood-brain barrier undetected.

The Action Group on Erosion, Technology and Concentration, a group dedicated to the advancement of cultural and ecological diversity and human rights, has raised awareness of nanotechnology. In a groundbreaking report, it says: "Fearful of a public backlash, industry attacked the theory that nanotechnologies could lead to the development of directed molecular self-assembly (nanoscale 'robots' capable of manipulating molecules and reproducing). Critics raised concerns that, unless perfectly controlled, human-created self-assembly could pose a major threat to global survival, analogous to uncontrolled cancer cells self-replicating until they destroy a living organism.

"The threat has been named 'global ecophagy' or, more simply and cinematically, 'Grey Goo'. Not an enticing image for venture capitalists or manufacturers thinking of going nano on the assembly line. But even if self-assembly could be controlled, the implications for the environment, the economy, labour, and democracy are enormous and need to be addressed openly. Now there is growing scientific evidence that directed molecular self-assembly is not only possible but relatively close at hand. If the industry's dismissals turn out to be short-sighted and/or self-serving, society will question whether or not scientists and industry cheerleaders can be trusted with so powerful a technology."

As Jeremy Rifkin puts it in *Biotech Century*: "Genetic engineering represents the ultimate tool. It extends humanity's reach over the forces of nature as no other technology in history... With genetic technology we assume control over the hereditary blueprints of life itself. Can any reasonable person believe for a moment that such unprecedented power is without substantial risks?" He warns:

A handful of corporations, research institutions and governments could hold patents on virtually all 100,000 genes that make up the blueprint of the human race, as well as the cells, organs, and tissues that comprise the human body. They may also own similar patents on thousands of micro-organisms, plants and animals, allowing them unprecedented power to dictate the terms by which we and future generations will live our lives.

6 Tying science to business

By the end of the 19th century, science in the service of production was an essential feature of capitalism, especially in the chemical and electrical industries. But the outright commercialisation of scientific knowledge and research, where such activity becomes a commodity, came to prominence in the last quarter of the 20th century. The integration of state-sponsored and funded research more directly into the needs of production is a major feature of the development of the market state in Britain and the United States.

In Britain, the state invests over £7 billion a year in research and development. Much of this is now tied to "outcomes" which demonstrate how they lead to further wealth creation by the private sector. Turning knowledge – scientific understanding – into products for the market place is seen as the key to economic success. The open commercialisation of this sector began as an objective of the Thatcher governments of the 1980s; the Blair governments have deepened and regulated this process. This is done to create the basis for new firms to develop in Britain but also to attract existing investment by transnational corporations (TNCs). A developed "science base", with potential new research staff available for employers, is seen as an essential requirement by the New Labour government. The net result is an intense commercialisation of science in all areas – from research to the publication of findings.

Under the Tories, more than 80 public sector research

establishments like the Medical Research Council and the Southampton Oceanography Centre were given commercial freedom while some were privatised outright. The first decade of Thatcher's government from 1979-89, saw a decline in the government's share of funding for research in universities from 81% to 72% of the total, with a corresponding increase in income from charities, industry and overseas sources. This trend has accelerated. Business and charitable foundations now provide universities with over 40% of their funding for research.

The state steps in

In 1993, the Tory government published a White Paper called *Realising our potential: a strategy for science, engineering and technology*. It was based on the premise that the primary function of science is to generate technological innovation in industry. This model has become explicit under the Blair government and other countries have copied it. In a strategy document published in July 2002, bearing an almost identical name, published by three government departments, New Labour declared: "Startling advances in communications, information, health and basic technologies are now converging to magnify the pace of scientific and technological change and the productivity of scientific research. Now more than ever before, investment in science accompanied by matching investments in technology and innovation offers the prospect of sustained social and economic dividends." The strategy added:

> The potential of scientific and technological discoveries will only be realised, though, if they can be effectively translated into innovation – new products, processes, services and systems. A vibrant innovation system is the key to reaping the gains from research, *connecting science and technology with developments in market demand and social needs*. The individual entrepreneurs, businesses, and investors are the essential catalysts who convert science and technology into new ways of meeting economic and social needs. They translate ideas into commercial reality... It is only through innovation that science and technology can benefit our economy and society. [emphasis added]

The Office of Science and Technology (OST) is based within the Department for Trade and Industry (DTI). It is responsible for all public sector investment in science. On its website, the OST talks of the need for "knowledge transfer" – the transfer of ideas, research results and skills between universities, other research organisations and business "to enable innovative new products and services to be developed". The OST says its aim "is to promote the transfer of knowledge generated and held in Higher Education Institutions (HEIs) and Public Sector Research Establishments (PSREs) to the wider economy to enhance economic growth".

A number of schemes exist that are aimed at "supporting entrepreneurship", training, commercialisation and development of links between the universities, the PSREs and business. These include the Higher Education Innovation Fund, University Challenge, Science Enterprise Challenge (SEC) and the Public Sector Research Exploitation Fund. The aim of the SEC is to establish a network of centres in UK universities, "specialising in the teaching and practice of commercialisation and entrepreneurialism in the field of science and technology". Twelve centres were established as a result of 1999-2000 awards. Another 39 are in the pipeline. The OST says: "Early measures of activity are encouraging with 5,900 science and technology graduates exposed to new enterprise teaching in the first two years, and over 850 at postgraduate and professional level. The centres have also helped to generate 400 new business ideas, over 80 of which have led to early stage businesses." The purpose of University Challenge is to enable universities to access seed funds in order to assist the successful transformation of *"good research into good business"*. [emphasis added] It is reported that in the first two years of operations 105 new "spinouts" were created.

Direct collaboration between public research institutions and business is fostered through the LINK scheme. The scheme "offers an opportunity to engage with some of the best and most creative minds in the country, to tackle new scientific and technological challenges so that industry can go on to develop innovative and commercially successful products, processes and services". LINK encourages innovative research "with good potential for eventual commercial exploitation, and offers opportunities for researchers from industry and academia to acquire knowledge and develop new technologies together which will help shape the 21st century". Companies of any size and research organisations throughout the UK can participate in LINK projects. Global corporations with a manufacturing and research organisation in the UK are also eligible. In 2004, it was reported that a number of major companies, including GlaxoSmithkline, AstraZeneca, Shell, Vodafone, Amersham and Rolls Royce, were in discussions with the government on how their commercial investment in research and development can "partner public investment in the UK science base".

The bulk of government money for research is distributed through seven research councils. It goes to the universities and to the research institutes that are nominally state-owned but increasingly run along commercial lines. Big business has a highly influential role in the most important one, the Biotechnology and Biological Sciences Research Council (BBSRC). Nearly one quarter of the BBSRC's committees are industry scientists. GlaxoSmithKline, one of the world's top pharmaceutical corporations, has no fewer than six representatives, including one on the governing council itself. There are also representatives from AstraZeneca, Unilever and United Biscuits. There are no consumer or trade union representatives.

The BBSRC's purpose is "to sustain a broad base of interdisciplinary research and training to help industry, commerce and Government create wealth". As a further sign of the merging of the public and private sectors, the BBSRC's chairman until January 2002 was Peter Doyle, a director of biotech giant Syngenta and the former executive director of GM company Zeneca (now part of Syngenta). Doyle originally took up his BBSRC post while still Zeneca's executive director. Doyle's replacement as chief executive is Professor Julia Goodfellow, the wife of geneticist Dr Peter Goodfellow, head of discovery research at GlaxoSmithKline.

There has also been a 300% increase in the grant given by the BBSRC to the Sainsbury Laboratory of the John Innes Centre

(JIC) in Norwich. The JIC is a plant biotechnology centre with major research alliances with Dupont. The BBSRC has been accused of instituting what has been called "a gagging order" that prevents all publicly funded researchers from speaking out on concerns about GM foods.

In a 2002 report called *Delivering the commercialisation of public sector science,* the National Audit Office examined the steps taken by the state-owned research establishments to attract commercial contracts and support. They cited with approval the example of Celltech, a biotechnology company created in 1980 which employed a total staff of 1,803 in the year to 31 December 2000, including some 1,150 research and marketing staff in the United Kingdom and abroad. This was built on science originating in Medical Research Council laboratories.

The MRC has since created a separate company – Medical Research Council Technology Ltd – "to lead the commercialisation of research outputs" for the organisation's work. The MRC was also instrumental in the creation of MVM Limited, a venture capital company managed by individuals from the private sector. This has two funds which invest in early stage life science companies. The first, UK Medical Ventures Fund, raised £40m in 1998 and the second fund raised a similar amount in October 2001.

Medical Research Council

The "mission" of the Medical Research Council is "to choose the most suitable commercial arrangement and the partner(s) judged most likely to develop Medical Research Council technology into products and services useful to society; to maximise the contribution to national wealth creation and UK industrial competitiveness; and to maximise income to the Medical Research Council in the medium to long-term."

The Treasury agreed in 1999 that research councils and research establishments could retain the financial benefits of their commercial activity and share this between them in whatever proportion they agree. The Medical Research Council income has grown from £150,000 in 1986-87 to some £7 million in 1999-2000 and £17.9 million in 2000-01.

Other research establishments have also obtained funds to develop commercial activity. The Babraham Institute, for example, obtained a £250,000 grant to refurbish laboratory and support facilities appropriate for use by "early stage companies". This attracted 19 companies to rent about 3,000 square metres

---

Scientists 'asked to fix results for backer'
Daily Telegraph, 14 February 2000
One in three scientists working for government quangos or newly privatised laboratories says he has been asked to adjust his conclusions to suit his sponsor.

Contracting out and the commercialisation of scientific research are threatening standards of impartiality, scientists claim. The survey was conducted by the union representing research scientists, which is campaigning against further privatisation of public laboratories.

The Institute of Professionals, Managers and Specialists says that public safety could be harmed by the Government's plans to bring private funding into the National Air Traffic Services and the Defence Evaluation and Research Agency. Privatisations over the last few years have included the Radio Chemical Centre, now Nycomed Amersham Laboratories, and the Atomic Energy Authority, which trades as AEA Technology.

Charles Harvey, the institute's spokesman, said an increasing number of scientists had privately raised concerns with the union so it had decided to include a question about the influence of sponsors in a survey about pay and conditions. Thirty per cent of the 500 respondents said they had been asked to tailor their research conclusions or resulting advice.

The figure included 17 per cent who had been asked to change their conclusions to suit the customer's preferred outcome, 10 per cent who said they had been asked to do so to obtain further contracts and three per cent who claimed they had been asked to make changes to discourage publication.

"Some were working for quangos and some for fully privatised laboratories," said Mr Harvey. "The piper is calling the tune and it raises worrying issues. We have seen the BSE crisis, food scares and the GMO debacle and the public is losing confidence in Government as an independent, fair-minded arbiter."

of space at their bio-incubator site and generated £680,000 from rents and services in 2000-01. But the NAO found that not all research sites were as enthusiastic and noted: "To meet the increasing emphasis on commercialisation, a culture that is also supportive of commercial activity, which helps staff to overcome barriers, such as the lack of recognition for commercialisation work, is needed. This will require change in many Research Establishments."

Catching the corporate bug

The Royal Society, which was set up in 1660 as a counter-weight to the anti-science, church-dominated universities of the time, boasts that its independent status allows it to play a "crucial role as the champion of top quality science and technology". It too, however, has caught the corporate bug. The Royal Society, has reported that recent donors included BP, Esso UK, AstraZeneca, and Rolls-Royce. Now the Society has introduced more formal processes to "encourage the commercialisation of the products of scientific research". It has a series of awards and in 2004 launched its Science, City, Industry Dialogue programme. The Society says it hopes that the scheme will allow scientists to discuss ways in which their work might be commercialised and industrialists to identify possible new academic research partners, products and funding routes. It also aims at helping "financiers to identify potential areas for new investment". So much for its vaunted independence.

Capturing the universities

The drive by successive governments to tie funding contracts to defined commercial outcomes has created stronger incentives for researchers to pursue projects leading to patentable results. Many universities have changed their rules and are encouraged to take shares in spin-off enterprises based on faculty research. For example, Oxford University now claims ownership of "works generated by computer hardware or software owned or operated by the university" and "patentable and non-patentable inventions".

Corporate influence on science is also exerted through direct funding of university research centres, which then have a significant say in policy and research nationally. One of the most notorious examples of this is Nottingham University's International Centre for Corporate Social Responsibility (!), which was set up with a £3.8m grant from British American Tobacco. Around 30 of the 200 professors at Nottingham hold sponsored chairs.

In *The Captive State: The Corporate Takeover of Britain*, George Monbiot says that there is scarcely a university that has not been compromised by its funding arrangements. He explains:

> Business now inhabits the cloisters of even the biggest and richest institutions. Cambridge University, for example, possesses a Shell chair in chemical engineering, BP professorships in organic chemistry and petroleum science, an ICI chair in applied thermodynamics, a Glaxo chair of molecular parasitology, a Unilever chair of molecular science, a Price Waterhouse chair of financial accounting and a Marks & Spencer chair of farm animal health and food science. Rolls-Royce, AT&T, Microsoft and the biotechnology company Zeneca have all set up laboratories in the university.
>
> In June 1999, BP gave the university £25m to fund work across five departments. In November 1999, Cambridge set up an £84m joint venture, funded largely by the British government, partly by industry, with the Massachusetts Institute of Technology. Its purpose is to "change the face of business and wealth creation in the UK" by stimulating "research spin-offs" and "training the business leaders of the future". Cambridge's vice chancellor explained: "We may once have been thought of as an ivory tower – today we are a tower of high technology and business prowess".

More recently, the pharmaceutical giant GlaxoSmithkline announced a £44m investment in Imperial College, London, to build and equip a clinical imaging centre. The vice-chancellor of Imperial College, Sir Richard Sykes who has led the campaign for university top-up fees, is a former chairman of GSK.

Britain is home to the headquarters of BP and Shell, two of the world's three largest fossil fuel companies. These companies, says

Degrees of capture, a report by Corporate Watch and the New Economics Foundation, have succeeded in capturing the allegiance of some of Britain's leading universities, through sponsoring new buildings, equipment, professorships and research posts. In return for corporate sponsorship and contracts, universities are encouraging oil companies to steer the research agenda, tailoring courses to meet corporate personnel demands and awarding high profile positions to oil executives. The director of the BP Institute at Cambridge University is one of the company's senior managers. The publicly-funded Engineering and Physical Sciences Research Council determines academic grants through a peer review council containing 12 oil or gas executives and just two renewable energy members.

According to the report, few universities have handed themselves over so completely to the oil and gas industry as Aberdeen, located in Europe's oil capital. Principal Professor Duncan Rice admits: "We are genuinely committed to trying to do all we can to help [the oil and gas industry] through contract work and through consultancy and, where possible, training programmes for people who are already in the labour force of the industry or moving towards it." In 2002 Heriot-Watt University was restructured into six schools and two institutes – one of these latter being the Institute of Petroleum Engineering. The Institute boasts that "we tailor our teaching and research to the needs of the petroleum industry and place considerable importance on the maintenance of close links with the industry". Principal and vice-chancellor of the university, Professor John Archer, himself a distinguished petroleum engineer, says: "At Heriot-Watt we have always made a virtue of the fact that over 50% of our income comes from our competitive endeavours in the market place – be it in research, in university businesses or in overseas markets."

The International Petroleum Research Directory (IPRD) lists about 1,000 research and development projects carried out in UK universities. Researchers Greg Muttitt and Chris Grimshaw say: "While the value of such research is protected by confidentiality agreements, we can estimate that it is worth about £67m per year. Almost half of this research is geological – finding where new fields are and how to exploit them. Most of the other research focuses on the development of new technology and drilling techniques, which enable the industry to extract petroleum from ever more marginal, difficult and expensive areas – such as the deep ocean – or to get more oil and gas out of existing fields. Thus most R&D serves to expand fossil fuel reserves."

Distorting the results

The commercialisation of science has other results too, including the concealment of poor performance. GSK is facing major legal actions in the United States over alleged covering up of negative trial results involving its anti-depressant paroxetine (marketed there as Paxil and in Britain as Seroxat). One action by New York state's attorney general, Eliot Spitzer, charged the drug company with "repeated and persistent fraud" in suppressing evidence that suggested that paroxetine was ineffective in treating depression in adolescents. Spitzer has an internal memo from 1998 which stated that it would be "commercially unacceptable" to admit that paroxetine did not work in children. It went on to say that the company would have to "effectively manage the dissemination of these data in order to minimise any potential negative impact". In August 2004, GSK settled with Mr Spitzer for $2.5m, without admitting liability, but there are still several class actions outstanding against GSK regarding the withdrawal side-effects from Seroxat.

Earlier in the same year, UK government scientists accused the drug companies of refusing to release evidence that anti-depressants can be harmful to children. Researchers preparing new National Health Service guidelines for childhood depression said they were astonished by the lack of co-operation from the manufacturers of SSRIs (selective serotonin re-uptake inhibitors). This family of drugs includes Lustral, Seroxat and Prozac. With five out of six SSRIs, the risks to children outweighed the benefits, the unpublished data showed. Previously published data suggested that the drugs were safe and effective in children. At that time, about 20,000 children were being prescribed the five drugs. SSRIs have never been approved for use with children in

Britain but have been used "off licence" by GPs. The National Institute for Clinical Excellence (NICE) had asked the National Collaborating Centre for Mental Health to investigate treatments for childhood depression.

Dr Tim Kendall, the co-director of the centre, which is supported by the Royal College of Psychiatrists, looked first at the published data on SSRIs and found they supported their use in children. When he and colleagues tried to obtain unpublished trial results, however, drug companies refused or ignored his requests. "We asked them for it and they would not give it to us," he told *The Daily Telegraph* (24 April 2004). Instead, the centre's researchers used unpublished data obtained by the government's Committee for the Safety of Medicines, which has access to confidential findings. Their analysis of all published and unpublished data showed that the side effects of all but one SSRI outweighed any advantages. Seroxat, for instance, increased the risk of suicidal thoughts, the team found. The only drug to have benefits in children was Prozac. Dr Kendall said the companies may have been unwilling to provide information because it had already been submitted to a peer-reviewed journal. Some data may have been commercially sensitive. He said: "But I think there is growing evidence to suggest that drug companies are withholding trials that are unfavourable. This is worrying because we do lots of work for NICE and we rely almost solely on published data. If we had seen only the published data, we might have concluded that SSRIs were worth prescribing to children."

Another way that industry influences the direction of science is by funding organisations which can lobby in their favour on science-related issues. For example, pharmaceutical companies fund some patients' groups to lobby for new drugs, while the Scientific Alliance was set up by money from the quarrying industry. Sense About Science seems a harmless enough name. But GM Watch, which analyses the underhand ways used by genetic engineering corporations to get their message across, has revealed the truth about this organisation. Sense About Science staff include Tracey Brown and Ellen Raphael. Both are also part of the extreme libertarian network behind the highly dubious

LM organisation, the *Spiked* website, and the "Institute of Ideas", to all of which Brown and Raphael have contributed. *LM* is the reincarnation of *Living Marxism*, a magazine that claimed atrocities in the Yugoslav civil war were invented by journalists.

According to GM Watch, most of the members of Sense About Science's advisory council and board of trustees are well known GM proponents. Funders include the Association of the British Pharmaceutical Industry (ABPI), Amersham Biosciences plc, BBSRC, BP plc, GlaxoSmithKline and the biopharmaceutical companies AstraZeneca plc, Pfizer plc and Oxford GlycoSciences. Sense about Science was created just in time for the UK's official GM Public Debate. After the debate had shown an overwhelming level of public opposition to GM crop commercialisation, Sense About Science launched a media campaign.

A Sense About Science article appeared in *The Times* under the headline "GM vandals force science firms to reduce research". Director Tracey Brown, was quoted as saying that: "The burden of trying to organise the research community to pre-empt and protect from vandalism is potentially disastrous". Articles in the *Times Higher Education Supplement* (*THES*) and elsewhere went still further, suggesting the debate had been hijacked by "activists" and that GM plant researchers were being subjected to physical and mental abuse, leading some to take jobs abroad. One *THES* article, headlined "Scientists quit UK amid GM attacks", included claims of intimidation by Chris Leaver (a Sense About Science trustee) and Mike Wilson (a Sense About Science advisory panellist). Fiona Fox and Tony Gilland, who both sit on a Sense About Science Working Party, are also both *LM* contributors. Indeed, Fox penned the notorious *LM* article denying the Rwandan genocide.

Scientists fight back

Scientists who obstruct the commercialisation agenda come in for systematic hounding by more pro-business scientists, who use learned journals to attack colleagues who do not conform to corporate agendas. A recent example is the case of Dr Andrew Stirling of Sussex University. He was not convinced about the case for commercialisation of GM crops. He is an expert on risk assessment at the Science Policy Research Unit and was a member of the government's GM Science Panel. He was privately warned by a senior pro-GM scientist that his research position would be under threat if he did not shift his position. The best known case in Britain was the attack on Dr Arpad Pusztai, who spoke out on the TV programme *World in Action* about the health effects of GM based on his research. Because he broke ranks with the way the scientific establishment publishes its findings, Pusztai was suspended, gagged for months and his research team was disbanded. At the time, he said of the scientific establishment: "Their remit was to screw me and they screwed me."

In May 2002, George Monbiot, in an article published by the *Transnational Corporations Observatory* website, exposed how the Bivings Group, a PR firm contracted to the biotech company Monsanto helped shape scientific discourse – and almost destroy the careers of independent scientists. In 2001, two researchers at the University of California, Berkeley published a paper in *Nature* magazine, which claimed that native maize in Mexico had been contaminated, across vast distances, by GM pollen. Before the publication, one of the scientists, Ignacio Chapela, was approached by the director of a Mexican corporation, who first offered him a glittering research post if he withheld his paper, then told him that he knew where to find his children.

On the day the paper was published, messages started to appear on an Internet discussion list used by more than 3,000 scientists. The trickle turned into a flood and the pressure on *Nature* was so severe that its editor did something unparalleled in its 133-year history: he published, alongside two papers challenging the findings, a retraction in which he wrote that their research should never have been published. Monbiot later tracked "Mary Murphy" and "Andura Smetacek", who launched the first attacks on the findings, to the same Bivings Group that worked for biotech corporations.

Monbiot noted: "'Sometimes,' Bivings boasts, 'we win awards. Sometimes only the client knows the precise role we played.' Sometimes, in other words, real people have no idea that they are being managed by fake ones." Chapela was eventually denied tenure by the University of California which had a controversial academic-industrial partnership with the Swiss agribiotech firm Syngenta, which ended last year. He appealed. The resulting report, issued on 28 June 2004, claims that Jasper Rine, a geneticist at the university who sat on a key committee reviewing Chapela's tenure, had conflicts of interest. It says that Rine had financial dealings with biotech firms, oversaw the Syngenta agreement and had cited Chapela's *Nature* paper as an example of poor science in one of his classes. Both the dean of Chapela's college and his department chair requested that Rine be taken off the committee four times; but Rine did not excuse himself nor did the committee chair ask him to leave.

In the United States, concerned professionals have formed the Integrity in Science project. In their founding statement, they say: "Although many have cheered partnerships between industry and the research community, it is also acknowledged that they entail conflicts of interest that may compromise the judgement of trusted professionals, the credibility of research institutions and scientific journals, the safety and transparency of human subjects research, the norms of free inquiry, and the legitimacy of science-based policy." The scientists say, for example, that:

▸ there is strong evidence that researchers' financial ties to chemical, pharmaceutical, or tobacco manufacturers directly influence their published positions in supporting the benefit or downplaying the harm of the manufacturer's product

▸ a growing body of evidence indicates that pharmaceutical industry gifts and inducements bias clinician judgement and influence doctors' prescribing practices

▸ there are well-known cases of industry seeking to discredit or prevent the publication of research results that are critical of its products

▸ studies of life-science faculties indicate that researchers with industry funding are more likely to withhold research results in order to secure commercial advantage

▸ increasingly, the same academic institutions that are responsible for oversight of scientific integrity and human

subjects protection are entering financial relationships with
the industries whose product-evaluations they oversee.

In July 2003, scientists and industry watchdogs gathered in
Washington to explore cases of industry-led manipulation and
distortion of scientific research, as part of the Integrity in Science
project. According to the speakers, several industries have made
so-called "junk science" – the publication of their own self-
serving research results – common practice. Also common are
suppressing or criticising research that does not support their
position and disseminating data or their own risk interpretations
directly to the lay press and policy makers. Many industries have
detailed plans in place to challenge scientific findings as soon as
regulations appear that could threaten their bottom line, said
David Michaels, a research professor of occupational and health
services at George Washington University.

Using the tobacco industry's own documents, Lisa Bero, a
professor of clinical pharmacy at the University of California,
San Francisco, described the ways in which tobacco companies
have intentionally manufactured doubt and controversy via their
own research findings in the hope of downplaying scientific

Research and profit

But increasingly over the years, and especially during the last 30
years since the Rothschild report, agricultural research has become
directed more towards commercial benefit (profit rather than
discovery), and in doing so it has become increasingly reactive,
having to respond to the perceived needs of industry and, indeed,
politics. As research has moved towards providing solutions for
industry, so industry has gained more control over the funding as a
customer paying for a service, with attendant controls over what is
done and how. Furthermore, as funding from government sources
has become more concerned with wealth creation and value for
money, it too has become increasingly responsive to pressures from
industry and, more or less directly, political influence.

Science, Agriculture and Research – a compromised participation?
William Buhler

evidence that illustrates the health risks associated with cigarette smoking and second-hand smoke.

Jeffrey Short, chief chemist for the National Marine Fisheries Service investigation of the Exxon Valdez Oil Spill, described a series of attacks on government science by Exxon. According to Short, Exxon manipulated data about the extent of the spill to support its claim that much of the seafloor near Alaska was already contaminated by natural oil seeps. Short also cited glaring abuses of scientific peer review, the manipulation of scientific meeting agendas, and abuses of the Freedom of Information Act. Exxon used these to make very broad requests – including requests for data associated with research still in progress – that slowed studies and interfered with their publication. "It has, in effect, reduced us to being field technicians for Exxon," said Short, who took leave from his job in order to speak out on the subject.

What are the results of this intense commercialisation of science? Dr Stuart Parkinson, director of Scientists for Global Responsibility – an independent British-based organisation supported by people like Stephen Hawking – believes that it leads to a bias towards research that produces commercial returns. In a speech in March 2004, he said:

> For example, the BBSRC [the research council mentioned earlier] is currently funding 26 projects concerned with growing GM crops, but just one involving organic production. One important reason for this is that cutting-edge science can lead to an avalanche of commercially valuable patents – much faster than that generated by more established science. For example, nanotechnology-related patents in the United States rose by 500% in the ten years to 2002. A knock-on effect from large amounts of funding going into hi-tech R&D is that we can get what is known as "technology lock-in". This is where society becomes so reliant on particular technologies that it becomes very difficult and expensive to change direction if they are found to be problematic. One classic example is nuclear power. Political decisions over the last half-century have meant that the lion's share of R&D funding for energy in industrialised countries has been directed towards this technology, while

alternatives like renewables have seen much lower levels of investment. Figures from the International Energy Agency show that R&D on renewables has rarely reached 25% of that spent on nuclear fission during the last 25 years. The consequence now is that attempts to phase out the technology due to concerns about, for example, links to nuclear weapons, vulnerability to terrorism or the dangers of nuclear waste are countered by the argument that we cannot afford to do without it because alternatives (eg renewable energy) are not sufficiently developed.

The second effect of industrial involvement is that more research is steered towards areas which can yield a commercial return, so that work developing a new product or process tends to be prioritised over, for example, work examining environmental or human health impacts of an existing product or process.

Capitalism and science

As socialists, we do not criticise the commoditisation of science in order to appeal for a return to times before science became a commodity... The commoditisation of science, its full incorporation into the process of capitalism, is the dominant fact of life for scientific activity and a pervasive influence on the thinking of scientists. To deny its relevance is to remain subject to its power, while the first step towards freedom is to acknowledge the dimensions of our unfreedom. As working scientists, we see the commoditisation of science as the prime cause of the alienation of most scientists from the products of their labour. It stands between the powerful insights of science and corresponding advances in human welfare, often producing results that contradict the stated purposes.

The Dialectical Biologist, Richard Levins and Richard Lewontin

Part 2
Ideas for the 21st century

7 Transforming the economy

In today's society, things are produced in anticipation of buyers coming forward to purchase at a price which results in a profit being made. Part of this profit is distributed to the shareholders, who provide the capital investment and become part-owners of the company. When a company's fortunes decline, or it makes a loss, its shareholders are likely to withdraw their funds and invest in one with better prospects. This is what defines capitalist society. Investors invest – buy and own shares – expecting to receive a proportion of the gains made. When stripped right down to its essence, in capitalist society the rule is: no profit, no production.

Of course many things are produced and many people do things which are not intended to be profitable or do not directly lead to a profit. But, in general, the tendency is always to subordinate these to the main line. Competition amongst companies in a capitalist economy requires them to make their products more attractive to potential consumers than those of their competitors. There are several tactics used: reducing the price charged; making broadly equivalent products appear different and more attractive; bringing new products to the marketplace to satisfy unmet demands, and stimulating new demands; or undermining, weakening and then either buying up or finally destroying the competitor. The giant transnational corporations (TNCs) use all these methods to their fullest extent.

The heart of the whole process of making profit is the ability of workers – including managers – to add more value to inputs during the working day than the total cost of their employment to the firm. The difference between the total cost of labour and the value added by workers is called *surplus value*. For example, steel, glass, upholstery and other materials and components enter a car plant as a variety of inputs. Through the blood, sweat, tears and skills of labour, they come out as higher value cars. The value added, which is the source of profit, comes from the hours of labour put in by the employees, managers, sub-contractors – all those who actively contribute to the production and distribution of the end-products which appear in the shops, market stalls, supermarket shelves, mail-order catalogues and websites. Part of surplus value is paid as rent to landowners and a part is profit, which in capitalist society is distributed to shareholders.

So the key to defending profits in an era of fierce competition is the pressure to reduce the cost of production. Costs of production include labour, which also means management, machinery, commodities bought from suppliers, distribution including holding stock, and communication. Obviously, reducing costs means paying less for inputs. This can be achieved in a number of ways: paying less for commodities bought in, increasing the quantity of commodities produced by the same labour force (productivity), through capital investment, training, pushing employees into a longer working day, cutting wages or a faster/higher rate of working. Other ways to achieve the same result include cutting benefits such as pensions, holiday pay, and by transfer of production to lower wage areas. Much of the drive to globalise production has come from these pressures.

Hence the unending search for ever-cheaper sources of labour and the leap-frogging of investment from developed countries like the US, UK and Japan, to Mexico, the Philippines, Malaysia, and Indonesia in the 1990s, and from there to China in the early years of the 21st century. Labour costs are higher in areas where employees have organised in trade unions. The concentration of workers which is taking place now in China is creating opportunities for them to become organised, but until this happens their working conditions and wages will remain far

---

What's in a brand

In 2004, HSBC, "the world's local bank", consolidated its advertising campaign as part of its drive to enter the first division of global corporations. In ten years it grew from a regional bank in Asia with 30,000 employees, to one of the most global of banks, with more than $1 trillion in assets, nearly 10,000 offices and 300,000 employees. It is now the second-largest financial institution, and the eighth-largest corporation in the world.

Now, in the intensifying pressure of globalisation, HSBC switched its $600m a year advertising account from more than 200 different agencies around the world to a single company able to handle all of its commercial communications in every one of the 79 countries in which it operates. Probably 90% of that $600 million will go to media owners, such as newspapers, magazines and TV stations.

HSBC's demand for a unified, global presence placed extraordinary pressures on the bidders. WPP the agency which eventually won, had 700 of its staff from New York to Kuala Lumpur involved in making the pitch, presenting a united front that showed that they could work together seamlessly. Hundreds or even thousands throughout the world will work on the account. WPP will make perhaps $8m profit on its $60 million fees and commissions. Its success in gaining HSBC's business threatened to destroy the InterPublic Group, parent of its competitor agency Lowe, and the world's third largest advertising group.

---

below those established elsewhere over many decades.

While pressure groups in the US and elsewhere have forced companies to pay some attention to the worst excesses, the irresistible demands of profit-making ensure that wages and working conditions can only be described as super-exploitation when compared to those previously won by organised workers in the older industrialised countries.

Though much of the cost reduction is intended to defend and increase profits, and keep the shareholders' hands in the till, the overall result is entirely the opposite. As productivity is driven up, and investment in automation replaces human labour, more and more commodities are churned out. For a while, as long as the market is large enough for the commodities to be sold, the

---

Doc Martens puts the boot in

Until 2003, Dr Martens' boots were made in Britain and sold to generations of punks, skinheads as well as their traditional market of manual workers and policemen. Now production is sub-contracted to factories owned by Pou Chen and Golden Chang, Taiwanese companies that moved to the mainland. Pou Chen's plants, one in Zhuhai and one in Dongguan, employ 110,000 people and churn out 100m pairs of shoes a year for Nike, Adidas, Caterpillar, Timberland, Hush Puppy, Reebok, Puma and others. Production on this scale requires buildings that would have challenged the most ambitious Lancashire mill owner during Britain's industrial revolution. Tens of thousands of young women hired from all over rural China work on bustling production lines that snake through a series of long, five-storey buildings. Dr Martens' Northampton factory used 20th century production techniques. Small groups of workers assembled complete shoes to reduce inventory costs. Pou Chen uses mass production techniques little changed from Henry Ford's days. In 2003, Dr Martens paid its 1,100 UK workers about $490 a week and had built a stadium for the local football club. Pou Chen was paying about $96 a month, or 36 cents an hour, for up to 69 hours a week. The migrant workers sleep in dormitories and must obey strict curfews.

Financial Times, 4 February 2003

---

individual companies can increase their returns.

But the general tendency throughout the global economy is for the rate of profit to fall. In attempting to overcome it, capitalist society tears itself apart, setting owners and managers against their employees, producing ecological disasters, provoking discontent and reaction and inducing fraud on a global scale. Without sales, the surplus value contained within the commodity is not realised. The cost of storing and in due course disposing of unsold stock, continues to add to the overall cost of production.

As competition intensifies, the commodities pour off the production line, warehouses become full to bursting as the unsold products amass, and so the pressure to sell builds up. Inevitably, marketing based on accurate information gives way to exaggerated claims and these in turn give way to fraudulent campaigns which endanger the health of millions. The pressure to sell more and more lies behind the increasing risk to health from the food we buy.

The need to reduce costs obliges competing firms to use all methods available. This drives them to research, seek out and adopt every new technological advance, and every step forward in management technique. In this way, the production process is constantly revolutionised. Huge leaps in productivity result in an ever-larger volume of ever-cheaper commodities.

So, the tendency of competition is to encourage increased investment in automation, and, consequently, in the part going into machinery and other forms of fixed capital in relation to the number of people employed (variable capital). This has serious and inescapable consequences for those shareholders expecting to benefit. The smaller proportion of people employed in relation to fixed capital reduces that portion of funds invested in labour, the source of surplus value, and so puts downward pressure on the rate of profit. This in turn requires further investment and another cycle begins. Increased productivity produces over-capacity, and the surge of cheap commodities overwhelms the available market.

This contradiction is both the motor of growth, and the cause of crisis. Globalisation – the escalating expansion of capital – is both the result of this contradiction, and the source of its own systemic crises and collapses. Gross Domestic Product (GDP) measures growth – the value of new goods and services produced within the borders of a country in a year. It is used as an indicator of the success or failure of an economy. For the world as a whole, therefore, global GDP can be used as a measure of the success of globalisation in resolving this contradiction.

For the period between 1961 and 2003, world GDP per capita growth has been slowing. It is striking that since 1990, the period in which globalisation has been most pronounced, growth measured by global GDP has been slower than in previous decades. In attempting to escape the consequences of falling profits, every route must be followed and new ones developed. Capitalist corporations do not just take scientific advances and new inventions and use them to improve existing commodities – goods for sale – or produce entirely new ones. They also turn freely usable things into commmodities. Everyday and extreme forms of this include water, genetic structures, and naturally-occurring life-forms. Bars in America have sold oxygen alongside the spirits, beer, wine and non-alcoholic drinks. The patenting of air cannot be far behind.

The China syndrome

Recent experience in China highlights the central paradox of globalising capital. The seemingly infinite availability of low-cost labour tempts TNCs to invest. Cheap capital from Chinese state banks from privatising state-owned utilities over the past few years has also encouraged the growth of local companies. The giant sell-off has resulted in mass sackings, tending to reduce the price of labour even further. Yet new and expanding companies have often found it cheaper to spend money on mechanisation than to recruit and train workers. This has resulted in a fall in the number of jobs created per percentage point in GDP growth, and the number of urban unemployed is rising.

Rapid growth in the designated enterprise zones and beyond is fuelled by inward investment as TNCs chase new opportunities for profit, transferring production from places as remote from each other as the US and Malaysia.

The world's boom has produced global shortages of oil, steel and other commodities including food staples. Prices of raw materials are driven sharply up, whilst low wages and efficient supply chains mean that prices of manufactured goods plummet. In 2003, the factories that are turning China into the new sweatshop of the world consumed 7% of global oil consumption, 27% of steel, 31% of coal and 40% of cement, 21% of the world's traded aluminium, 24% of its zinc, 28% of its iron ore and 23% of its stainless steel.

In a bizarre reversal of fortunes, the country is obliged to fund the purchase of its output. Just as the governments of more advanced capitalist countries favour less wealthy nations with "aid" to buy arms and other products, today China buys government bonds from the US, by far its largest market.

In 2003, China surpassed the US as the world's top destination for foreign direct investment, attracting £32 billion. In 2004, it became Japan's and South Korea's largest trading partner. If official figures are accurate, the annual growth rate of 8.6% of gross domestic product since 1980 registers a pace that constitutes the most striking economic transformation in human history. Its scale and rapidity towers over the British Industrial Revolution of the 19th century.

China today provides an object lesson in the essentials of capitalist production. Through uncontrolled expansion and self-reproduction, massive over-investment produces and reproduces a supply of commodities which flood world markets. Unconscious, unplanned expansion fuelled by finance capital in a helter-skelter chase after profit, demonstrates and proves the insane and anarchic logic of globalised capitalism. Chronic oversupply has created a cauldron of industrial competition which pits Chinese manufacturers against competitors both at home and in South East Asia.

Price wars produce falling profit margins on their core products and push many companies into scattergun efforts to diversify. Midea, an air-conditioner maker, launched six new product ranges: bread-makers, coffee pots, refrigerators, dishwashers and smoke extractors. Lifan, a big motorbike maker has expanded into buses, mineral water, paint thinner, imported wine, newspapers, a football team and duck-down garments. It also wanted to open a bank. The wastefulness of such competition-driven investment is eloquently expressed by a single statistic: of all Chinese manufactured products, 90% are in oversupply, and there is a shortage of nothing, according to the National Statistics Bureau.

The inevitable wave of bankruptcy is postponed, temporarily, as the government fears social chaos. But two measures indicate the scale of the looming debt crisis waiting to detonate the banking sector. Officially, non-performing loans – a polite expression for when borrowers are unable to make repayments – amount to 20% of the total. But the international rating agency, Standard and Poor puts the figure much higher – at 45%, which accounts for more than 80% of commercial lending.

When, not if, the financial plug is pulled, millions more workers will be sent to join those cast out of the privatised previously state-owned industries as social priorities have changed. Out of a population of 1.3 billion, there are already an estimated 30 million unemployed in the cities. A further 150 million transients, former rural residents are thought to be roaming at any one time from job to job in booming urban areas, unable to compete for the best jobs, unable to get access to good health care, or provide their children with a good education. At least 200 million people remain on the land, abandoned, with virtually no work. Whilst Shanghai and Beijing now have

---

China's ecological crisis

China's own environmental record is so lamentable that if it were ever to import Western consumer habits, we might all suffer the consequences. Imagine, for example, what would happen if coal production were to double. China relies on coal for 75% of its energy and already spews out 19 million tons of sulphur dioxide a year, compared with 11 million tons for the United States. It would soon rival the US as the world's largest source of greenhouse gases – although as a "developing nation" China is exempted by the Kyoto treaty from cutting its carbon dioxide emissions. The implications for global warming hardly bear thinking about.

Environmentalists point out that China's "ecological footprint", though large and increasing, is considerably less per head than that of either the US or the UK. Even now, however, the inhabitants of roughly two-thirds of the 340 Chinese cities, where air quality is monitored, breathe air that fails to meet national air-quality levels (which are considerably less stringent than World Health Organisation norms). Indoor pollution from coal burning takes more than 700,000 lives a year.

Then there is water. Two thirds of China's major cities are now seriously short of fresh water, and as many as 700 million people drink water that is contaminated with human and animal waste and that doesn't come close to meeting government standards (also below world norms).

Jasper Becker *Independent,* 8 May 2004

hospitals similar to those in developed countries, the universal rural system of health care created by Mao Zedong's 1949 revolution is fast disappearing, leaving wide swathes of the country with care worse than was available before the revolution. Just as in the US, in conditions of such extreme competition, capitalist production is unable to provide social support for people without work.

Agriculture fares no better

The methods of manufacturing and of industrialisation have also revolutionised agriculture. The application of science and new technology has shifted food production from a reliance on manual labour to a dependence on mechanisation. Just as in manufacturing, the continual competitive pressure to purchase

---

The global glut

The world economy is now facing a widening deflationary gap created by deficient global demand. There is a global glut in both labour and product markets, with too many goods chasing too few buyers and too many workers chasing too few jobs. Intense price and exchange-rate competition among major exporters have been adding to instability and deflationary pressures, while many developing countries facing tight payments positions are being forced to curtail imports. These difficulties are similar to those that the Bretton Woods Institutions were created to resolve. If decisive action is not taken to restore stability in financial and currency markets, to start a global recovery and reverse the rapid rise in unemployment, there is a real threat that trade imbalances and the coexistence of continued rapid growth in some parts of the world with stagnation, decline and job losses elsewhere could deepen the existing discontent with globalisation among a wide section of the world's population, triggering a political backlash and a loss of faith in markets and openness, and leading to international economic disintegration with the burden falling disproportionately on the poor and underprivileged. This is perhaps the first real test for economic policy in a post-Bretton Woods globalise world.

Trade and development report 2003, UNCTAD

---

the latest equipment, the most potent chemical inputs, and the highest-yielding seeds places farmers firmly on the technological treadmill. Advances in technology may raise single-crop yields, but they also often lower the farmer's net income: capital expenses, debt service and production costs eat up a higher proportion of the farmer's proceeds, while overall increases in output merely cause the price of global commodities to drop.

In the US, for example, factory farming techniques – including carefully controlled heating and lighting, specially formulated feed and heavy doses of antibiotics – enable the average poultry

---

Milking the farmers

In Wales, in 1945, there were 27,000 registered milk producers producing an average of 21,000 litres per producer each year – a total of 567m litres. By the early 1970s the number of producers had fallen by nearly 50% to 15,000 producing an average of 81,500 litres per producer. By 2004, the number of registered producers had plummeted to 3,000, producing a staggering 500,000 litres each – a total of 1500m litres. This increased volume has been achieved with little increase in the number of animals.

Productivity increases derive from improved grasses, fertilisers, scientific breeding techniques, and disease control. And the days of hand-milking are long gone. In the most advanced units the cows present themselves to be milked several times a day by robot machines which automatically attach to the cows' teats.

The resultant reduction in the value derived from milk production together with, in recent years, increasing competitive pressure from supermarkets has contributed dramatically to the falling price paid to farmers relative to farm asset values. From the early 1930s to the present day, the milk price paid to producers has increased six-fold; from an average of 3p per litre to 18 ppl in 2003. During the same period land prices increased 100-fold, from £40 per acre in the early 1930s to around £4,000 today. And the average price of a farmhouse has increased more than 130-fold from £995 to £130,000.

Gwlad, the magazine of agriculture and rural affairs information from the Welsh Assembly, Issue 30, July 2004

producer to raise 240,000 birds each year. But after expenses this prodigious (and cruel) production earns the farmer only $12,000, or five cents per bird. Such technological techniques typically do nothing to help farmers, while providing a boon to the manufacturers and marketers of the technologies.

Meanwhile, the global economy's emphasis on free trade often forces farmers into competition with producers in countries where costs are lower due to more favourable climate and geography, lower labour costs, or less stringent standards. Farmers are pressured to become still more "efficient" by increasing the size of their farms, becoming more narrowly specialised and adopting newer technologies. The treadmill speeds up, and farmers inevitably fall further behind.

Farmers in the poorer countries face similar problems. Those still embedded in a local economy can feed their families with their diversified production, selling the remainder in local markets. But those who have been drawn into the global food system must specialise their production for export, using the income from it to buy food. A farmer in South America or Africa

---

Crisis in the countryside

In *A rough guide to the UK farming crisis*, Corporate Watch reported that in 1939, Britain had almost 500,000 farms, most of them under 40 hectares, employing 15% of the population. Today, a third of the farms have gone, with the pace accelerating in recent years. Some 87,000 farmers and farm workers left the industry between 1993 and 2001, and a further 18,000 in 2002. The government predicts that by 2005 another 25% of the remaining farms in the UK will have gone bust or merged, with a further 50,000 people forced to leave farming. UK dairy farmers are in great difficulties because of the pressure exerted by the big supermarket chains. The farmgate milk price has plummeted by over 30% since 1995, falling to below production price. Between 1970 and 2000 the number of dairy farms in the UK fell by 70%. The resultant crisis in rural areas has taken its toll on social and economic life. There are now fewer than 12,000 rural shops left in Britain, with 300 closing each year. Banks and post offices have closed in large numbers. Six village pubs close each week.

can easily be destroyed by a recession in Europe or a bigger-than-expected harvest in Asia.

The total income from UK farming fell by 70% from its 1996 high to a low of £1.8 billion in 2001/2 in the year of foot and mouth. It has since recovered slightly, rising to £2.36 billion in 2002 and to £3.23 billion in 2003. Despite the recent recovery, the underlying pattern is of a long-term decline in farm incomes. The total income generated by agriculture has declined in real terms by around 40% over the past 30 years.

Annual surveys by Deloitte & Touche show that the average net farm income fell dramatically from £80,000 in 1995-96 to £8,000 in 2000 and to £2,500 during 2001, the year of foot and mouth. Incomes recovered somewhat, to £12,500 in 2002/03. But for some, predominantly small farmers, they remain well below the minimum wage. An increasing number of farmers now also work part-time off the farm.

Fictitious capital, fictitious profits

The increasing failure of production to yield a sufficient rate of profit obliges capitalist producers to seek ever more funds for expansion, far beyond the amounts provided by shareholders. The escalating demand for credit led to the rise of the financial sector. This was especially marked in the 1980s. It provided the source of funds for investments abroad, and the acquisitions and mergers which continue to characterise the trajectory of corporations.

As the financial sector has grown, its expansion became a magnet for investors, speculators and assorted gamblers. In the decade up to 2001, the numbers employed in banking and finance in the UK rose by 1.7 million people, as 500,000 manufacturing jobs were lost. The British economy has become massively over-dependent on exporting insurance and financial services, together with a surge in speculation on overseas markets. In June 2004, the Bank of England warned that a flood of speculative cash into hedge funds run by "less-experienced" managers brought the risk of a sudden correction that could trigger instability in financial markets and push the world deeper into recession. In the same year the financial sector was providing around 37% of all domestic profits in the United States, having risen from a mere 7% in 1948. Calculations suggest that financial shares are overvalued by between 58 and 80%. With growth declining globally, a new downward spiral cannot be far off.

Whilst the complexities of the world financial system can seem remote to many people, the growth of personal and household debt looms larger by the day. In June 2004, the Bank of England warned that the overall mountain of debt of £1 trillion pounds held by UK consumers was the major threat to the stability of Britain's banking system. But as the volume of commodities cascading onto the high streets continued, and prices continued to drop, the TNCs increased their marketing budgets.

Besides shoes and clothing, the dominant commodities are based around the silicon chip. Millions upon millions of chips pour out of plants day by day in search of a home. For more than 30 years, an inverse law has operated in computing – power increasing and price decreasing. This particular expression of the law of the tendency of the rate of profit to fall is as hard at work here as everywhere else. There is no end in sight to this process. PCs, laptops, games machines, mobile phones, phone cards, cars, washing machines, bread machines. Everything that can host a chip, will. But for profit to be realised, commodities must not just be made. They must also be sold. And for people whose wages are held down by competition, to be able to buy they must have access to credit. So the ultimate chip-based commodity is the chip-and-pin credit card that makes borrowing from the future an essential part of life.

As this book went to print, interest rates had begun to rise again. Realisation of the distinct possibilities of collapse began to appear in the financial pages. It was not a question of if, but when. The impact on the finances of all those tempted into credit-card debt by the life-style marketing campaigns, and seduced into large mortgages by the meteoric, seemingly endless rise in house prices is inevitable. Assets will overnight be turned into so-called "negative equity". Millions more pensions will evaporate. Jobs will disappear. Uncontrolled meltdown will produce incalculable social and political consequences.

This is an account of a social, economic and political system out of control. It has created forces so monstrous, that is impossible to bring the system to order. This is the motivation for change.

History demands change

We have tried to show that the means, capacity and potential for satisfying human need in the shape of goods and services is distorted, held back and turned into something oppressive by a productive system that is driven primarily by profit. Our proposals are aimed at liberating human achievement from the straitjacket of capitalist social relations.

This is both possible and necessary. The means are already to hand, as we will show. The great achievements in terms of science, technology and human organisational skills are immediately in front of us. Yet they remain beyond conscious, human control because they are owned privately, dependent on capital and its narrow objectives before they are brought into use. Alternative forms of ownership and work on a not-for-profit basis already exist within capitalism. Yet they are marginalised and isolated forms that stand no chance of becoming the dominant form within the existing order of things. They are all subject to the overwhelming pressures of market forces and the demands of capitalist states and governments.

Historical forces are on our side, adding to the possibilities and potential already described. Despite its appearance of permanence, which it tries to reinforce whenever and wherever it can, capitalism is a relatively small blip on the timescale of 12,000 years of social history. It grew within feudalism and emerged through social and political revolution and the violence of the industrial revolution. History demands that the system of private ownership itself is transcended in order to liberate the potential that it contains – and to halt the ecological destruction that actually threatens life itself. This force in the shape of human aspirations is knocking at the gates, demanding that they are opened. The means of production have outgrown the way the economy is organised. We have to break the bonds, the chains that hold humanity back and create the conditions for a new type of society to evolve.

One of the enduring myths of capitalism is that it is not possible to produce without private ownership. Co-operatives and other not-for-profit enterprises show that is simply not the case. Furthermore, the actual owners of industry and commerce absented themselves from the scene in a practical sense way back

---

At a certain stage of their development, the material productive forces of society come in conflict with the existing relations of production, or – what is but a legal expression for the same thing – with the property relations within which they have been at work hitherto. From forms of development of the productive forces these relations turn into their fetters. Then begins an epoch of social revolution. With the change of the economic foundation the entire immense superstructure is more or less rapidly transformed. In considering such transformations a distinction should always be made between the material transformation of the economic conditions of production, which can be determined with the precision of natural science, and the legal, political, religious, aesthetic or philosophic – in short, ideological forms in which men become conscious of this conflict and fight it out. Just as our opinion of an individual is not based on what he thinks of himself, so can we not judge of such a period of transformation by its own consciousness; on the contrary, this consciousness must be explained rather from the contradictions of material life, from the existing conflict between the social productive forces and the relations of production.

"No social order ever perishes before all the productive forces for which there is room in it have developed; and new, higher relations of production never appear before the material conditions of their existence have matured in the womb of the old society itself. Therefore mankind always sets itself only such tasks as it can solve; since, looking at the matter more closely, it will always be found that the tasks itself arises only when the material conditions of its solution already exist or are at least in the process of formation.

Preface to a Contribution to the Critique of Political Economy 1859, Karl Marx

in the 19th century. With the development of credit, joint stock companies and other means of raising finance, the actual owner of capital became increasingly remote and unnecessary. As Marx remarked, the capitalist is actually a "mere manager, administrator of other people's investment, a mere money-capitalist. Ownership of capital is now entirely divorced from the function of capital in the production process". All the actual work is done by salaried employees

The aim of a classless society through the abolition of capitalism would be to:

▸ ensure the majority have access to the benefits currently only available to the few
▸ ensure survival of the planet, ecosystems and humanity
▸ create a society based on co-operation, satisfying need and not profit
▸ release the potential of automation, reducing working hours substantially
▸ overcome alienation of people from their work, what is produced and society as a whole
▸ use the abundance of products to alleviate poverty and need world-wide
▸ allow and enable people to fulfil their potential and aspirations
▸ make health and well-being the single dominant social objective for the world's population.

Alternatives that beg the question

Over the past decade, millions of people have taken to the streets throughout the world in massive demonstrations against the institutions and policies of corporate globalisation. Seattle in 1999 brought together a coalition of workers and activists from the industrialised and developing countries against the World Trade Organisation. A growing global consciousness formed in response to the power of the transnational corporations was transformed into militant protest. The WTO confirmed its undemocratic nature by moving its 2001 ministerial meeting to Qatar, ruled by a feudal monarchy where public protest is ruthlessly suppressed. In April 2000, police shut down much of Washington so that a World Bank-IMF meeting could take place free of disturbance. A subsequent meeting of IMF and World Bank directors in Prague closed a day early and a planned meeting in Barcelona was cancelled. The Italian state brutally suppressed opposition to the G8 Summit in Genoa, killing a protester and injuring many more. Thousands from all over the world have gathered in Porte Alegre, Brazil, each year since 2001 for the annual World Social Forum, entitled "Another World is Possible". Similar gatherings have taken place in India and in France.

World Bank-IMF projects like water privatisation in Ghana have met resistance from the trade unions and community groups. Tens of thousands have struggled against dam projects in India, which are driven by global corporate interests. In countries like Britain, there is widespread opposition to genetically-modified (GM) food because of the justified suspicion that companies like Monsanto put profits ahead of scientific probity. In poorer countries, small farmers have led the movement against GM because of the threat it poses to their livelihoods and health.

In September 2000, representatives of peoples' organisations in Cambodia, India, Indonesia, Laos, Malaysia, the Philippines and Thailand joined in a 12-day mobile campaign for biodiversity. The participants declared that:

> Biodiversity can only be protected and properly managed by local people. Importantly, Asian communities do not perceive biological resources as commodities for agribusiness and industry. Instead, they have a sacred and spiritual value to sustain our lives and our survival.
>
> Our biological resources have been destroyed on a massive scale with colonialism. It was exacerbated by the Green Revolution, which was imposed by our governments in co-operation with international agriculture research institutes. The great pressure towards genetic engineering and the use of genetically modified organisms (GMOs) by agricultural transnational corporations (TNCs) led by Monsanto and Novartis will inevitably exacerbate destruction of the world's biodiversity and rapid genetic pollution.

The development of GMOs, the promotion of GM food and products as well as the intellectual property rights system imposed by the industrialised countries all stand against religious and ethical principles and faith of Asian people. All this violates the rights of farmers, consumers and entire nations. The self-reliance and sovereignty in the Asian region will be threatened to the point that we all become slaves of giant international corporations.

As human beings, we are both part of and highly dependent on biodiversity. Rice, corn, and other staple crops, food crops, medicinal plants and all other life forms are significant genetic resources that shape our culture and lifestyle. We oppose any plan to transform these into genetically modified organisms.

Every day, activists and ordinary people engage in struggle against ecological degradation, the results of industrialised food production, the movement of jobs from one country to another, and the ruthless exploitation at work that is the hallmark of globalisation for profit. This resistance has found its reflection in a set of "alternatives" to corporate-driven globalisation, put forward by organisations like Oxfam, the International Forum on Globalisation (IFG), the World Development Movement (WDM) and social scientists like David Held.

The IFG points out that groups have waged public campaigns against the operations of TNCs on numerous fronts – ranging from world-wide boycotts against Nestlé on dried baby milk and bank loans to South Africa, the battles against Union Carbide over the Bhopal disaster in India, the repression of Coca-Cola workers in Guatemala, the promotion of bio-tech milk products by chemical companies like Monsanto, and clear-cut logging and deforestation by Mitsubishi and MacMillan Bloedel. "Through these and many other corporate campaigns, workers, environmentalists, consumer, church and human rights groups have cultivated important strategic capacities and skills for challenging TNCs. At the same time, a variety of legal and social action centres on corporate issues have been developed bringing valuable profiles and data on specific TNCs. Today, these resources need to be refocused and retooled for the task of building a broad-based global movement aimed at the new realities of corporate rule."

The IFG's *Alternatives to Economic Globalisation,* set out 10 organising principles for "democratic and sustainable societies". These include creating a "new democracy", local production, ecological sustainability, the protection of the commons – resources like water, air, land, fisheries and forest – from corporate domination, the right to a livelihood, an emphasis on human rights, diversity and "greater equity both among nations and within them" to "reinforce democracy and sustainable communities". Few could disagree with these sentiments – but that is all that they remain. The one, very important, word that does not figure in the IFG's analysis is "capitalism". The absence of an analysis of the inner dynamics of how the system functions makes it impossible to put forward serious alternatives. We are left to guess how the transnational corporations have accumulated such power and influence. Ultimately, the IFG appeals to the status quo to mend its ways, declaring: "As the Bretton Woods institutions are dismantled, the countervailing institutional power required to reform the global financial system and end global corporate rule can come from strengthened states and a reformed United Nations."

There is a call for the replacement of the World Bank, the IMF and the WTO with new institutions created under the auspices of the United Nations. This is the same UN that itself is in hock to big business through alliances at every level of the organisation. It is also the body that proved toothless when the United States and Britain launched their illegal attack on Iraq.

The IFG is right to cite the growth in popular movements that challenge corporate power, such as Living Democracy in India, which urges democratic community control of resources and that in Canada hundreds of organisations have "joined in alliance to articulate a Citizens' Agenda that seeks to wrest control of governmental institutions back away from corporations". There are similar movements in most countries, particularly in South America where the Zapatistas in Mexico have inspired movements of the landless poor. But their aspirations cannot be met by a tinkering around with global capitalist institutions, even if it were possible to do that.

Non-governmental organisations (NGOs) like Oxfam, Christian Aid, Greenpeace and Jubilee 2000, have mushroomed over the recent period of globalisation. Many have joined government delegations at global summits. They have also become key agencies in the delivery of rich country "aid" and humanitarian assistance. Deeply concerned about the course of corporate globalisation, many have suggested a better way of doing business that will make the corporations more acceptable to the rest of society. Christian Aid, for example, has called for the legally-binding regulation of transnational corporations. In a briefing document for the World Economic Forum and the World Summit on Sustainable Development in 2002, it advocated "minimal standards to govern corporate behaviour" in terms of employment conditions and protection of natural resources in order to "stop the worst TNC abuses". The charity's somewhat amazing conclusion was that legal regulation would turn the corporations into "a positive force for development". Well intentioned as these thoughts are, they defy reality in a massive way. The summit duly despatched the notion of regulation to the waste paper bin.

Oxfam's campaign, which is supported by many other like-minded organisations, is to make trade between rich and poor countries "fair". If this happened, it would make a "real difference in the fight against global poverty". Oxfam rightly points out:

> Large parts of the developing world are becoming enclaves of despair, increasingly marginalised and cut off from the rising wealth generated through trade. Shared prosperity cannot be built on such foundations. Like the economic forces that drive globalisation, the anger and social tensions that accompany vast inequalities in wealth and opportunity will not respect national borders. The instability that they will generate threatens us all. In today's globalised world, our lives are more inextricably linked than ever before, and so is our prosperity. As a global community, we sink or swim together.

The charity's view is that the international trading system is managed by rules and institutions that "reflect political choices".

In a rational world, where resources were commonly owned and controlled, this would be true. In the world of global capitalism, this is a far-from-accurate analysis. In fact, the opposite is true. Political choices actually reflect dominant, objective economic forces which are based on exploitation and profit, not fair trade. In the end, Oxfam's call for "a new model of inclusive globalisation" will fall on deaf ears and does nothing to bring out the real issues confronting poor countries in the international trade system.

In the end there is simply no such thing as capitalism with a human face. Held, author of a number of books on globalisation, believes that the present course is full of dangers and that alternatives are needed. In an article for *opendemocracy.net* he rightly says that "Washington-led neoliberalism and unilateralism has failed the world" and that "it is urgent that we find a way beyond its legacy". He observes the coincidence of the crisis affecting the global economy, ecology, political rule and the fate of poorer nations. He too, however, cannot bring himself to write of *capitalism*. This is because Held observes trends and patterns very well but refuses to see their relationships. In his book *Global Transformations*, he writes that globalisation is best thought of as

> a highly differentiated phenomenon involving domains of activity and interaction as diverse as the political, military, economic, cultural, migratory and environmental. Each of these domains involves different patterns of relations and activities. These can be thought of as "sites of power" – interaction contexts or organisational milieu in and through which power operates to shape the action capacities of peoples and communities.

Held calls for a "new global covenant". This is based on the rejection of the "Washington consensus" in favour of a "free and fair global economy which also supports a human security agenda" so that globalisation is "steered for the benefit for all". His five essential goals are: the promotion of the rule of law at international level; greater transparency in "global governance"; a "deeper commitment to social justice in the pursuit of a more equitable distribution of changes; the "reinvention" of community and the regulation of the global economy. This is supposed to be a framework for a "global social democratic consensus". In fact this is a humanist illusion and is clearly no alternative to corporate-driven globalisation.

The International Labour Organisation is supposed to represent and advance the interests of workers throughout the world. You would not think so after reading *A fair globalisation: creating opportunities for all*. In 190 pages of text, analysis and graphs, the ILO unbelievably fails to apply the term *capitalism* even once to the study of globalisation and its social impact. Yet the report acknowledges that public debate on globalisation is at an "impasse" and that the will for consensus is "weak". International development commitments go largely unfulfilled, it notes, without asking why. The fact is that, as we have shown, capital is locked into a dynamic of its own and will only modify its operations in so far as this does not affect the main purpose of its existence – capital accumulation and profits. Ignoring this reality allows the ILO to dwell on ways to "harness the potential of globalisation itself" in order to "extend the benefits" to more people.

There is a clear acceptance of the status quo and even praise: "The global market economy has demonstrated great productive capacity. Wisely managed [!], it can deliver unprecedented material progress, generate more productive and better jobs for all, and contribute significantly to reducing world poverty." This could easily have been written by the World Bank or the chief executive of one of the more "socially responsible" corporations. As a result, the ILO puts forward proposals that are essentially meaningless. The report calls for: "a focus on people"; a democratic and effective state; sustainable development; productive and equitable markets; fair rules; globalisation with solidarity; greater accountability to people; deeper partnerships and an effective United Nations. This presents no challenge to corporate globalisation and will do nothing to help the cause of the workers for whom the ILO claims to speak. In fact, by tying them into working in partnership with big business, these proposals can only make conditions worse and erode still further trade unions' independence.

There is a growing school of thought that proposes an alternative form of capitalism based on limiting growth. The New Economics Foundation argues that it "isn't growth so much as the quality of our lives that counts". A briefing paper describes economic progress as a "cultural myth" that helps bind society together. The NEF admits: "There is, in the current climate, no real alternative to economic growth that doesn't involve the risk of greater hardships for the most vulnerable in our society." So it proposes to reformulate "sustainable objectives" and other measures in order to redefine what constitutes progress as an alternative to using economic growth as a yardstick.

Growth is also author Clive Hamilton's target. In his *Visions of the Future – the post-growth society*, he argues that: "Growth not only fails to make people contented; it also destroys many of the things that do. Growth fosters empty consumerism, degrades the natural environment, weakens social cohesion and corrodes character." It seems as if growth has an almost autonomous power and significance, which is then projected onto society in terms of its effects and impact. For Hamilton it is not the dominant role of capital which defines the character of growth. Instead growth defines the role of capital, the market and the alienating ideology of consumer capitalism. This means it is growth, not capitalism which is considered to be the opponent of potential social change and progress.

This standpoint results in subjectivism, which is expressed by an emphasis upon the importance of attitudes and opinions as the basis for understanding the relationship between reality and thought. Because growth is considered in ambiguously psychological terms as what makes us unhappy as human beings it must be replaced by a situation that makes us happy. Hamilton claims: "The politics of the transition to a post-growth society does not call for the overthrow of the state or the destruction of capital; it starts from where we are." He sets out a vision of society which represents a radical rejection of the ideology and social structures of growth fetishism.

So the aim of this "post-growth society" is an ethical

capitalism that has somehow rejected the significance of economic growth. It will be a society that, because it is still based upon capitalism, will also have capital accumulation and an expansionist logic, and yet will also not emphasise the role of growth! This is untenable because, as we have shown, the imperatives of capital accumulation are based upon the increase of material wealth, in the form of an expanding production of commodities and services. In reality therefore, the process of accumulation cannot be differentiated from growth. The very connection between growth, accumulation and consumerism exists, because the act of purchasing a commodity facilitates the possibility of realising the surplus value within a commodity.

Hamilton essentially argues that material goods themselves are the representation of alienation. But while it can certainly be argued that the quantity of material goods that a person owns is not identical with happiness, it is not possible to disconnect the satisfaction of human wants from the actual goods of consumption. It is not the action of consumption that contributes to alienation, but instead the character of the process of consumption. For example, is it possible to have an over-consumption of books, or musical CDs? Both can represent a contribution to the development of our imagination and intellectual capacity.

Is a person who spends a lot of disposable income on books adapting to consumerist ideology and deliberately trying to create a sophisticated identity for themselves? The answer to this question could be "yes" if virtually none of these books were read, but in general the very act of buying books – which are still commodities and consumer items – represents a use value that contributes to the realisation of profound cultural and intellectual needs. In contrast the inability to be able to buy books because of poverty (and there may be limited access to a public library which have been run down by cuts) is a denial of the possibility of satisfying cultural wants. The result is a form of alienation from the intellectual processes of cultural development because of an inability to consume the use value of books. In contrast, the buying of goods as a sign of prestige and power over others is alienating, not because the goods themselves are alienating, but because they come to represent the social power of some humans over other humans. This alienating situation is ultimately an expression of the social relations and the complex historical development of the capital-labour relation.

The basic objective content of consumption in order to meet human needs remains a constant aspect of historical development. In this context the production of a greater variety of goods is generally an expression of social progress because humans have enhanced their capacity to meet their needs. The role of advertising has distorted this process of realising needs, and brand images have created many unnecessary goods, but still this expression of the ideology of commodity exchange is secondary in importance to the objective connection between the process of consumption and the meeting of human needs. Thus even in the contemporary consumer society the role of consumption is not to satisfy the subjective motive of selfishness, egoism and greed but is instead a generalised expression of fulfilling human needs.

Hamilton's analysis shows the importance of alienating ideology in the act of consumption. For example, advertising creates dissatisfaction with what a person has got and makes consumers aspire to want more and therefore purchase new products. The purpose of marketing and brand identity is to sell an illusory identity to the consumer, (sense of family togetherness or the power of sexuality) but real human needs are not realised. Only the sense of desire remains: "Products and brands can never give real meaning to human lives, so modern consumers lapse into a permanent state of unfilled desire. This, of course, is the essential state for consumers in modern consumer capitalism."

To overcome alienation in the process of production and consumption it is necessary to revolutionise social relations so that they facilitate the producers' and consumers' capacities and abilities. They could then realise economic growth in terms that represent their power over economic and social activity.

Hamilton takes the view that people can make a voluntary decision to change lifestyles by reducing income and consumption patterns. This is a utopia for the comfortably affluent majority. It is not a feasible and practical option for the majority of people who are compelled to work long hours in order to maintain a reasonable standard of living. Most people may actually want to reduce the amount of hours they work, and have more leisure time, but the alienated conditions of their economic activity mean that they have no option other than to work long hours. Only the transformation of these alienated conditions that dictate the character of people's work patterns will create the possibility for people to extend their choices about income, levels of consumption and hours worked. Hamilton has understood that an important problem within capitalism is that it undermines the realisation of human potential. The challenge is to create conditions that liberate this potential.

Not-for-profit working already exists

There are many examples within capitalism of not-for-profit forms of ownership and economic activity. They show that it is possible to run enterprises and services without the profit motive. They include major state-owned bodies like the National Health Service, which is one of the world's largest employers with a 1.3 million strong workforce. Although NHS activities are increasingly commercialised and parts of it contracted out, and while it lacks democratic control, for over 50 years it has proved that something as crucial as healthcare does not need a profit incentive.

Another not-for-profit group of organisations is known broadly as the voluntary sector. These are mostly charities which are run by trustees, who are responsible for the assets of the organisation. Increasingly, they carry out a range of services formerly provided by the public sector. It is estimated that there are more than 150,000 active charities in Britain with a total annual income of £20.8 billion, assets totalling £70 billion and more than 500,000 paid employees. Half are engaged in social work while 12,300 work in museums.

More than 750,000 co-operatives of different types serve some 760 million members in more than 100 countries. They are either consumer, producer, worker or purchasing/shared services co-operatives. Their story probably begins with the 28 pioneers who in 1844 opened a co-operative store in Rochdale. A co-operative can be established as a partnership. There are model partnership agreements which can be used to ensure that the partnership is established on a fair and co-operative basis with the rights and responsibilities of each partner clearly defined. Most co-operatives are established as companies limited by guarantee. This legal format allows for limited liability for the members, democratic management structures, and for a mixture of commercial and social objectives.

In just 25 years, over 11,000 employee-owned companies have been established in the US, employing more than 1.5 million workers. Tens of thousands of employee-owned enterprises have been created in the former Soviet Union and Eastern Europe. Other examples include Publix supermarkets, with 119,000 employees, which is currently the largest employee-owned firm in the US, and Journal Communications, publisher of the *Milwaukee* (Wisconsin) *Journal,* where 3300 current and retired employees are owners of a wide array of firms in the communication business.

In Europe, Italy is reported to have the largest concentration of producer co-operatives in the western world – around 16,000, employing over 300,000 workers. In North America, Canada is particularly rich in co-operatives, claiming around 5,000 co-operatives of various kinds, including credit unions and consumer co-operatives, with 151,000 employees for 14.8 million members, and assets of $167 billion in 1996. Co-operatives have been especially successful as farmers' organisations. Farmers organise to efficiently purchase supplies or services and to process and market their products.

It is reported that worker co-operatives employ more than 300,000 in Spain. The country is home to 11,079 large and small labour firms, employing 62,567 as well as the large and diversified Mondragon Co-operative, formed in the impoverished Basque area in 1956. Today Mondragon is an industrial, banking, management and marketing giant in Spain, with 34,400 employees, 70% of them members of the co-operative, exporting 46% of its industrial production.

Credit unions and mutual savings associations may be the second most common kind of co-operative. They are owned by their depositors, who can receive loans at preferred rates and benefit from dividends as well as interest.

According to the Association of British Credit Unions, in September 2003, there were 444 ABCUL credit unions, providing financial services to around 365,100 people, who between them had saved around £293m and were borrowing £240m. At the same date, there were a total of 665 registered credit unions, with a total membership for Britain of over 460,000. At the other end of the spectrum are giant credit union co-operatives like the Desjardins Credit Union of Quebec, with more than 15,000 employees and $83 billion in assets.

The Landless Workers Movement (MST) is attempting to "redemocratise" the land in Brazil. It is now the largest social movement in Latin America. In a struggle against absentee landlords, more than 300,000 families have won land titles to over 20 million acres through MST land take-overs. In 1999 alone, 25,099 families moved on to unproductive land. There are currently almost 100,000 families in encampments throughout Brazil awaiting settlements. The MST has also created 60 food co-operatives, as well as small agricultural industries. The movement has also set up a literacy programme.

A housing co-op is where members (tenants) control and manage their homes. Many co-ops also own their properties. There are over 250 registered housing co-ops in England. Most date back to the 1970s and 1980s. Many are fully mutual, which means that all their tenants are members and have a right to be involved in the co-op. Most co-ops elect a management committee which organises the day-to-day business. In the US, more than 1.5 million families of all income levels live in homes owned and operated through co-operative associations.

The Community Land Trust (CLT) idea has been developing in the US and Canada over the last 30 years, and is now being applied in several projects in the UK. It provides mutual ownership of land for the benefit of the community. CLT schemes take land off the market and place it into a system of trusteeship. CLTs are often characterised by dual ownership, in which the CLT itself keeps ownership of the land while the users of the land own or rent the buildings on the land on a long leasehold basis, which is paid through modest ground rent levels.

A major development of the last 30 years is "open source". This is the term used to describe computer software that is collectively owned and voluntarily developed. The "contract" that accompanies the software is called a General Public Licence. This dictates that any new source code – which is needed to make software function – will remain free and available to anyone who wants it. The contrast is with proprietary software like Windows, which Microsoft protects by licensing the copyright and legal threats against "pirates". The movement started when the University of California, building on work done by AT&T, developed the Unix operating system and began giving it away for a nominal fee, along with its source code. The increasing dominance of commercial software and Microsoft led to the decline of Unix, which was not suitable for small PCs. The baton was picked by a Finnish student, Linus Torvalds who in 1990 asked via the Internet for help in developing a free operating system he had started work on. The system became known as Linux and marked the start of the open source revolution. In his book *The Success of Open Source*, Steven Weber writes that

> by the end of the decade, Linux was a major technological and market phenomenon. A hugely complex and sophisticated operating system had been built out of the voluntary contributions of thousands of developers spread around the world. By the middle of 2000 Linux ran more than a third of the servers that make up the web. It was making substantial inroads into other segments of computing, all the way from major enterprise-level systems (in banks, insurance companies, and major database operations) to embedded software in smart chips and appliances.

> Modern bourgeois society, with its relations of production, of exchange and of property, a society that has conjured up such gigantic means of production and of exchange, is like the sorcerer who is no longer able to control the powers of the nether world whom he has called up by his spells.
>
> *Communist Manifesto* 1848

Our proposals

Building on the results

Capitalism has already developed an array of methods and technologies, many of which constitute the basics of a fully-integrated, socialised system of production and distribution. Much of what has been developed is currently concentrated in a few countries and benefits a small percentage of the world's population, whilst the majority suffer inhuman and degrading conditions. A new democratic society serving the needs of the majority will ensure that the beneficial results of capitalist production are made available to all. These include:

▸ a globally interconnected communications infrastructure
▸ scientific systems of management
▸ highly-skilled workforces in many countries
▸ integrated methods of supply, production and distribution
▸ the continuing scientific and technological revolution
▸ a global financial system.

Communications infrastructure

A truly globally distributed network is beyond the capability or interest of capitalist corporations. While some in the developed countries carry two or even three mobile phones transmitting text and pictures as well as voice, a large proportion of the world's population has never seen a phone let alone made a call. But in an equitable society focussed on need, the benefits of the computing and communications revolution will be made universally available.

With a global spiders' web of optical fibre and satellites, enhanced with mobile telephony, personal wireless devices, and the continuously increasing speed and power of networked computer systems, a new generation of the Web will draw the wealth of data, information and knowledge management systems into an interconnected layer of intelligence encircling the planet. Application of this technology is virtually limitless. Its uses will benefit humanity in ways which we can only dimly perceive. Knowledge will be widely shared and cultural diversity expanded. Through unlimited, intelligently-guided access to every kind of intellectual product, every individual will have boundless opportunities for self-development. Scarce, specialist expertise can be shared across the globe. Remotely controlled surgery and many other less spectacular aspects of telemedicine already open pathways to the future. Unprecedented social connections will develop around communities of common interest.

In a fully integrated network using multipoint tele- and video-conferencing, the majority will be full participants in policy-making, planning and decision-making. In this way, participative democracy will extend far beyond the primitive forms of registering votes electronically currently under test.

Networks of geostationary satellites provide the basis for global positioning systems (GPS) which greatly simplify navigation in three dimensions. GPS devices are now routinely installed in many types of vehicles and give spoken directions to drivers. With roadside devices providing electronic track, accurate mapping, and built-in safety precautions, automated, driverless, clean fuel, door-to-door public transport systems are now on the horizon.

Air traffic control systems will become better able to deal with the proliferation of planes in the sky. New generations of high, medium and low speed trains, trams and hybrid vehicles using new fuel systems (liquid petroleum gas, electric, solar, hydrogen) will be drawn together into an integrated transport system.

With radio frequency and biometric identification devices taking the ubiquitous barcode several steps on, any tagged object can be tracked as it moves. The potential exists for real-time information to be made available on any object or process on the planet. Repressive governments with a huge and increasing number of discontents and opponents eye these technologies as the ideal means of social control, using ID cards and electronically-tagged irremovable bracelets or anklets as a prison without walls. In a democratic society bent on satisfying the needs of the majority, the emphasis will be on control of objects not people.

Scientific systems of management

In manufacturing, from the moment of an object's first appearance in a production plan, or in response to an individual customer order, the most advanced systems now can and do track its progress through the various stages of fabrication, assembly and delivery. Some, like computer manufacturer Dell, and components supplier Dabs, make stage-by-stage progress on orders available to customers on its website, as do parcel collection and delivery companies.

Transnational and global corporations were made possible by these kinds of technologies. But as these organisations enlarged, becoming more and more complex, they began to outgrow the old deeply hierarchical forms. Many layers of management became unnecessary as routine decision-making fell to automation. Mergers and acquisitions brought dissimilar organisations together, with the need to overcome problems of different, often incompatible systems and cultures. Central, common, duplicated functions led to rationalisation, standardisation and integration within and across company and national borders. Business units were developed to provide common services across the heterogeneous parts of the diversified corporation. The profit centre emerged as the dominant means of control.

Management based on company-wide, rigid organisation structures with strictly allocated roles and responsibilities became increasingly unworkable. These old forms had grown up in the age of Newtonian, mechanical, reductionist science and engineering, and were designed to resist change. But the new technological revolution destroys the old certainties. Mechanics had to give way to uncertainty, relativity, and a new understanding that the previously isolated, independent, unchanging objects are all subject to development and change as participants in an evolving web of interconnected processes.

Attempts to accommodate to change produced a period of value chain analysis, process redesign and re-engineering, automating many manufacturing and some management processes but keeping, even strengthening the bureaucratic machine. Through the 1980s and 1990s the profit-driven drive to continuously revolutionise the technologies of production accelerated as the crisis deepened. To survive, all organisations were obliged to introduce means of adapting to change, whilst retaining their identity and sense of purpose. Mission statements were agonised over, and all subscribed, at least in words, to the need to adopt the principles of the "learning organisation". These techniques will prove invaluable in constructing a new, democratic economy.

The new science of chaos and complexity has begun to offer a new philosophy for developing organisations which is changing the basis of management. Rather than acting to preserve stability, new-style organisations will welcome the instability and change which characterises complex, living, social systems. In *Leadership and the New Science*, Margaret Wheatley insists:

> In response to changing external conditions and their own internal development, these *dissipative structures* dissipate or give up their form in order to recreate themselves into new forms. Faced with increasing levels of disturbance, these systems possess the innate ability to reorganise themselves to deal with the new information. For this reason, they are called *self-organising systems*. They are adaptive and resilient rather than rigid and stable.

Order in the newly emerging social system will develop from, and be based upon dynamic, fluid, inter-related, interdependent networks of autonomous self-organising, self-*re*organising, self-managed structures/units linked by thousands of connections into a new continuously evolving whole, but sharing a single, collective vision and purpose – contributing to the well-being of all.

Highly-skilled workforces

A key demand and impact of the technological revolution is the development of highly-skilled, IT-literate workforces, with individuals able to easily move from job to job as production methods change, entire industries disappear and new ones arise. In the countries which have been drawn into the globalised economy, the rapid re-division of labour demands flexibility and literacy from its workers. The growing number of firms using flexible workplace practices (such as team work and multi-skilling), tend to have more highly skilled and better educated workforces than firms organised along more traditional lines. Under capitalism, these skills are deployed to serve the enhancement of profit and alienation of the worker from production and distribution. In a radically new framework, these skills will form the basis of a new approach to production.

Integrated production and distribution

Many TNCs are giant holding companies characterised by a diverse range of products, highly responsive supply chain management; globally distributed planned production systems, automated production (robotics), and a broad range of marketing techniques.

Some aspects of production are highly efficient, requiring less and less labour to produce high volumes of products. Others are hugely destructive – of people, and of the environment. Many of the characteristics of highly efficient production will be carried forward into new production systems. Those which are destructive and unsustainable will be discarded.

The scientific and technological revolution

This has much to contribute to the tasks of clearing up the mess resulting from the old capitalist system of production and building the new. The new sense of purpose will replace the distorting impact of the bottom line as the means of determining the direction and pace of technological innovation. Knowledge in all the major fields will advance in leaps and bounds as the recent trend to the commercialisation of intellectual property rights is ended. New technologies will be subject to rigorous testing, and the risks of early introduction assessed against their contribution to improving the well-being of the population and of the ecosystem.

Early action on energy conservation and the development of sustainable energy systems will supersede the destructive thirst for oil. Cleaning up and recycling emissions from coal and gas-fired power stations are high priority, as are safe solutions for decommissioning nuclear installations and disposing of wastes. With current health warnings recommending limits on eating fish due to the presence of toxins, rapid progress will be needed to find and deploy antidotes for the heavy metals and other pollutants such as PCBs and dioxins which have been dumped in lakes, rivers and seas for decades.

A society which can use technology constructively will encourage the maturation of areas such as synthetic biology, currently at the stage of experiment and demonstration. Scientists are already using kits of synthesised parts (BioBricks) to construct living machines which will help dispose of nuclear waste, biological and chemical weapons and to fabricate anti-malarial drugs cheaply.

The potential impact of unintended consequences of genetically modified crops, bacteria, insects, and any organisms resulting from the study and application of genomics and proteomics will cease to be seen as a threat. The removal of the competitive pressure for early implementation will be replaced by strict application of the precautionary principle – first do no harm.

The benefits of genetic counselling in reducing the impact of diseases which are inherited, and gene therapy – both for inherited conditions and those which arise from random mutation – are already beginning to be realised. As more knowledge of the interaction between external and internal factors becomes available, the relative importance of social, preventive action and individual healthcare interventions will become clearer and can be acted upon.

When monopoly profits on herbicides such as glyphosate are removed from the equation, the marketing hype surrounding the contribution of new seeds to eliminating world hunger will subside and objective assessment will prevail.

As research into the applications of nano- and bio-technologies bears new fruit, such as self-constructing and self-repairing machines, new and even more spectacular leaps in the power, speed and availability of computing are coming on stream. Much of the accelerating acquisition of knowledge in these fields is itself attributable to the deployment of computer-based techniques and robotics – a phenomenon observed in the race to map and publish the human genome. This dialectic of development, with each branch of science feeding the other, will deliver unimaginable contributions to the collective future of humanity when the new social paradigm comes into play.

A global financial system

In the 1990s the computing and communications revolution paved the way for the globalisation of financial markets. Innovative financial products and services changed the way that banks monitor and manage credit risk, market risk, and operational risk. The global financial system consists of financial markets, domestic and international, that are used by transnational corporations, government agencies and banks in the conduct of their business. The global financial markets include the market for foreign exchange, the Eurocurrency and related money markets, the international capital markets, notably the Eurobond and global equity markets, the commodity market and last but not least, the markets for forward contracts, options, swaps and other derivatives. But crisis after crisis has left the global financial system reeling. With the abolition of speculation on the money markets, the techniques developed by global capitalism can be used to clear payments between enterprises within and between countries. The drive to a moneyless society will become possible.

Act globally – start locally

What we have described above are amongst the highest achievements of capitalism in its three and a half centuries of rule. The new social framework will spread their benefits throughout society and to every country. But the two world wars, and the more recent attacks on Afghanistan and Iraq by the Bush-Blair coalition, show that capitalism tolerates no limits to its destructiveness. To protect these resources we have to change society along the lines set out below.

As capitalism has subordinated the sovereignty of national economies with globally inter-connected enterprises and a world financial system, so our proposals for moving beyond capitalist-driven globalisation are based on the needs of the whole of the world's population. Our aim is to extend the gains and advances that capitalism has given the few, to all people in all countries through the development of a global, socialist society. This is the only alternative. We put forward the following principles as a way to act globally by starting locally:

▸ the social ownership of land, banking and finance, transport and communications infrastructure
▸ ownership of production facilities of the major corporations through a variety of forms of co-ownership
▸ democratic control and self-management of economic and financial resources, including public services
▸ steering the development of productive capacity towards satisfying need
▸ ecologically sustainable production and distribution
▸ encouraging and supporting small-scale enterprises, creative workers and farmers
▸ favouring local production for local needs
▸ facilitating the development of the "conscious market".

These changes can and will begin to reverse the alienating effects of capitalist production. They will create the conditions for the release of the natural altruism of people, building on, for example, half a century of experience of people working in the UK's National Health Service.

Identifying and setting priorities for need
Society will have to
1. solve urgent economic, social and ecological problems generated by capitalism through emergency programmes of action
2. set an agenda for addressing unmet needs for food, clothing, housing, health, energy, communication, transport, education, arts, entertainment, sport, recreation, safety, social support, security in older age and self-development
3. In the longer term, address new problems and challenges as they emerge and respond to new needs identified by people

through the democratic process.

Actionable first steps

There are some immediate steps we could take to release and redeploy resources to meet urgent need in housing, healthcare, education and transport.

Shareholders' dividends. Capitalist firms distribute £20 billion a year in dividends. With firms collectively owned, these resources can be used to tackle urgent social questions.

Pension funds. Almost one half of the stock market is actually owned by pension funds and insurance companies, who have invested the contributions and premiums of millions of workers. Their value at the end of 2003 was about £650 billion. Many funds are in a state of collapse following mis-investment and their misuse by companies. In future, these funds would be used to develop self-managed and collectively owned enterprises. The value of existing company pension schemes would be guaranteed under these new arrangements.

Bank/building society deposits. These funds are mostly used to speculate on foreign exchange markets and in all sorts of financial schemes. While guaranteeing their security and value, a not-for-profit economy could use these funds to advance sustainable production for need.

Government spending. Large parts of present government spending are either wasteful or are used to prop up capitalist firms. A major part of the NHS budget, for example, is used to buy drugs from the major pharmaceuticals. Government spending is also wasted on the private finance initiative and subsidies to railway companies or on arms budgets. Housing benefit is used to keep people in poverty when the funds could be used to slash rents to affordable levels.

Switching to production for need

These first steps will set in motion the reshaping of society. The priority will switch from production for profit and the accumulation of capital to an approach based on assessing the usefulness of products for meeting socially-agreed needs. The new priority will stimulate and encourage changes in the market.

The most advanced techniques will be adapted to reflect new patterns of consumption and demand.

In the medium-term this could work in the following way:

Planning. Regional plans will reconcile expected needs, balancing the potential of local, self-managed production against purchase of fairly traded goods. The coincidence of overproduction and famine will recede into history. Part of this process will be a rigorous assessment of the relative social benefits and costs of local production versus acquiring what is needed through trade.

Production and distribution. There will be full-cost accounting, taking into account the cost of recycling of resources, increased use of technology to increase productivity to reduce physical and mental labour, scientific and public assessment for safety of proposed new products, location of production and distribution as close as possible to the market, to minimise ecological impact.

Fair trade. We will not acquire things to the disadvantage of those we are acquiring them from. This leads to fair trade with other countries and producers, paying prices for goods that help towards the equalisation of standards of living throughout the world.

Conditions at work. The objective is to reduce hours and stress through the use of automation and the elimination of employer-employee relationships in favour of self-management and control. Wage differentials will be based on skills rather than market scarcity. There will be an emphasis on health, safety and job satisfaction as opposed to working simply to earn a living, whatever the nature of the task. Unattractive tasks should be shared by all.

Co-producers. An economic approach based on co-operation will put the needs of the consumer first in terms of safety, life of the product, ease of upgrade and maintenance. Consumers' representatives will be involved as co-producers in decisions about production, which will also involve responding to new needs and wants drawn from how people live their lives.

Self-management: making it work

At present, the food chain is under the control of agribusinesses, processing corporations and a handful of supermarkets. The pressures they exert have contributed to severe ecological damage, the decline of rural areas, a sharp fall in food safety, the promotion of nutritionally poor food, low wages and, of course, massive profits for a handful of firms. Given the social ownership of all these elements of the food chain, a new approach based on self-management and co-production for need will revolutionise the way we eat.

All the existing enterprises – supermarkets, distribution facilities, processing plants, food producers, and farmers will co-operate in inter-dependent, *self-managed* networks. Each separate enterprise would contract with purchase/supply partners. Prices will be determined by the costs of production, taking into account sustainable methods of agriculture and processing, and the livelihoods of those involved in production, distribution and retailing.

Each enterprise will be run by an elected *workers' council* with access to a wide range of expert, financial, technical and scientific advice. The responsibilities of those involved in self-management could include:

▸ working locally with representatives of consumer households, hospitals, schools, social services and other large users to ensure local needs are identified and met
▸ taking advice from experts in the fields of nutrition, food economics and safety
▸ identifying with consumers what new products can be developed and supplied to meet both local and national needs
▸ ensuring that food hygiene, safety and nutritional qualities meet agreed standards
▸ identifying what can be produced locally and what needs to be acquired from elsewhere
▸ formulating proposals on their own working conditions, hours and salaries
▸ ensuring that revenues generated from these activities are accounted for and that contractual obligations in the supply

chain are fulfilled
‣ producing a democratically-arrived at plan for food supply in
  the short, medium and long-term as proposals to Assemblies
‣ working with and being accountable to local, regional and
  national Assemblies.

Many of these tasks are already carried out in a haphazard and
often uncoordinated way within capitalist society by salaried
workers. The aim here is to set them within a new framework of
social responsibility and accountability. This approach to self-
management and democratic planning could become a model for
all branches of industry and services.

The role of Assemblies

Local and regional Assemblies (see Chapter 8) will be responsible
for ensuring that commitments given by self-managed enterprises
are carried through in terms of financial probity, supply of goods
and so on. At national level, the Assembly will have to ensure
that sufficient capacity exists to satisfy needs, based on
demographic and other trends. It will have to make strategic
assessments on all the major categories of need. The Assemblies
will encourage an approach to production that leads to an
increase in well-being. For example, regional and local
Assemblies will make funds available to self-managed co-
operatives of farmers, food processors and distributors to
encourage local food production.

  Many approaches to replacing Gross Domestic Product as the
main measure of wealth, growth, and the rise and fall of stock
markets are already being tried. Community accounting systems,
genuine progress indicators, and local indicators initiatives, are
all showing ways to measure social progress in new ways. A
broad range of measures and indicators are in use to assess the
well-being of a community, or the sustainability of a production
process, for example. Accumulating expertise in all of these areas
will provide a firm foundation for the new direction of the
Assemblies.

  The Assemblies will have to set down the minimum earnings
that are required for various kinds of households and put

forward suggestions about the range of earnings that will reflect relative skills levels without reproducing the excesses paid to senior managers in the capitalist system.

Redefining the market

History saw the early development of the market and money as the means of exchanging the surplus produce of settled communities and artisans. As surplus, the products were no longer useful to the producer, but the market made them accessible as useful items to others. Traders who travelled from place to place were able to accumulate wealth by buying cheaply in one place, and selling elsewhere at a higher price. As the market gained in importance, some producers began to exploit their own ability to produce beyond their own needs. They began to concentrate on producing primarily for sale in the market. The harder they worked, and the more they developed their technique, the more they were able to accumulate wealth. This accumulating wealth took on a life of its own, tempting competition, and as explained earlier, created its own need for expansion.

For little more than three and a half centuries, expanding value through production of a ballooning volume of commodities for exchange in an ever-widening marketplace has dominated social development. Profit-driven competition leads to overproduction and ecological calamity. Economic collapse, social and political crisis follow. Regulation of market relations by the WTO has been subject to direction by the growing power of profit-driven corporations. The myth of the invisible hand of the free market providing the best possible means of organising the production and distribution of goods on the world market has been exposed many times over.

A new start

In the 20th century, first attempts at a new start by the fledgling revolutionary government in Russia replaced the anarchy of capitalist production. The aim was to bring socially owned property and conscious planning to the fore, whilst retaining the market system. Instead of the much-needed replacement of the capitalist system worldwide, the early beginnings of the socialist system became isolated. With the infant society under siege, conditions ripened for the defeat of the revolutionaries by the rising layer of state functionaries with Stalin at its head. The internationalist, democratic and gradualist approach to developing a socialised economy and society was replaced by the forced building of "socialism in a single country". All property became state property, and all production was determined by an obsessive, all-encompassing bureaucratically-conceived, and hopelessly inadequate national plan. Democratic self-management of enterprises was replaced by production quotas. Distribution of peasants' surplus agricultural produce through the market was outlawed and replaced by seizure by the state.

As a consequence, food production collapsed and millions died through famine. Eventually, the contradiction between the bureaucracy, an isolated economy and the world capitalist system was impossible to reconcile and the Soviet Union collapsed in 1991. In Yugoslavia, a system of socially-owned, self-managed enterprises operated successfully for many years – until it too became entangled in the debt-and-crisis-ridden nets of the predatory capitalist financial system.

Lessons learned

We are obliged to learn the lessons from 20th century history:

▸ capitalism is a world system. It must be replaced with a new world system. There is no national solution to the crisis. We must act globally, but we can start locally
▸ we have to appeal for solidarity and support by workers in other countries, encouraging them to seize control of the TNCs in their countries
▸ distribution of useful products through the market pre-dates capitalism and will outlive it
▸ property must be owned collectively and locally, rather than by some remote state body
▸ production for need based on planning is possible, but cannot and should not completely replace the expression of consumer preference through the market.

Bringing these lessons together with the technical advances made by capitalist, transnational corporations provides the basis for the thinking, conscious market.

The 'thinking' market

Advanced methods of needs analysis and market research, incorporating predictive demography will inform strategic, long-term planning. The results will consist of guidelines for building sustainable production and distribution capacity worldwide. Those employed in this planning process will be accountable to the delegated authority of the elected global Assembly.

Methods of measuring consumption developed further from the most sophisticated existing loyalty card plus market information databases will be deployed to ensure that short-term production and distribution is responsive to individual wants, within the limits of possibility agreed collectively. Producing on-demand to satisfy individual taste has already become normal in some industries. Many cars and computers are assembled only when an order has been placed. While satisfying needs already agreed, the conscious market will expand to respond to many more individual expressions of want. So, for example, web-based facilities for registering an individual's preference profiles will become universal. Everyone would be able to store and update their measurements and holographic images as the basis for virtually designing, "trying on" and ordering customised clothing.

At the shortest response-times, production to restock supermarket shelves is already triggered automatically by registering purchases at the check-out. But the purchasing and supply systems are driven by competitive instinct. The result is that many production workers in food processing and packing live in tents, shacks and hostels close to the plant, available for work at the whim of the employer, and paid – if at all – only for the hours that they do. This dehumanising result of the profit-driven application of technology will easily be ended. With a system of planned production for need, the haphazard consequences of the unconscious market will be drastically reduced.

Used sensitively, the combined techniques of planning for need and measured consumption can be used to ensure that the needs of all vulnerable people are monitored and met. They can also be used to inform and manage public health campaigns around nutrition, for example.

Distribution of wealth

The distribution of profits to disinterested shareholders – the current private owners of capital, will cease. Stock, currency and other markets for speculation will be closed. The wealth generated by workers realised from sales of their products will be distributed according to the following principles:

1. A part will be paid to the workers in the enterprise. An individual's income from employment will be set in relation to the basic living wage, supplemented by skill and performance-related amounts. The level of the basic living wage will be determined from the numbers of hours of work required to generate the value of products and services needed to meet basic needs. It will be reviewed regularly.
2. A part will be retained for reinvestment in, and further development of the organisation.
3. The value generated by an organisation, over and above the wages paid to workers, and the amounts retained for reinvestment, will be divided amongst the Social Needs Funds to support education and research; health and social care; recreation and the arts; infrastructure development including energy, communications and transport; pensions, and incomes for those unable to work through disability or illness.

The proportion of the social surplus allocated to each of the various Social Needs Funds will be determined through planning rounds controlled by the democratic process. Social Needs Funds will be administered according to rules established through Assembly structures. The IMF, World Bank and WTO will top the list for replacement by new institutions directly accountable to the World Assembly. These will take measures to ensure that incomes and the standard of living are progressively equalised around the world.

Debt

The burden of repayment imposed on the people of the heavily-indebted poor countries by the IMF, the World Bank and the regional banks, as the price of forced entry into the world market, will be cancelled. The status of personal debt in the transitional period will be subject to assessment by committees of the local Assembly. Loan-sharking will be outlawed. Personal credit and debt will be administered by local credit unions and mutual funds.

Housing

Private housing for owner-occupiers will continue, but strict limits will be imposed on the ownership of multiple properties by individuals. Increased capacity will eliminate cycles of price inflation and collapse. Plentiful supplies of collectively-owned, rented properties will be available for temporary occupation, as well as long-term stewardship.

The future

As the socialised system matures it will identify, measure, and satisfy all the basic needs of people throughout the world, according to criteria agreed through the democratic process. In a system focused on producing for need rather than on an endless profit escalator, society will offer the potential for reducing working hours for those now in work, and, for the hundreds of millions without work, the opportunity to provide for their families for the first time. Society will move forward decisively to the time when manual work becomes a smaller and smaller part of life and when everyone can live in the fullest sense according to their needs.

Cars as socially useful objects

At present, car production and sales are based solely on the need to generate profit in a competitive market, open up new markets and persuade government to build roads. But their use value, which is freedom of movement, is declining rapidly and is being overwhelmed by the ecological and social consequences of mass car use. Even capitalism recognises these problems – although it only reinforces the problem or offers market-led "solutions" like car pricing which ignore the basic problems. Car production for social need would establish the car's place in holistic, integrated affordable transport systems, with people living closer to their work, and a full-cost assessment of pollution. Price will have to take account of all these factors. Car pooling, giving people access to shared cars when they need them, would be rapidly developed as an alternative to private ownership, since most cars remain idle for the majority of the time. Extending dial-a-ride and community transport systems would be boosted alongside research into eco-friendly fuel systems. There would have to be agreements about limiting the use of cars in built-up areas.

* * *

News from the future: when health comes first

These questions and answers come from interviews by our health correspondent. Set at some future date in the not too distant future, they look at the way health care has changed since the power of the global corporations was broken.

Q. What triggered the transfer of pharmaceuticals to social ownership?

A. Problems with the big drug companies had been steadily making themselves felt in the public consciousness since the 1980s. By 2002, although around half of the world's top ten pharmaceuticals were formally based in the US (Pfizer, Merck, Johnson & Johnson, Bristol-Myers Squibb and Wyeth) and the other half in Europe (British GlaxoSmithKline, AstraZeneca, Swiss Novartis and Roche, and the French Aventis) but all had become global enterprises. Their enormous power came into sharp conflict with mounting health care funding problems.

A series of studies revealed some unacceptable truths: for more than two decades, pharmaceuticals had been a colossal industry, with total world sales of prescription drugs in 2002 calculated at around $400 billion. And they were making colossal profits. By charging far higher prices at home, than was possible elsewhere, it had become the most profitable industry in the United States.

In 1990 the world's top ten drug companies had profits of nearly 25% of sales. In 2002, their combined profits ($35.9 billion) were more than those of all the other 490 businesses put together ($33.7 billion).

Q. These are astounding figures. So how did they do it?

A. These enterprises had something really special. In the age of the so-called free market they were protected from competition. The international system of licensing gave them exclusive marketing rights and the use of patents protected them from competitive products.

The general tendency to privatisation promoted by the

corporations through the WTO and national legislation established a restrictive system of patents and intellectual property rights. These anti-competitive measures meant that the huge profits could be defended against even small-scale defiant attempts at generic drug production by companies which had sprung up in Asia and South America. There was a huge public outcry when hundreds of millions of people with AIDS, particularly in Africa, were left to die without drugs because neither they nor their governments could afford the artificially high prices. The deal that resulted from the campaign meant that a few million began to receive treatment. But the titanic power wielded by the corporations meant that the issue disappeared from public view – for a time.

With minor changes to products, frequent legislative changes in favour of protecting profits, and teams of highly paid lawyers to exploit them, patents could be extended for many years beyond the original 20 year limits and stratospheric prices maintained. Changes in the law meant that the companies began to claim intellectual property rights over medicines derived from plants by forest-dwellers and people living in tribal societies. Collective, freely available knowledge developed over thousands of years suddenly passed into the hands of private, for-profit corporations.

Q. So how did it all change? What went wrong for the drug companies?

A. Well, on the surface, it was a combination of things, really. You couldn't say it was down to just one cause. But underlying it was the general downturn in the economy that set in around 2003-04 before the whole thing unravelled. The downturn meant that funding health, education and social care had become increasingly difficult as tax revenue declined, and the turn to privatisation diverted more and more tax money into shareholders' pockets. In countries with work-based health insurance like the US, employers started reducing benefits, and in countries with a more general form of insurance, and even in the UK with its tax-funded health care, the governments started passing more costs to the individual. Ironically, previous successes in reducing morbidity and mortality in the industrialised countries meant that there were relatively more older people placing additional burdens on the care services. In China, with the world's biggest population, the policy that attempted to slow population growth by allowing only one child per couple had a similar effect. And despite the vast power of the drug companies, patents on several of their blockbusters, the source of much of their profits, ran out.

But things turned really nasty in the US, the world's richest, and most indebted country when many older people – seniors – more than a quarter of the population by 2004, could no longer afford the over-priced drugs they needed. They were forced to decide between drugs and heating or food. Some would take the drugs less often than prescribed, or share them with others. Others failed to take the drugs they were prescribed altogether, but were too proud and embarrassed to admit it. So their doctors were sometimes misled into thinking that the previous prescription was inadequate and unknowingly compounded the problem by either increasing the dose, or prescribing another combination of drugs. Some people turned to the Internet, illegally buying from cheaper sources in Canada and Mexico. Others living near the border took buses, and organised coach trips. Of course the drug companies pressured the government to make even this illegal. Anger and frustration grew, and the previously conservative older generation took to the streets.

Q. How did the transfer to publicly funded research change things?

A. Just as soon as research was freed from the constraints imposed by corporate interests, the Global Health Alliance began to set priorities according to need. Many of the so-called "lifestyle" programmes that Big Pharma had been running were stopped, much to the relief of the scientists they had employed. Major innovations followed quite swiftly. Malaria, bilharzias, and several of the major killers and disablers in the previously neglected countries of the South soon succumbed to a multi-pronged attack. The insects and other carriers which spread those diseases were eradicated or controlled through drainage and similar relevant schemes, and new drugs put into mass production to treat those who had been infected before the preventive measures took effect.

HIV/Aids was more difficult to deal with. Treating the symptoms became much easier as the drugs were produced and distributed cheaply, but the social and psychological problems took quite a while to resolve until the civil wars died down and the use of rape as a weapon of repression ceased. We developed a combination of education and counselling programmes which built on local cultures – and these are still being used. Fortunately there were hundreds of thousands of people, highly skilled in the art of persuasion, and well-informed about health issues, who became available for retraining just at the right moment.

Q. Who were they?
A. They had previously made up the pharmaceutical corporations' armies of marketing and sales forces. Nowadays, as soon as a new drug has been approved, it and the dosage regimes for all indicated conditions are entered into the GHA's prescribing database which is referenced every time a clinician records a diagnosis, or even a set of signs and symptoms into a patient's record. So there's no longer a requirement for a separate process of informing clinicians about new developments. They simply become available for use. And there's no longer any need for the big teams that competed to push an array of virtually identical drugs. Many of them are now delighted to be doing something useful with their skills.

Q. How is research funded and organised now?
A. Contributions are provided to the GHA by all participating countries, regions and states. The amount each country provides is determined partly by its population, and partly according to its ability to pay. There is still significant inequality left over from before, but this is now reducing, year by year, and we expect to be able to drop the ability-to-pay clause quite soon.

There are global programmes to deal with universal problems – travel has become much more widespread as, these days, people are much freer to live and work where they want. So infectious diseases have much greater potential to spread.

Research groups in both the universities and those operating independently are invited to bid for funds for projects that are on the list, and they can also put forward their own suggestions for things that excite them. The committee meets three or four times a year to allocate awards, and to consider new proposals. The members of the committee are elected – some through the academic network, and some from the participating countries' care receivers and providers. The quality of research units is assessed by regular audits, and these are available to the committee along with the project bids.

Q. What happens to the results of the research projects?
A. Now that science is publicly funded, the results of all research can be properly checked and confirmed by laboratories in different countries, before being released into the public domain. When we got rid of the old laws on intellectual property rights, the old competitive secrecy dissolved, collaborations between centres developed very quickly and progress in most areas has become much more rapid. Unlimited bandwidth means that global teleconferencing is now the normal means of sharing knowledge. But there is still no substitute for direct human contact, so study centres and research groups regularly exchange members and expertise around the world.

Q. Without intellectual property rights, how do people get recognition for their work?
A. Most people are more than happy to have their results taken up widely and put to use and they are usually credited in further research. There are still some occasions when later researchers "borrow" the work of others and fail to acknowledge the source, but the background infrastructure technologies which support the global research programmes make this easy to spot. When the people who do this are discovered, it is widely publicised, and they tend not to get any more funding for quite a while!

Q. What benefits have come from the results of the Human

Genome Project and follow-on activities?

A. As you know, DNA samples are taken from all babies – normally at birth. If there is something in the biological family's history to suggest a potentially avoidable problem, a sample may be taken from the foetus in its sixth month. There are now many inheritable diseases which we can inhibit by switching off the genes responsible, though we've a long way to go in understanding the full complexity of gene interactions, and the unwanted effects often mean that continuing care is required. From the genetic profile of a foetus we can advise the parents much more accurately about the likely health career of their baby, and jointly consider the options available. For every baby we can identify many of the vulnerabilities they exhibit, and set up a range of plans to avoid or deal with at least the most likely of the external threats. So, the information is available if parents want to take advantage of these plans from or before birth. If they don't, the information is kept until the child achieves the level of competence necessary to make their own decisions.

Of course, all of this was subject to years of debate. Until we got rid of insurance-based, self-funded health care, and the other inequitable systems, there were understandable concerns about discrimination, job insecurity, and the like. Some people are still worried about privacy and confidentiality – again with good reason. So all access to genetic data is restricted according to the patient's wishes, and if they want, they are notified whenever access is made.

But, the most important thing to remember is that these developments must be seen in the context of the major shift of emphasis to preventing disease. Genomics has made a contribution to this, but it has been relatively small when compared to the elimination of inequality, the move to sustainable manufacture, the adoption of clean engine technologies, global action on clean water, healthy eating, education, and not least housing.

Q. How has the pattern of disease changed globally?

A. We'd known for decades that the links between poverty and disease are very strong, but only when conditions changed and we introduced a society built around satisfying needs and the principle of equality did it become possible to do anything more than attempt to deal with the consequences. We're now much more focussed on preventing disease, though of course people don't always follow the advice, so some still get sick and accidents continue to happen. And there are – and always will be – new threats of disease from mutating viruses which have to be spotted and stopped in their tracks before they make any headway in the population.

Nowadays people everywhere have, or are close to getting access to clean water and sanitation, education and greatly improved housing. Child mortality from diseases like diarrhoea has become something you read about in history books. Tuberculosis does recur occasionally, but is mostly eradicated. Polio was finally beaten, once the mistrust in Nigeria and other countries about the real intentions of the vaccination programme was overcome.

We'll still be dealing with the burden of cancer for years to come, but the shocking rise in new cases in the latter part of the 20th century is now in reverse. The build-up of carcinogens in the atmosphere is clearing faster than the residues in the oceans, and these continue to make their way up through the food chain.

Q. What about the connection between food and health?
A. In the places which had been relatively better off – like the former United States of America, and some of the countries in the former European Union – it took quite a while to break the addictions to the deadly fat, sugar and red meat diets which had been so profitable for the big corporations like Coca-Cola, McDonald's and the old supermarket chains. But now the objectives of food production put nutrition, and taste top of the list.

The connection between good health and good food always seemed so obvious to most people in health care, but when the transnationals started organising disinformation campaigns trying to distort and misrepresent the best scientific advice, it became clear that their time had come.

As is general in most branches of production now, land is held by Community Land Trusts, or variations on the theme in different countries. The organisations which produce and distribute food are jointly owned by co-operating groups of suppliers, producers, and consumers. So, all profits are recycled back into improving production and reducing the working day. We no longer depend on the exploitation of cheap labour which used to be an essential part of food production; producers get a fair price for their produce, whereas before, the competition between giant supermarket chains and their vast purchasing power forced prices down below the cost of production. It was the drive for profit which filled our mouths and arteries with hydrogenated fat, and the same drive that, for a while, broke the traditional agricultural practices like seed-saving.

In places like Sub-Saharan Africa, where the majority of people had been severely malnourished for decades with millions starving to death, the food aid programmes were dramatically increased – but without the accompanying debts which had previously further impoverished them and many other countries. This was only necessary whilst land reform was carried out, and domestic food production could get going. Nowadays, life-expectancy there is approaching the norm. And the wide variation which used to separate the rich and poor has narrowed quite dramatically.

8 Reconstructing the state

Week by week, sometimes day by day, the British and American governments have built the foundations of an authoritarian state. The terror attacks on the US on September 11 2001 only led to an intensification of the attack on democratic rights that was already well under way. Since then, the "war on terror" has served as a flimsy pretext for greater and greater assaults on rights and freedoms at home and abroad.

The arrest on 27 May 2004 of Muslim cleric Abu Hamza, a British citizen, signalled the implementation of a treaty signed with the United States in March 2003, which was agreed without consultation or warning. This treaty allows the removal of suspects from Britain to the US without the American authorities first having to make out a case for extradition in British courts. Abu Hamza faced extradition merely on the basis of the indictment drawn by the US Attorney-General. When he signed the treaty, Home Secretary David Blunkett did not even bother to ask for reciprocity when it comes to US citizens who might be wanted in Britain.

In area after area – from whittling away the rights of defendants in criminal cases to the detention without trial or charge of alleged terror suspects – New Labour has undermined the limited liberties that have come to be associated with capitalist democracy. The story of how this happened is recounted by Helena Kennedy QC, a New Labour peer who, after a brief flirtation with the Blair government, suddenly realised that it was trampling all over the principles she held dear. In *Just Law*, she takes New Labour to task for a "wholesale assault on the underpinnings of the rule of law".

By the rule of law she means, in the area of crime for example, having clearly defined laws, access to lawyers, circumscribed police powers, an open trial process, rules of evidence, the right of appeal and the presumption of innocence. "It stands for the fundamental principle that every state actor must conform to certain basic requirements of acceptable behaviour set down not by the actor itself but by some independent body," she maintains. But under New Labour, which enacted more than 700 new criminal laws in eight years, the state has assumed greater and greater powers at the expense of defendants.

There are severe limitations on the right to silence, repeated efforts to reduce trial by jury, an acceptance of the retrial of those already acquitted and allowing the disclosure of any previous convictions during a trial. There are mandatory sentences set down by ministers and the imprisonment of more people as a result of government directives. This is done, says the government, to "rebalance" the criminal justice in favour of the victims. As Kennedy remarks:

> The rhetoric of "rebalancing the system" as between victims and the accused disingenuously presents the criminal trial as a contest between these two parties, thus denying the central role of the state. We are beginning to see a semi-privatisation of the criminal justice process, with the victim, the private individual, being used to disguise the reality of the powerplay.

The presumption of guilt runs through the Terrorism Act 2000, enshrining as it does a reversal of the burden of proof, with accused persons having to show beyond reasonable doubt that they did not have items for terrorist purposes. Suspected terrorists can be stripped of their citizenship, a move that Abu Hamza was challenging through the courts before he was arrested on the extradition warrant. Further laws passed in the wake of the September 11 2001 terror attacks allow the state to detain indefinitely, without charge or trial, non-citizens deemed terrorists by the Home Secretary. Before introducing the law, the New Labour government had to opt out of part of the Human Rights Act on the spurious grounds that there was a continuing state of public emergency in Britain. In June 2004, there were 14 people detained indefinitely in Belmarsh Prison, south-east London. It is unlawful to disclose even their names.

New Labour's anti-terror laws also deny the right to proper representation by lawyers. A detainee can appeal to a tribunal against the Home Secretary's decision that he or she is a threat to security. But detainees and their legal representatives are excluded from any part of the hearing which deals with the alleged intelligence on which the detention order has been made.

From time to time, Kennedy refers to the globalisation process dominated by transnational corporations and the changes that have resulted in the way people live. She notes: "Law is seen as an encumbrance to liberal free marketeers, save in the ways it protects commercial transactions, provides remedies for default and makes the world safe for global capitalism. The minimalist state wants minimalist law."

What Kennedy shows is that the rule of law developed under capitalism is itself coming to grief at the hands of the New Labour regime. In this view she is not alone. On 3 March 2004, the Lord Chief Justice, Lord Woolf, in an unprecedented speech, attacked the government for encroaching on judicial independence. His anger was particularly directed at a clause in a new Asylum Bill which sought to prevent the courts from hearing appeals against decisions from immigration tribunals. He warned that he was

> not over-dramatising the position if I indicate that, if this clause were to become law, it would be so inconsistent with the spirit of mutual respect between the different arms of government that it could be the catalyst for a campaign for a written constitution. Immigration and asylum involve basic human rights. What areas of government decision making would be next to be removed from the scrutiny of the courts? What is the use of courts, if you cannot access them?

Asylum seekers have become an easy, identifiable target and the pretext for yet more ruthless laws that undermine long-standing international rights. New Labour found time for three major pieces of legislation between 1999 and 2004 which curtailed the rights of asylum seekers. The 2004 Act was nearly twice as long as the Bill when it was originally published. The new Act makes it a criminal offence to turn up in Britain without documents and curtails the right of applicants to appeal to the courts. Another clause compels those who lose their claims, but cannot return home, to do community work for no pay in return for benefits. Earlier legislation introduced the dispersal of new asylum seekers to often squalid accommodation throughout the UK. They were denied the right to work while awaiting a decision. The lucky ones could claim £37.77 a week – 30% below Income Support levels. The latest plan is to deny failed applicants the right to medical treatment pending their removal from the country. Doctors will be told to ask for a person's status before making a diagnosis.

In May 2004, the Court of Appeal ruled that the denying of any support or shelter to asylum seekers who applied late was a breach of their human rights. The Refugee Council has long campaigned against this provision. In April 2004, it published *Hungry and homeless* which revealed that many asylum seekers were sleeping rough. The Mayor of London's office estimated that 10,000 refugees were destitute.

At European and international level it is a similar story. The new European arrest warrant does away with almost all of the checks and balances of the existing extradition procedure. For a list of 32 offences there will now be no legal test in the requested state. The requesting state simply has to say that a person is wanted for one of the listed offences and this person can be arrested – their homes searched and property seized – and deported to stand trial. There is no habeas corpus, no appeal, no rights for the suspect, says Statewatch, the organisation that monitors civil liberties in the EU. At the same time as governments are overriding the conventions of the rule of law, they are strengthening the administrative power of the state at national and EU level. Surveillance of people and the interception of electronic communications are now established as routine.

In the United States, a sweeping attack on democratic liberties followed the September 11 attacks. Soon after the attacks, Attorney General John Ashcroft sent to Congress a proposal containing the Justice Department's wish list of new police powers. The far-reaching law was passed almost without dissent, with only a cursory debate. Ashcroft was handed virtually all the powers he sought and several he had not even asked for. Almost immediately hundreds of Middle Eastern and South Asian men were rounded up and detained without trial or charge. According to the American Civil Liberties Union report *Insatiable appetite*, the law's most far-reaching provisions:

▸ permit the Attorney General to incarcerate or detain non-citizens based on mere suspicion, and to deny re-admission to the United States of non-citizens (including legal, long-term permanent residents) for engaging in speech protected by the First Amendment

▸ minimise the power of the courts to prevent law enforcement authorities from illegally abusing telephone and Internet surveillance in both anti-terrorism investigations *and* ordinary criminal investigations of American citizens

▸ expand the authority of the government in both terrorism and non-terror investigations to conduct so-called "sneak and peek" or "black bag" secret searches, which do not require notification of the subject of the search

▸ grant the FBI – and, under new information sharing provisions, many other law enforcement and intelligence agencies – broad access to highly personal medical, financial, mental health and student records

▸ permit law enforcement agents to investigate American citizens for criminal matters without establishing probable cause based on an assertion that the investigation is for "intelligence purposes"

▸ put the CIA firmly back in the business of spying on Americans by giving the Director of Central Intelligence broad authority to target intelligence surveillance in the United States

▶ contain a broad definition of "domestic terrorism", which is
so vague that the government could designate lawful groups
such as Greenpeace as terrorists.

The Patriot Act conferred on the President powers to deem
people "enemy combatants" without any rights whatsoever. This
term was developed to avoid the provisions of the Geneva
Convention about prisoners of war. On this spurious basis,
detainees are held in cages in Guantanamo Bay, Cuba, and
routinely abused by their guards. Taken from Afghanistan and
other countries, the detainees face military tribunals without
even the right of legal representation. Meanwhile, the US
commission that investigated the September 11 attacks
concluded that the intelligence agencies were not paying
attention to the threat from al-Qaeda. Naturally, their answer
was to recommend the creation of a National Counterterrorism
Centre to co-ordinate all the state bodies and deepen the assault
on civil liberties.

It was the verdict of the vast majority of experts that the
invasion of Iraq by the US and Britain was illegal under
international law. There were no grounds made out for a pre-
emptive strike against a sovereign state. In Britain, Elizabeth
Wilmshurst resigned as the Foreign Office's deputy legal adviser
because she believed the invasion violated international law. She
told BBC Radio on 13 June 2004: "There was a tremendous and
passionate debate about the legality of this. Most international
lawyers I met were of the view that the conflict was unlawful
under international law. The issue is whether the Security
Council authorised the use of force in Iraq. There is no question
that there was no basis for the use of force in self-defence. I took
the view that participation by the UK in the conflict in Iraq was
contrary to international law." Lord Goldsmith, the Attorney-
General, has refused to publish the advice he gave to the
government.

These attacks by governments on the rule of law have other
dimensions, as Sophie van Bijsterveld explains in *The Empty
Throne – Democracy and the rule of law in transition*. She relates
the continuous undermining of law with the "the profound

inability of the state to fulfil its classic functions". What she cites in particular is the growth within globalised capitalism of self-regulating, quasi-state bodies which "stand on the divide between law creation and law enforcement, combining regulation and supervision". This has resulted in an area of law outside of the existing structures. She says:

> The closed, monocentred, and self-contained decision-making procedures governed by mechanisms of national constitutional law are broken open and the fiction that they can all be traced back to sovereign enactment and one source of power... is no longer adequate.

The requirement of a legal basis for the exercise of public power has lost substantive meaning as a result of delegation, she believes, asking:

> What significance does the principle have when public decision-making takes place in complex processes in which parliamentary involvement is minimal, or when areas to which the principle of legality is applicable are taken up at the international level? What does it mean when those areas are transferred to the market, where no prior 'legality' principles applies at all?

These questions get to the heart of the matter. The legality of the capitalist state is the issue that is posed. Its increasing lawlessness adds to the case for revolutionary change.

Alternatives that ignore the state

The question is, then, what is the way forward? A range of people, from academics with a profound knowledge of globalisation and international financiers to anti-corporate activists, agree that the state is in crisis. They propose a series of reforms that at international level are intended to improve the "governance" of the political system and return some legitimacy and authority to the state.

George Soros, the international financier who famously drove the pound out of the European Monetary System by speculating

Arrested for sketching

Ron Dare (Letters, 25 June) says the majority in this country wants a Home Secretary who "will take whatever legal measures are required to protect them"; but the evidence which would legitimate the detention of those imprisoned in Belmarsh (and therefore the proof that acts of terror have been averted) has not been made public. Mr Dare may suppose that there is no smoke without fire and that if so far no bombings have occurred in the UK since 9/11, it is thanks to Mr Blunkett's detentions.

On Easter Monday I was in central London sketching locations of South Bank entertainment sites on the Waterloo South Bank footbridge in preparation for a meeting with a client to whom I hope to sell a signage system. The two police officers who approached and asked what I was doing did not believe me in spite of the product brochures and client contact lists I said I had in my bag. They did not ask to see them but called another half dozen constables, then helped themselves to a bag search. On finding philosophy texts in my bag (a subject I happen to write on) whose authors were Iranian-Islamic (12th and 16th century!) they then marched me to Waterloo police HQ.

Following an hour-long conflab over the contents of my bag (which included a foreign language newspaper of all things) the officers emerged to announce my arrest under the terms of the Prevention of Terrorism Act "on reasonable suspicion that I was engaged in activities constituting a risk to public security". Small circles in my sketch indicating bollards along a footpath were taken to be intended bomb placements.

I spent four hours (having already been detained for three and a half) in a cell in Kennington police station wondering whether I might not be joining those in Belmarsh where Mr Blunkett could detain me without explanation and, in the interest of public security, refuse to divulge the alleged evidence. If the majority in this country need protecting, they had better ask who the enemies of democracy currently are.

David Khurt, *The Independent* 6 June 2004

against it under the Tories, is also a student of globalisation. He has warned against the dangers of rampant, free-market capitalism. In his latest book he writes: "Markets are designed to facilitate the free exchange of goods and services among willing participants, but they are not capable, on their own, of taking care of collective needs such as law and order or the maintenance of the market mechanism itself. Nor are they competent to ensure social justice. These 'public goods' can only be provided by a political process." He adds: "I consider the present arrangements in which capital is free to move around but social concerns receive short shrift as a distorted form of a global open society." Soros calls for measures to contain the instability of financial markets and correct the bias in international trade that favours developed countries. He wants "powerful international institutions devoted to… poverty reduction and the provision of public goods on a global scale".

The noted anti-capitalist globalisation campaigner George Monbiot's concern, expressed in his new book, *The Age of Consent*, is to re-establish the democratic process, but globally rather than nationally. He favours a parliament of 600 representing the world's population of six billion elected on the basis of one person one vote. The parliament would have moral authority but command no police or armed forces. His intention is that "through the deployment of a modified species of capitalism to create the conditions in which capitalism can be destroyed". He suggests reforming the UN, replacing the 15-member Security Council with a weighted voting system of all states, "until nation states cease to exist".

Monbiot is critical of the World Social Forum series which he describes as "the dictatorship of those who turn up", proposing instead that the self-establishing World Parliament would be representative of the whole population, and therefore carry legitimacy and moral authority. It would provide a system which can hold the global and international powers to account and stimulate an accelerated fusion of human interests which will propel us towards a change in the way human beings think. The parliament would constitute a revolutionary assembly, which, with no connection to existing national governments would be truly global rather than international.

The major merit of his book is that it is looking beyond capitalism. Unlike most he sees that, like everything else, capitalism too has its limits. "The dictatorship of vested interests is succumbing to entropy. We can hasten its collapse, but only if we are to turn our intermittent campaigns into a sustained revolt." He acknowledges that capitalist-led globalisation "has created the means of its own destruction", showing how

> simultaneously, it has placed within our hands the weapons we require to overthrow the people who have engineered it and assert our common interest. By crushing the grand ideologies which divided the world, it has evacuated the political space in which a new, global politics can grow. By forcing governments to operate in the interests of capital, it has manufactured the disenchantment upon which all new politics must feed. Through the issue of endless debt, it has handed to the poor, if they but knew it, effective control of the world's financial systems. By expanding its own empire through new communication and transport networks, it has granted the world's people the means by which they can gather and co-ordinate their attack. The global dictatorship of vested interests has created the means of its own destruction. But it has done more than that; it has begun to force a transformation of the scale on which we think, obliging us to recognise the planetary issues which bear on our parochial concerns. It impels us, moreover, to act upon that recognition. It has granted us the power to change the course of history.

Having left the camp of "the dictatorship of those who turn up", and rejected anarchist "anti-power", Monbiot is opting for "a global democratic revolution". But, and this is a clear weakness, he has little or nothing to say about the need to confront and defeat the brutal application of force wielded by the defenders of capital. Will Bush and Blair, or their successors, simply melt away in the face of a world government, even a revolutionary assembly, with "moral authority" but no forces of its own? How does his proposal for a one adult-one vote system of election to a world parliament involve the growing number of people who are active in the struggle? Monbiot nods his head in their direction and, in passing acknowledges the need for conscious revolutionary action, declaring that "it requires the active engagement of a network of insurrectionists who are prepared to risk their lives to change the world". But he fails to follow this up, replacing the confrontation for power with a kind of parliamentary leapfrog. The merit of Monbiot's contribution is that he thinks beyond the status quo; the weakness of his analysis is that it ignores, avoids or sidesteps a series of fundamental issues. These centre on the nature of the capitalist state and the driving forces that compel globalised capitalism to act the way it does. Without an understanding of these related phenomena, the proposals for world government by the people for the people have absolutely no possibility of becoming a reality.

All these perspectives assume that the present state system, at national and international level, is neutral and will yield to pressure for reforms that, if implemented, would undermine the basis of its own power. What we have attempted to show is that, on the contrary, the existing state at national level and global institutions like the WTO, are inextricably bound up in countless ways with the destiny of capitalism as an economic system of production and exchange.

The real alternative

The capitalist state is bringing down the curtain on a period of history that began in the 18th century. Transformed by the march of global capitalism, the state is unable and unwilling to uphold or sustain the democratic forms that have allowed it to rule over the majority for this long period. The state has lost its legitimacy and authority by:

‣ merging its identity with corporate interests to rule more directly on their behalf
‣ facilitating the commercialisation of civil society by market forces
‣ undermining the independence of the legal system
‣ trampling all over the rule of law at home and internationally
‣ taking away long-established democratic rights

▸ using state violence and war in a bid to enhance its role
▸ devolving more and more power to unelected, unaccountable bodies
▸ allowing the media to fall into the hands of a few corporations
▸ targeting the poor, migrants and the youth for special treatment
▸ declining to meet social need and abolishing the welfare state
▸ undermining the significance of the right to vote
▸ rendering parliamentary systems more redundant than ever before.

Our proposals are aimed at creating the conditions where the state as a special body alienated from society begins to disappear, where it becomes unnecessary. The first step along this road is achieving state power, with the purpose of abolishing what is oppressive, secretive and unnecessary, and reordering the remainder so that it serves the interests of the majority.

A *transitional state*, basing itself on an economy producing for need, which can swiftly satisfy needs, both in Britain and internationally, will institute a truly democratic society for the first time. The principles for a transitional state should include:

▸ self-organisation throughout society where possible
▸ involving as many people as possible in government and administration
▸ an end to special privileges and incomes for state officials
▸ total accountability and subordination of all officials to elected bodies
▸ elections for all public offices
▸ complete transparency and openness at all levels
▸ a new legal system based on community control and self-policing.

The major impediment to a democratic society remains the unbridled power of the corporations and their relentless drive to expand and accumulate. Just as capitalist economic relations are a barrier to human progress, so too is the state that gives political expression to the profit system. No more democracy can be squeezed out of capitalism. Regime change is the goal. The moment is opportune because the state has lost legitimacy and authority which it can never recover. It is divided against itself, as the internal disputes over the invasion of Iraq and other issues have shown. By openly endorsing and promoting free-market capitalism, the state leaves capitalism politically naked. In so doing, it exposes capitalism to a direct assault on its rule in ways that the state has set out to prevent and divert.

Without parliamentary democracy, capitalism could not have developed; without it capitalism cannot sustain itself. This is the opportunity we must seize to take history in a new direction. We have to extend the right to vote and give it a new significance. This requires us to create new forms of democratic representation. The great advances won in the 19th and 20th centuries must be *reclaimed* and taken further through a revolutionary development.

The political system

The parliamentary system in Britain masks and mystifies the reality of where real state power lies and how it is exercised. As a consequence, the system is democratic in name only. Executive power, the power to make and carry through decisions, lies outside of Parliament. Decisions made are then brought to Parliament for ratification, in the same way as a rubber-stamp is used to signify "approved". Window-dressing is something done extremely well in Britain and the "show" that Parliament puts on is certainly impressive. There are debates and votes, committees for legislation and investigation, elections and resignations. Why, the Prime Minister even has to answer questions once a week in the House of Commons. But MPs do not even have the power to choose or approve a Prime Minister after an election. Before Parliament is called together, the Queen, of all people, sends for the leader of the majority party who automatically becomes Prime Minister. He or she then chooses a Cabinet without reference to Parliament, or even the party that won the election. Such is "representative" democracy in Britain. The "sovereignty of parliament", a concept loved by constitutional historians, is of course weaker still in the context of the European Union. Laws drawn up by the equally undemocratic EU take precedence over British parliamentary law.

From time to time, the veil is drawn in such a way as to expose Parliament in front of everyone. Such was the case over Iraq. The decision to invade Iraq was, for example, made by George W. Bush and Tony Blair more than a year before it actually took place. Parliament was not informed. This followed the decision by the US administration, late in 2001, to plan for war. A book by Bob Woodwood, the journalist who uncovered the Watergate scandal, highlights the importance of Blair's support for Bush as the "driving force in all of it". Not even the British Cabinet was party to the secret agreement to invade a sovereign state. More than a year later, Parliament was asked to endorse a *fait accompli*, with British and American troops already in place to launch an invasion. The advice of the Attorney-General on the legality of a war was never made available to Parliament – or anyone else for that matter. A majority of public opinion was opposed to the invasion and, on 15 February 2003, Britain saw the largest anti-war demonstration in its history. There was barely a majority for war in the House of Commons, with half of Labour MPs not actually in the government voting against. The dossiers about "weapons of mass destruction" were a work of fiction. Yet the invasion was launched, rendering public opinion meaningless.

In effect, whatever power Parliament possessed in the 18th century it long ago gave up to the government of the day. In turn, government, as we showed in Part 1, is increasingly centralised around the powers assumed by the Prime Minister, a few close advisers and the heads of the military and intelligence services. The overwhelming majority of those involved in decisions are unelected, unknown and unaccountable, either to Parliament or the electorate in general. The "corridors of power" are closed to all but the most privileged of political, business and financial circles. Occasionally, we are allowed a glimpse of the real matrix of executive power. The Hutton Inquiry in the summer of 2003, into the death of government scientist Dr David Kelly, inadvertently lifted the lid on the murky world of real political power. It revealed how secretive, virtually conspiratorial, select groups set Kelly up and essentially drove the civil servant to suicide. Finally, the primary purpose of the state and government today is to create the most favourable conditions demanded by transnational capitalism. That is ultimately where accountability lies – this is the real power behind the throne.

The parliamentary system is, therefore, a façade that increasingly undermines and devalues the right to vote that was won in bitter struggle against the ruling classes. A single vote every four or five years in a general election cannot alter the fact that this form of democracy is limited and curtailed in so many ways that reform is impossible.

Our proposals

Alongside democratic ownership and control of economic and financial resources (see Chapter 7), we should build on the formal democratic rights we have achieved and give them real meaning and content through a new political framework. This would replace the House of Commons, the totally unelected House of Lords, the system of monarchy left over from feudal times, the secretive Privy Council and the presidential-type powers of the Prime Minister. A new democratic Britain could involve:

‣ a national system of government built from the bottom up in contrast to today's hierarchical regime imposed from the centre
‣ national, regional and local Assemblies with executive as well as deliberative power
‣ local and regional Assemblies to decide on how best to meet a range of needs in their own areas and to send delegates to a national Assembly
‣ a national Assembly with executive and legislative powers over major issues such as health, housing and education budgets and overall economic objectives
‣ committees, making use of expert advice, to draw up plans to reflect the national Assembly's decisions. The chairs of the committees could form the government

‣ delegates to local, regional and national Assemblies to reflect diversity in our communities

‣ distinct voices, for example, for women, minority ethnic citizens, older people, young people, workplaces, students and small businesses

‣ all matters to be discussed, debated and decided upon with full public access to proceedings, putting an end to secretive methods of existing politics

‣ delegates to be paid no more than the average national income with no special privileges

‣ all delegates subject to recall and removal by local/regional voters at any time

‣ information and communication technology available free to every household to encourage and stimulate mass involvement in the new democratic process

‣ full information on proposed decisions to be made available and extensive consultation with voters *before* decisions are taken at any level

‣ freedom of political representation and the right to organise politically.

State administration

The state bureaucratic administrative machine is composed of departments, executive agencies and quangos. Its form has emerged, evolved and changed over 150 years in response to the developing needs of British and later global capitalism. The essential characteristics of state administration remain the same, however:

‣ the state bureaucracy is inherently conservative and remote
‣ there is the minimum of accountability
‣ secrecy is the norm
‣ expertise is used to reinforce the status quo or vested interests
‣ preservation of special privileges is demanded.

Even a cursory look at departments like the Home Office shows that they function to maintain social control. Most of the time and resources are spent on matters like reinforcing the crude punitive penal system, curtailing our civil liberties, increasing surveillance, punishing and demonising asylum seekers and increasing the powers of the police and control of the courts. Some 67,700 people are involved in carrying out the functions of the Home Office – 58,000 attached to the prisons and asylum systems.

The Ministry of Defence spends billions on armaments to use against other countries, or to sell to poor nations where rulers deploy British-made weapons to keep their own populations down. Some ministries have names that totally belie their purpose. For example, the Department of Work and Pensions ensures that the welfare system is used as a stick to beat people with, and that older people are left to survive on a meagre state pension. The Department for Environment, Food and Rural Affairs looks after the interests of major agribusinesses and is allowing life in the countryside to become increasingly difficult for those who live and work there. What about the Department for Trade and Industry? Its "mission statement" says: "The DTI drives our ambition of 'prosperity for all' by working to create the best environment for business success in the UK. We help people and companies become more productive by promoting enterprise, innovation and creativity."

A host of so-called agencies exist outside of the central state, making them even more remote. The Food Standards Agency, for example, is supposed to be in charge of food safety. Yet it has become a body that mostly concentrates on telling you how much nutrition there is in different foods rather than examining the dangerous way most food is processed on behalf of a handful of supermarkets. The FSA also promotes genetically-modified food as "safe" – it calls them "novel foods" – and is partisan against organic food producers. So much for its independence. Another FSA – the Financial Services Authority – is supposed to regulate the finance industry on behalf of consumers. In fact, its main task is to make sure that financial businesses stay within the law and do not go bankrupt. When it comes to things like the mis-selling of mortgage endowment policies, the FSA is on the side of the industry.

Then there are "quasi-autonomous non-governmental

organisations" – quangos to you and me – and other types of
public bodies. These carry out a series of functions on behalf of
government and range from the BBC and national museums to
the Housing Corporation, which funds and regulates housing
associations. There are also numerous scientific and advisory
bodies. Their collective budgets run into many billions of
pounds. There were almost 850 of these types of organisations in
2003, run by boards and committees appointed by ministers.
There were 22,000 appointments, many of them well-paid
positions. For example, the chair of the Housing Corporation
was paid more than £40,000 for a part-time post. There is a
whole industry out there of people collecting paid positions on
quango boards. Nice work if you can get it.

There is a human cost to this too for many of the staff
employed in the state bureaucracy. Consumed by a nightmare of
paperwork, reports, target chasing, endless meetings and inertia,
those who joined thinking they would do "something to help
society" are soon disabused. The whole process leads to a waste
of people's talents which could be better deployed elsewhere on
behalf of society as a whole, rather than on preserving the
narrow interests of the status quo.

Our proposals

A revolutionary government could not make use of the
machinery of state as it is presently set up and run. We should
aim to transform these state bodies from an apparatus that is
superimposed on society to a body that is subordinate to civil
society. As there would be no narrow class interests to represent,
many of the existing functions could be abolished straight away.
There would be no need, for example, for an immigration and
nationality division of the Home Office that currently employs
13,500 people with the task of driving asylum seekers and
refugees away from Britain. What is the point of the Financial
Services Authority in an economy that has abolished
speculation? Many other organisations that regulate aspects of
capitalist economy, like Ofcom for phone companies, would also
be abolished as unnecessary. A DTI that brings together
privately-owned corporations, university research and

commercial "opportunities" could not serve a society based on collective ownership and co-operation.

In their place would come new bodies that are totally under the sway and control of national, regional and local Assemblies. For example, a new department concerned with trade and industry would not have the primary task of stimulating the market economy through deregulation and competition. Instead, it would encourage self-management in the workplace, help create an audit of productive resources, stimulate ideas about new technology with the purpose of reducing workloads and cutting working hours and turn scientific research institutes away from commercial priorities in favour of solving pressing problems facing society. Furthermore, all departments would devolve not just staff but also their functions, to regions and cities to help ensure that bureaucratic inertia does not dominate.

As far as state administration is concerned, the principles for the future could be:

▸ the subordination of bureaucracy to society through accountability to Assemblies
▸ the replacement of existing structures with those better suited to new purposes
▸ new state bodies as facilitators and supporters of the new society
▸ the elimination of state administration wherever possible
▸ an end to special privileges and making a career out of bureaucracy
▸ payment of staff to reflect general levels of incomes in society
▸ complete public transparency in the work of the bureaucracy
▸ making other public bodies accountable to those who use services and to Assemblies.

The legal system

The legal system in Britain, although it is an inseparable part of the state machine, fulfils a number of often contradictory roles. It can, for example, often come into conflict with other parts of the state and government. We have seen a number of examples of this, both under the Tories and New Labour, where the judiciary has argued for the protection of democratic rights and the rule of law. There is, in fact, a deep crisis within the capitalist state over these issues. The state is proving increasingly incapable of and unwilling to protect or even advocate legal rights. We need to take forward what human society has achieved in terms of law while rejecting the existing class-biased framework in favour of a revolutionary, new approach.

At one level, the legal system – with its judges, courts, lawyers and prisons – is clearly an expression of the dominant power relations and ideology in society. It is based on hierarchy, authority and the ability to deprive those who do not "obey the law" of their liberty. These are all expressions of the power of the state. The judiciary sits as representatives of the "Crown" – which in 21st century Britain means the state and not the monarchy. Judges are appointed by the government in the person of the soon-to-be abolished Lord Chancellor. Much – but not all – law in Britain is handed down by the state in the form of legislation. Lawyers are accredited by bodies that owe their powers to the state. Prisons lock people up on behalf of the "Crown", which is why they are known as Her Majesty's Prisons. From this standpoint, the legal system has no essential independence from the capitalist state.

But while the legal system, which has Anglo-Saxon origins, derives its powers from the state, it does not simply represent capitalist interests in a crude and direct way. Of course, the legal system constantly reinforces the status quo in a variety of actions and activities. It upholds private ownership of property and contract law as the cornerstone of capitalist society. The emphasis in the legal system is on an individual and their rights, which denies a person's existence as a social being. Challenges to the basis of laws on the grounds that you might object to the protection of privilege are not allowed or accepted in courts.

As society is based on class division and conflict, there is a need to moderate and mediate between warring groups and the legal system provides just such an outlet. Because the ruling classes do not rule in a direct fashion, the legal system has developed a relative autonomy. The legal system in Britain thus reflects within it both the dominant nature of capitalist rule and the struggle for rights against arbitrary state power that stretches back many centuries.

The modern legal system emerged during the transition to capitalism in Britain. Historians such as E.P. Thompson date the transition from the Black Act of 1723. This law was introduced unopposed and rushed through in days to legislate the death penalty to deal with "wicked and evil-disposed men going armed in disguise". These were men who were involved in running battles with royal forest officials over the protection of their land who, allegedly, blacked their faces in order to avoid recognition. A range of offences were set out for which the death penalty was the consequence. Thompson explains in his brilliant study on the origins of the Black Act that:

> The Act registered the long decline in the effectiveness of old methods of class control and discipline and their replacement by one standard recourse of authority: the example of terror. In place of the whipping-post and the stocks, manorial and corporate controls and the physical harrying of vagabonds, economists advocated the discipline of low wages and starvation, and lawyers the sanction of death. Both indicated an increasing impersonality in the mediation of class relations, and a change, not so much in the "facts" of crime as in the *category* – "crime" – itself, as it was defined by the propertied. What was now to be punished was not an offence between men … but an offence against property. Since property was a thing it became possible to define offences as crimes against things, rather than injuries to men. This enabled the law to assume, with its robes, the postures of impartiality: it was neutral as between every degree of man, and defended only the inviolability of the ownership of things.

The Black Act lasted almost a century and became the arena for a series of battles between the propertied and the propertyless. In many cases, people were executed; in others, juries refused to convict and set defendants free. These struggles coincided with the expropriation of common land through enclosure, actions that were legalised by Acts of Parliament.

"Justice" is said to be blind and all enter the system with the same rights. At a superficial level, this seems to be true. High ranking members of society like Lord Archer can get sent to prison as well as the homeless. But decisions like these cannot obscure the real nature of relations within the legal system. Judges, for example, are drawn from a narrow, elite social class. Whatever their claims to impartiality and their attempts to free themselves from prejudice and bias, they inevitably come to court with the preconceptions and general approach to issues that is common to their class in society. Until quite recently, for example, they refused as a point of principle to believe that the police would lie under oath or fabricate evidence. In the remote world of judges, none of this seemed possible, whereas in the society inhabited by the rest of us, it all seemed quite probable and somewhat inevitable.

Access to the best legal representation usually requires substantial independent resources. While the wealthy can afford to hire a battery of top lawyers to defend them in court, the rest have to make do with lawyers assigned by the state. These can easily be the least experienced, or those who do not make the case a priority. As a result, defendants in criminal cases may be put under pressure to plead guilty in order to speed up the case and allow the lawyer to move on to more lucrative work. In civil cases, extreme restrictions on access to legal aid exclude a wide range of people from taking action.

And people do not all appear as equals except in the most abstract sense. They come before courts as individuals of a social class. They have differing backgrounds, opportunities and wealth. While people have a right to own property, this makes little difference when it comes to major issues. The capitalist has, in law, not only a right to own workplaces, but also the right to retain profits made out of the labour of others. This is equality capitalist style, the freedom to be unfree. That is why most people in the criminal system have "offended" against property (see below) and are from the working class.

The law, as it has evolved under capitalism, has resulted in a system with its own interests and development, alongside – as well as in direct relationship and conflict with – the state and its representative institutions. One of the outcomes is a contradictory set of rights, which the capitalist state itself is finding increasingly restrictive, as we shall see. Thompson says in *The Black Act*:

> If the law is evidently partial and unjust, then it will mask nothing, legitimise nothing, contribute nothing to any class's hegemony. The essential precondition for the effectiveness of law, in its function as ideology, is that it shall display an independence from gross manipulation and shall seem to be just. It cannot seem to be so without upholding its own logic and criteria of equity; indeed, on occasion, by actually *being* just. And furthermore it is not often the case that a ruling ideology can be dismissed as a mere hypocrisy; even rulers find a need to legitimise their power, to moralise their functions, to feel themselves to be useful and just.

Our proposals

It would be easy just to denounce every aspect of the current legal system as simply an extension of capitalist rule, which should be dumped in its entirety. That, however, would be a simplistic conclusion, paying no regard to the nature of revolutionary change. A new society cannot but begin with much of the baggage of the old. It is not possible – and in fact is extremely dangerous – to start from a blank sheet. That would rule out drawing on any aspect of human achievement in history in a positive way. No one would suggest reinventing the wheel; neither should we seek to do so with law.

Law is a contradictory phenomenon under capitalism, used both as a method of enforcing the status quo, and as a way of offering some form of protection along the lines of individual rights. It is capitalism that restricts justice, lending the legal system a class bias and reinforcing unequal access, while political agendas dictate issues like crime and inter-personal behaviour. Says Thompson:

> I am insisting only upon the obvious point, which some modern Marxists have overlooked, that there is a difference between arbitrary power and the rule of law. We ought to expose the shams and inequities which have been concealed beneath this law. But the

rule of law itself, the imposing of effective inhibitions upon power and the defence of the citizen from power's all-intrusive claims, seems to me to be an unqualified human good. To deny or belittle this good is, in this dangerous century when the resources and the pretensions of power continue to enlarge, a desperate error of intellectual abstraction.

Historical experience shows that if law is taken simply as a means of class rule, then it is open to abuse against individual citizens. That was the case under Stalinism in the Soviet Union. Once a privileged bureaucracy had seized control of the state, it set about creating a system of rule that had legal sanction but was in fact totalitarian. Law was used to destroy the opponents of Stalinism, including the leadership of the 1917 Revolution and those who developed independent social and political views.

We must start from the fact that capitalism is increasingly finding law and the legal system an impediment to its rule. What capitalism will not defend, we should take forward in a new way. Law must guard against corruption of the new regime by bureaucrats, political opportunists and other interests.

The struggle for democratic and legal rights in Britain in any case goes back much further than capitalism. In 1215, the barons forced King John to sign the Magna Carta or face a civil war. Arbitrary rule and punitive taxes imposed to finance the Crusades led the barons to draw up a charter of rights. Article 39 stated: "No freeman shall be seized, or imprisoned, or dispossessed, or outlawed, or in any way destroyed; nor will we condemn him, nor will we commit him to prison, excepting by the legal judgement of his peers, or by the laws of the land." In the English Civil War between parliament and Charles I, the Levellers demanded the right to vote for all men, irrespective of their wealth, and were brutally suppressed.

The American Revolution of 1776 and the French Revolution of 1789, led to statements of individual rights that were heavily influenced by the struggles against tyranny in Britain, led by Tom Paine and others. The struggle for the right to belong to a trade union and to vote for representation in Parliament lasted for much of the 19th century, resulting in death, exile, imprisonment and hardship for countless men and women. After the Russian Revolution of 1917, new types of rights emerged – social rights concerned with, among other things, employment, housing and education. After World War II, colonial countries fought for, and won, the right to self-determination. This history and its achievements are not to be given up lightly. They should form the basis of a new framework for law that goes beyond the limitations set by capitalist social relations.

Preserve and enhance the rule of law

The rule of law is now undermined by the degeneration of the capitalist state. In future, the rule of law must embrace published laws that apply universally, laws that are never retrospective, freedom from arbitrary arrest and defined limits to the powers of the state. Christina Sypnowich argues in *The Concept of Socialist Law* that

> the practical effect of these principles is to set limits to the discretion of judges, legislators and the police. The rule of law ensures that political interference in legal affairs, and the arbitrary power which is often the result, is impermissible. Detention without charge, conviction without sufficient evidence, unduly harsh punishment: all would constitute violations of the standards of consistency and coherence integral to a system of law.

Today, the judiciary is a distinct part of the capitalist state, as we have demonstrated, even if it has a relative autonomy in its day-to-day workings. Its much-vaunted independence and impartiality is subject to many restrictions and influences under capitalism, which taken together undermine the principle in practice. Moreover, its ultimate role is to uphold the status quo based on capitalist property and social relations. Today, the state is more and more overriding any independence the judiciary has, while building up police and administrative powers.

Our proposals

If law is to serve society as a whole, all links between the legal system and the state must be severed. Judges must be allowed to judge on the basis of the law alone and not some overriding principles set down by the state. The selection of judges at all levels must be a transparent process free from interference by the state and involve judges, lawyers and ordinary people, who would get special training to help them in their task. Judges must reflect regional, social and economic groups in society. Lay judges should sit alongside professionals, and legal officials must be answerable to the communities they serve.

A special commission would investigate and report back to Peoples Assemblies on what laws inherited from capitalism need scrapping or amending in the light of the framework of the new society. For example, the whole area of company law, with its emphasis on the rights of corporations covering all their activities, would not apply to a society based on common ownership. Present oppressive laws and regulations on asylum and refugees would be another example of redundant law. Employment and trade union law would have to be revised in the light of the new circumstances, reinstating the unqualified right to strike taken away by Tory/New Labour laws. The anti-terror laws would be scrapped.

ID cards will be abolished and there will be explicit rights to:

▸ *habeas corpus,* requiring people arrested to be brought to court and charged or released
▸ free and equal legal representation
▸ freedom from state surveillance
▸ inspect freely all data held by the state and other bodies.

Extend democratic rights

The rights capitalism allows are extremely narrow. For example, the European convention on human rights, now part of the Human Rights Act, restricts itself to restating principles that mostly relate to arrest and detention, the expression of opinions, freedom from torture and the right to assembly and to join a trade union. All are heavily qualified and allow the state to modify, or opt out of the convention, when it is deemed necessary. New Labour has done this, as we have seen, in order to imprison foreign citizens without trial or charge. While these rights are important and must be preserved, they are based on the status quo of capitalist social relations. While there is a right, for example, to join a union, there is no stated right to strike. There is no mention of the right to vote whatsoever, or of the question of elections.

The right to express an opinion has a sub-clause which states: "The exercise of these freedoms, since it carries with it duties and responsibilities, may be subject to such formalities, conditions, restrictions or penalties as are prescribed by law and are necessary in a democratic society, in the interests of national security, territorial integrity or public safety, for the prevention of disorder or crime, for the protection of health or morals, for the protection of the reputation or rights of others, for preventing the disclosure of information received in confidence, or for maintaining the authority and impartiality of the judiciary." These conditions give the state carte blanche when it is deemed necessary to crack down on rights.

Our proposals

Today, individual rights to justice, like the ability to elect for trial by jury, are under constant attack by the state. We need to restate them in a fresh way. Individual rights to liberty and freedom from arbitrary arrest will be reaffirmed in unconditional and positive terms. Social rights established in law, within a framework of the abolition of the capitalist exploitation of labour, should include the legal rights to:

- decent housing at affordable cost for everyone
- free education for students at all ages
- employment for those who can work and average pay for those who cannot
- equal pay and job opportunities for women
- free child care for single parents
- equality for black and minority ethnic citizens
- asylum with equal status to those already resident
- free health care at all levels and types of treatment
- dignity in old age through pension provision at average income, and free care

‣ safe and nutritious food at affordable prices
‣ equal access to cultural and personal development
   opportunities.

Crime and punishment

The most evident class bias in the legal system is in the area of
crime. Laws setting out offences all derive from legislation drawn
up by the state and imposed on the legal system to implement.
The concepts of individual responsibility, guilt and punishment
that lie at the heart of criminal law express both the hostility of
the state and the atomisation of the individual in capitalist
society. Offences are dealt with out of social context. The reasons
for committing an offence are not allowed to become part of a
defence. Only the "facts" in relation to a specific charge are
taken into account.

   The criminal law system is not so much about delivering
"justice" or even "fighting crime" as a way of reinforcing
existing forms of social control and authority. Although it is
constructed in a language of formal equality, criminal law and
punishment is selective and unequal. The whole notion of what
constitutes serious crime and a "danger to society" is narrowly
drawn, so as to exclude much of what many consider harmful
behaviour. For example, prosecuting a company for
manslaughter is next to impossible, as the relatives of the victims
of rail crashes have found out to their cost. The intense
exploitation of workers in Britain and abroad, which shortens
lives and makes people ill, is considered "good" although it
adversely affects people more than existing crime. While terrorist
bombings are dealt with as crimes, the dropping of bombs on
civilians by state-employed pilots is legally sanctioned. Pollution
is destroying the planet's ecosystems and making people ill, yet
those responsible are not considered criminals. These are the
crimes of the powerful and the rich, but they are free to commit
them while others are prosecuted and persecuted.

   The rapid changes of the last 25 years have shattered many of
the forms of social relations that developed after 1945 in the
period of economic boom and the welfare state. Market forces
have produced far less stable households, urban degeneration,

the growth of extreme wealth alongside deprivation, the marginalisation of sections of young people, burgeoning individualism, and a manufactured craving for consumer goods. The decline of informal social control through relatively stable communities has coincided with the dramatic fall in the price of drugs to produce whole inner-city as well as rural areas of decline and despair. Young men, in particular, have seen their traditional status and social role challenged and this has deepened their alienation. Increasing numbers of young women have struggled against the odds as lone parents. This is the background to contemporary crime, much of which is committed by the poor against the poor. More than two in three of all prisoners are unemployed when they go to jail.

Under New Labour, the courts have been instructed to deal harshly with offenders while the rehabilitation aspects of the system are downgraded. The Probation Service, which for most of the post-World War II period played a role in helping offenders, has lost any notional independence and is being merged into a National Offender Management Service (NOMS).

Any ideas of justice in the system are replaced by managerialism, cost-cutting and the "targeting" of a specific group. In an article in the September 2001 magazine of the Legal Action Group, Professor Ed Cape, director of the University of the West of England, Centre of Criminal Justice and Professor Lee Bridges, Chair of the School of Law, University of Warwick, noted:

> The fact that the policy of 'targeting' has the effect of concentrating criminal law enforcement on the socially excluded and ethnic minority sections of the population serves a wider political purpose. It is not the rights of the 'ordinary' citizen that are being threatened in this process, but those of an identifiable, even 'alien', minority. In other words, it is not just law-abiding citizens who are portrayed as having separate interests from 'criminals', but the minority of 'persistent offenders' can be further divided off from other offenders for special treatment without raising the spectre of a general erosion of citizens' rights.

Statistics compiled by the Prison Reform Trust (PRT) highlight
the increasing use of imprisonment – amongst the crudest forms
of punishment, and deteriorating conditions for those
imprisoned. When New Labour came to government in May
1997, the prison population was 60,000. In March 2004, the
prison population in England and Wales stood at 75,000, its
highest ever recorded figure and an increase of almost 2,500 over
the past year. For the second consecutive year, England and
Wales had the highest imprisonment rate in the European Union,
at 141 per 100,000 of the population. The number of prisoners
in England and Wales has increased by more than 25,000 in the
last ten years. Previously it took four decades (1954-94) for the
prison population to rise by 25,000. Overcrowding has led to
appalling conditions and a sharp rises in suicides. In August
2004, 14 prisoners took their own lives, the highest total ever
recorded for a single month in British jails.

The number of women in prison has increased particularly
dramatically. Ten years ago in 1994 the average female prison
population was 1,811. In March 2004, there were 4,549 women
in prison, an increase of 151% in the last ten years. The offences
for which women were most often sent to prison in 2002 were
theft and handling stolen goods. Just over 2,500 women were
received into custody for these offences, of which the most
common crime is shoplifting. They accounted for 40% of all
female receptions into prison in 2002. There were more than
11,000 under 21 year olds in prison; of these, 2,565 were under
18.

Most of the rise in the prison population over the last decade
can be explained by the significant increases in the proportion of
offenders sent to prison and the length of sentences, particularly
the increased number of long-term prisoners, says the PRT. At
the end of September 2003, there were 28,250 prisoners serving
sentences of four years and over. This compares with 14,750 in
1994, an increase of 92%. In terms of custody rates, ten years
ago one defendant in 26 would have gone into custody. Now it
is one in 13. First time domestic burglars are almost twice as
likely to receive a custodial sentence today as they were eight
years ago and at the same time the average sentence length for

burglars has increased from 16 months to 18 months.

The punishment system is inherently racist. At the end of February 2003, one in four of the prison population was from a minority ethnic group. This compares to one in eleven of the general population. The imprisonment rate for black people is 1,140 per 100,000, ten times higher than the imprisonment rate for South Asians or whites, which are 166 per 100,000 and 170 per 100,000 respectively. If white people were imprisoned at the rate of black people, England and Wales would have half a million people in prison. Black people are five times more likely than white people to be stopped and searched. Once arrested,

---

The overcrowding crisis in our jails means that some offenders no longer attend appeals because they fear that by the time they return to prison, their cells, will be allocated to another inmate.

Lord Woolf, Lord Chief Justice, speaking at the annual Perrie Lecture Awards, 6 June 2003

---

black people are more likely to be remanded in custody than other offenders charged with similar offences. Black and Asian defendants were less likely to be found not guilty than white defendants.

Our proposals

What is self-evident is that the prison and criminal justice systems produce criminals rather than addressing or tackling the issue of criminality. It is yet another example of the inability of capitalism to deal with the problems it creates. It would rather spend an average of £36,000 a year keeping someone locked up than face up to the root causes. Thus, the issue reduces itself to one of "crime management", New Labour style, which embraces the law-and-order, authoritarian agenda set by the Tories in the 1980s. The way the approach to crime is framed by traditional political parties serves to disguise the real relations and concerns in society. As criminologist John Muncie put it in a paper to British Criminology Conference 1999

The power to render certain harmful acts visible and define them as "crime", whilst maintaining the invisibility of others (or defining them as beyond criminal sanction) lies at the heart of the problem of working with notions of "the problem of crime". Notions of "crime" offer a peculiarly blinkered vision of the range of misfortunes, dangers, harms, risks and injuries that are a routine part of everyday life. If the criminological intent is to reveal such misfortunes, risks and harms then the concept of 'crime' has to be rejected as its sole justification and object of inquiry. The first stage in decriminalising criminology (or to decentre crime) is to recognise that any number of damaging events are far more serious than those that make up the 'crime problem'. Moreover, many of these incidents (such as petty theft, shoplifting, recreational drug use, vandalism, brawls, anti-social behaviour) would not seem to score particularly high on a scale of serious harm. Despite this it is often these "minor" events that take up much of the time and preoccupation of law enforcement agencies and the criminal justice system. Conversely, the risk of suffering many of these crimes defined by the state as 'serious', would seem negligible compared to such everyday risks as workplace injury and avoidable disease.

This shows the urgent need to reframe the whole concept of crime and how to deal with it. With the abolition of the alienated social relations of capitalism, communities will have greater opportunities to explore what defines crime from a totally different standpoint. Instead of naming and shaming, retribution, vengeance and punishment, we should emphasise reparation and community self-control and influence. There are grounds for replacing the body of existing criminal law, with its thousands of offences, with law based on making offenders face up to their responsibilities and their impact on communities.

The existing prison system belongs to the Middle Ages. Prison does little to prevent reoffending. It is designed to brutalise and shame and should be scrapped. Where it is unavoidable to detain offenders, a new approach would make rehabilitation its sole priority. Formal court structures that presently deal with crime could be replaced with neighbourhood/community courts that would start from compensation and reconciliation rather than retaliation. There would be more use of arbitration, adjudication and conciliation in place. In this way communities would come to accept that it has a responsibility for the personal and social development of all of its citizens.

The police and state forces

The police force in Britain is incapable of serving communities because of the way it is run and controlled. At one level, the police force is the servant of the state and charged with preserving "law and order". At times, this means the police are sent out to prop up governments by attacking demonstrations and strikes. In most recent history, the police were used by the Thatcher government to attack miners and printworkers in the mass struggles in defence of jobs that took place during 1984-86. They also violently suppressed the anti-poll tax demonstrations in London in April 1990.

More recently, the police have used anti-terror laws against protesters outside an arms fair in London, in September 2003, when 144 people were arrested. These laws allow the police to abandon the need to show cause when stopping and searching someone. In addition, the police Special Branch works closely with MI5, the British secret police, to spy on and infiltrate those considered to be a "threat to national security". This goes far beyond the alleged terror networks, to militant trade unions, left-wing political organisations and protest groups opposed to government policy.

At another level, the police are clearly incapable of dealing with crime. The clear-up figure has fallen to only 23% across all forces despite increases in personnel. In London, and Somerset and Avon, the figure for 2003 was only 15% per cent. The bureaucratic, secret world of the police means they are often closer to the criminal fraternity than ordinary people. In fact, often their behaviour mimics aspects of the most backward social behaviour in the shape of racism, corruption, indifference and lying when it comes to obtaining convictions. As a result, many vulnerable and innocent people end up serving long sentences for crimes they did not commit.

Society should not have to rely on a professional police force

divorced from day-to-day accountability and control to deal with
real life problems and issues. Spending more money on police
numbers, equipment and computers, and giving them more
powers makes no difference. The problems are beyond their
capacity to deal with. Instead, the community should learn to
police itself, relying on professional help where necessary. That
would require the abolition of the police force as presently
constituted and its reorganisation to support community self-
policing.

Responsibility for preserving and enhancing collective and
personal property and security would fall on the shoulders of the
entire community, who would now be in overall social and
political charge. A range of mechanisms – from the formal to the
informal – would be introduced. Even in Britain today, there are
communities that have had to act themselves to drive out drug
dealers, for example. Taken together with the new approach to
dealing with crime, the reorganisation of the justice system and
the scrapping of the existing prison system, these proposals offer
a chance for society as a whole to develop a collective cohesion
that is patently absent today.

The secret intelligence agencies, MI5 and MI6, together with
the police Special Branch would also be abolished. The army,
together with the navy and air force, which is used to fight wars
on behalf of the capitalist state, would be reorganised as a
defensive force. All their weapons of mass destruction will be
scrapped. Altogether, the new, transitional state would advance
society towards the day when the administration of people is
transformed into the administration of things by the people.

* * *

Education and the future: a transatlantic dialogue

*Glenn Rikowski is a Senior Lecturer in Education Studies in
the School of Education at University College Northampton.
Rich Gibson is a co-founder of the Rouge Forum, and an
associate professor of education at San Diego State University,
California. This dialogue was conducted by email between 19
July and 8 August 2004.*

GLENN: First of all Rich, I think that it's best to acknowledge
that there are problems regarding the two of us talking about
education in socialism. One is that there is no agreement
regarding the nature of socialism, and so trying to outline an
education for socialism is a non-starter. Secondly, it could be
argued that a couple of teachers like us outlining "the education
of the future" runs against the notion that any programme for
education in socialism (or in a transitional epoch) must be the
result of *collective* and *democratic* discussions, educational
practice and political action. Are we not just a couple of teachers,
educational activists and thinkers spinning ideas about education
in socialism? Why should anyone take notice of what we say? A
third point is that education in socialism, like socialism itself, is
simply unimaginable. We are both locked into capitalist society,
and our capacity to visualise anything beyond it, such as socialist
society and an education for socialism is impossible. However, I
would like to think there is a way through at least some of this.
A friend of mine, Richard Shepherd, argued that after the fall of
the Berlin Wall and the transformation of the Soviet Union and
Eastern Bloc from state socialist or state capitalist (take your
pick) societies into a capitalist ones, folks would want detail
about what socialism would be like. They would want to know
more about what they were committing themselves too. What
are your thoughts on these issues, Rich?

RICH: Geeze, Glenn! Those are four big questions. First, on
socialism: I think it failed and we need to build a critical

understanding of what went wrong. What will be can only come from what has been, with some imaginative leaps, so the huge struggle for socialism, which cost the lives of millions of honest people and which despite its failure still stands as a high-watermark of humanism, is key to understanding where we want to go.

GLENN: But Rich, this implies that we need to say what we think socialism was, or is – and where actually existing forms of socialism, or attempts at creating socialism, took a wrong turn.

RICH: Yes Glenn, and for me socialism was 1) the continuation of the state, in the form of the dictatorship of the proletariat, as a site of class struggle 2) with the party in the lead, purportedly acting in the interest of the working classes and the peasantry 3) as a result of a revolution (meaning I do not think there is a way to vote away capitalism), for the purpose of winning a more humane, free, egalitarian, and democratic world. Because brevity must be a concern, let me compact history a great deal and say I believe the key efforts for revolution were the Paris Commune, the Russian revolution, the Chinese revolution, and the Cuban revolution. Each of these battles built on the other.

The Paris Commune, brief as it was, set up the principles of socialism in practical ways (smashing the existing state, no elected officials paid more than average workers, immediate recall of elected officials, a working – as opposed to a bureaucratic – government, quasi-soviets in power, the necessity of an armed people, etc.). The Russian revolution demonstrated that a socialist revolution could rise up in the midst of an imperialist war, face massive attacks, and sustain itself – if briefly. The Chinese revolution again demonstrated the relationship of imperialist war and revolution, and deepened 1) the idea of a mass party, 2) the role of a peoples' army, fairly egalitarian and democratic, and peoples' (guerrilla) war, 3) questions about dialectical materialism and making the philosophy of praxis a mass issue, and 4) the role of class struggle, and consciousness, post-revolution. The Cuban revolution showed that a revolution was possible even at the fingertips of the empire, and the potential role of socialist education for a new kind of humanity. Each revolution elevated human history. Yet each, I think, collapsed. Each failed to address successfully the production and appropriation of surplus value, to overcome capitalist economic relations.

GLENN: And what about my second point Rich, on why people should take any notice of us?

RICH: Well Glenn, to paraphrase the other Marx, Groucho, I am not sure I would want to pay much attention to anyone who paid too much attention to me. That said, however, let us look at concrete circumstances. This is a world whose major powers are promising their youth perpetual war. Inequality is booming, as are many forms of irrationalism (racism, nationalism, religious fundamentalism, sexism, etc). An international war of the rich on the poor is producing new forms of fascism on every continent. At the same time, the world is more united than ever before, through systems of production, exchange, transportation, technology, and communications. Everything is there for all to live fairly well, if we chose to share. This contradiction is not acceptable. Indeed, there is no alternative but to discover a path to get rid of capitalism, to create a humane world where people can truly lead reasonably free, creative, connected lives in sharing communities.

GLENN: How does education come into this project, Rich?

RICH: Education is key, not only in creating the base of understanding, through critical analysis of existing social relations, to offer a ground for a leap of imagination beyond daily life, but also because education, schooling, is now structurally pivotal to some of the most powerful imperial players, like the US.

GLENN: What are the relations between schools and imperialism in your view, Rich?

RICH: Well Glenn, in de-industrialised North America, I believe schools, not industrial work places nor the military nor the tax system, are the focal organising places of most peoples' lives. Of course, schools offer skill training (literacy, etc), and ideological training (nation building). Schools are huge markets. They involve billions of dollars of exchange (textbooks, salaries, architects, buses, buildings, etc), and they warehouse kids, a vital tax free corporate benefit in a society whose economy created one-parent families, or requires two people working to win the salary of what one person earned 25 years ago. Most importantly, schools are centres of hope which is probably the main reason people send their kids to us strangers.

GLENN: But from what I've read of your work, teachers can make a difference, right?

RICH: Absolutely! What I've outlined above is not *all* that goes on in schools, or need go on. Good teachers swim against the current every day, teaching from the understanding that students are capable of comprehending and changing the world. Teachers do not have to be missionaries for capitalism and some, though far too few, are not. These are, after all, *capitalist* schools and they are not semi-autonomous sites, though they are contested sites of class struggle, every day. Even so, it is capitalism that is semi-autonomous. Its schools are not.

So, education is key to things as they are, and to changing things to what they *might be*. Education is integral to sustaining any changes that might be won by poor and working people. Education has also been key to revolutionary projects in progress, as in South Africa, or perhaps more modestly, in the Mississippi Freedom Schools in the early 1960s, the Black Panther Party schools connected to their free breakfast programs, etc.

GLENN: So Rich, coming round to the really tough one: what might an education system look like in a future society?

RICH: Well Glenn, I suppose that depends on how that society has developed, what it is and wants to be. If it is a society that has just experienced a successful uprising, education will look much different from a society that has achieved real community – as the earlier society will certainly be under extreme internal and external military, economic, political, and social pressure. Yet Glenn, I think either education system must address the question Marx raises in his third Thesis on Feuerbach:

> The materialist doctrine concerning the changing of circumstances and upbringing forgets that circumstances are changed by human beings and that it is essential to educate the educator himself. This doctrine must, therefore, divide society into two parts, one of which is superior to society.
>
> The coincidence of the changing of circumstances and of human activity or self-changing can be conceived and rationally understood only as revolutionary practice.

I believe this addresses the issues of *transformation* and *self*-transformation that educators face every day quite well.

Both Georg Lukacs and Paulo Freire wrote highly significant last books. Lukacs' *Tailism and the Dialectic*, drives home three key ideas that Freire's last work, *Pedagogy of Freedom*, takes up as well. In each instance, two things are clear from the two writers. First, overcoming the contradiction of subject and object – the self-actualising person making their own history, in circumstances they did not make – requires the conscious action of the critically curious subject. Second, justice demands organisation. Only through a revolutionary political organisation can such conscious actions become truly a *movement*. Third, within this, "revolutionary passion", is vital, key. However Glenn, I do not share Lukacs', or Freire's, sense of what the organisation should look like – or at least not Lukacs' tacit support of Stalin's Russia, and Freire's leadership in the Workers Party of Brazil, about to recreate all the old problems of socialism. Still, I think their common idea is correct. The *negation of the negation*, the idea that things change and what is new is always in re-creation, and that the profound optimism built within it requires organisation.

GLENN: Perhaps you could elaborate on why teachers' power is so crucial, Rich.

RICH: Well, it's not just power in relation to organising for big events, public events (demos, protests, etc.), though it is also that. But the more power we have, by organising the chess club, by being a coach, by taking on unwanted tasks, the more freedom we have to teach what reason is, critical thinking, that is, dialectical materialism: how to think of things as they change, the view that we can understand and change the world. So, we teach the scientific method of knowledge, in social studies and physics.

GLENN: And there's an ethical dimension here too, a question of *values*, I believe.

RICH: This is crucial: we teach love, both as a fact of sensual pleasure, and a question of species survival, evolution, and we discuss how sensual love is distinct from exploitative sex, how we can tell lovers from Bill and Monica. With our power and freedom, we restore the study of work, labour, production, labour history, Marx – and revolution – to the curriculum, showing how over time people have made gains, wittingly and not so wittingly, and how we have been betrayed as well. Anything but class, as James Loewen says, is the rule of teaching in US schools, and we need to get the power to break the rule – which the work of the Rouge Forum demonstrates is possible.

GLENN: What about the social context in which schools, teachers and students operate?

RICH: Clearly, we must address the immediate issues in schools: curricula regimentation, high stakes tests, militarism, demands for cutbacks and de-funding via marketisation. We should show the historically factual ties of these issues to the needs of an imperialist society. What is our immediate goal in this? I think our goal should be, simultaneously, the ability to control our workplaces, schools, in conjunction with kids and parents – and revolution. The struggle for control of the processes and products of work is incessant and necessary on any job, and it should be our understanding on ours. Control of the work place is proved by our ability to shut it down. Between today and shutting it down, we should lead boycotts of the tests, protests, drive the recruiters off the campuses – urge people into more and more direct, self-actualising, collective action against the boss – and against capitalism. This is not a call for action that is manufactured out of the air. These actions have already happened. Our job is to make sense of them, to encourage and organise more of them – to lead.

GLENN: Becoming *educators* in this much wider and deeper sense that you have outlined?

RICH: Yes, I think we should shut down the schools, as many as we can, as often as we can. Does that mean I want to destroy public, or more exactly not so "public", education as no nation has a truly public system? No. It means I want to overturn the social relations that make unpublic education rotten, and I want to build a lasting social movement that can create a better world. If we should do that, we will have a responsibility to begin, and maintain, freedom schools in the midst of very serious struggle.

GLENN: Rich, I would venture to say something about the *kind* of schooling we have and might have for a socialist future. If schooling is an aspect of the "real movement of society", then what does this entail? I would argue that there are at least three moments within this movement. First, in relation to capitalist schooling, the key point is *critique*. This would be the critique of capitalist society, its forms of schooling and training, its markets, and so on. This first moment attempts to push to the fore the *negativity* of all that passes for the "positive" in capitalist society, especially in education and training. For example, mainstream education researchers and theorists here in the UK are all too quick to grasp the latest "good idea" emanating from Policyland: the learning society, social capital, personalised learning and so on. Though under New Labour there have been so many of these that a reluctant scepticism has developed. But this misses the point. These policies sound appealing in a way. Who could be against lifelong learning, for example? But in capitalist society these "good ideas" can only ever be perverted and inverted moments (the opposite) of what they purport to represent. Thus, as I have explained in the case of lifelong learning, in capitalist society this is transformed into a kind of "learning unto death" in the form of labour-power production. So, the moment of critique is essential – and we need to encourage our students to be critical of all aspects of society.

But if critique was all we had to offer, that would be insufficient. And for the second moment Rich, I would like to draw on something that you mentioned earlier, and which Peter McLaren has talked about in relation to Paulo Freire: *love* – which I think, in its broadest sense, must be linked to *human needs*. An education for the future must be about meeting human needs: not just of the students, but also of the communities in which they live, and beyond. Of course, we must be on our guard that these needs are expressed and considered in truly democratic sites and that students' and teachers' efforts to meet them are not hijacked by capital or the state. But this may be less of a danger if the state has been smashed already and capital is a battered social force, on the wane! Yet I would not want people to get the impression that the education of the future is just about critique and educating to meet, and in fact meeting, human needs. It must not be entirely negative nor self-sacrificial, but should also point to the *realm of freedom* – the freedom that Marx was talking about in his brief sketch of the communist impulse in the *Economic and Philosophical Notebooks of 1844*. The education of the future has also to speak to desires, wants and dreams.

RICH: Critique (through negation), love, and the realm of freedom; that is not only a fine ground for any classroom, but for revolution. In our current epoch, resistance and the revolutionary struggle are key to freedom, and to understanding. So, as you say, these moments work in relationship to each other, to the whole of capitalism, and they can operate in similar ways in the everyday classroom as well.

9 Culture for all

Love it or hate it, culture in our time is technology based. While it expresses the achievements of human history, at the same time, it is not socially or class neutral. As writer and self-confessed computer nerd Bob Hughes writes:

> The machine on which I write this was massively subsidised by the sweat, tears, taxes and poisoned aquifers of the people of Taiwan, Malaysia, Thailand, Singapore and China... Its chips have consumed 700 times their own weight in water, hydrocarbons, toxic gases and solvents... It has perhaps 30 capacitors containing tantalum: very likely part of the spoils of Congo's civil war, which has killed around 4 million people.

The Internet is an outstanding example of the contradictory nature of today's culture. Ranged against the corporate interests of media giants and companies like Microsoft, Amazon, Google and Sony are those who create content, value and social significance – the artists, technicians and users. They are the countless musicians, writers, professional and amateur photographers, editors, technicians, including hackers, web-builders, researchers, readers, fans, campaigners for rights and freedoms and students, as well as those looking for long lost relatives or even a recipe for dinner. Not to speak of fraudsters, criminals, pornographers and credit card cloners. The corporates want tollbooths on the information highways and seek to make every form of creative labour into something they can exploit, while on the other side, the desire is to preserve the Internet commons as an area free from state or corporate control. Thus the Internet is a symbol of the great possibilities that exist for human creativity while at the same time showing how this comes up against corporate interests.

The Cyber-Rights and Cyber-Liberties organisation explains in a *Short history of content regulation and content blocking technology* that:

> Until the 1990s there were no restrictions on Internet content... Despite the largely serious and academic nature of most material, a sub-culture also flourished of odd sexually-oriented, politically-oriented, and other materials often considered "wacko" (insane). The presence of such materials was tolerated by all users and even considered a sign of the health of the medium. In particular, few people were bothered by the presence of pornography in a community made up of over 90% of male users.
>
> When the Internet became more widespread and governments began to take notice, the *first stage* in Internet content control began, consisting of heavy-handed and repressive forays in censorship. The US Communications Decency Act 1996 was a part of this trend, as are more recent but similar proposals by the Australian government...
>
> The *second stage* in content control thus began with the introduction of rating and filtering products that claim to permit users to block unwanted material from their personal systems. The most sophisticated and widely recognised of these systems is the Platform for Internet Content Selection (PICS), introduced by the World Wide Web Consortium. European governments were especially interested in this hoped-for solution. They backed away quickly from incidents in the first stage of direct suppression and put forward PICS and rating systems as a proposed standard, both through national governments and the European Union as a self-regulatory solution to Internet content.

The Internet Content Rating Association (ICRA) was adopted by the media giants, AOL-Time Warner, Disney/ABC, Bertelsmann

(BMG), Microsoft, BT and Bell Canada. Content filters are now being adopted by Internet service providers (ISPs) without users' knowledge. They may block out all but rated sites, which eliminates areas of cyberspace on the grounds that they are "unrated". The sponsors of the content standards are also suppliers of browsers, which reinforces the big corporations' control over access to the Internet. Other forms of control include "cookies", which place a unique small file on your computer which allow your browsing habits to be followed and even directed without your knowledge.

One of the most successful global companies in recent years is the Google search engine, which has outstripped its earlier rivals such as Yahoo. "Googling" is an activity engaged in by millions of Internet users daily, to find everything and everybody, from travel packages to cooking recipes, long lost relatives and childhood friends, academic and scientific research results. But as we innocently surf the waves of the web, thrilled by the ease of communication, we do not realise how our every click is being monitored.

One of the reasons for Google's financial success is that by tracking users' surfing patterns on the net, it can offer prime spots for advertising merchandise.

Google's immortal cookie: Google was the first search engine to use a "cookie" that expires in 2038. This was at a time when federal websites were prohibited from using persistent cookies altogether…

Google records everything they can: For all searches they record the cookie ID, your Internet IP address, the time and date, your search terms, and your browser configuration. Increasingly, Google is customising results based on your IP number. This is referred to in the industry as "IP delivery based on geolocation."

Google's toolbar is spyware: Google's free toolbar for Explorer phones home with every page you surf, and yes, it reads your cookie too.

www.google-watch.org/bigbro.html

Creativity goes corporate

The distinction between cultural activity and commerce is increasingly obscured. To enhance their image and to sell their products, the corporations increasingly embrace "creativity". It is all part of the "media and entertainment business", a seamless unity of global capitalist enterprise. All aspects of culture are now included, from advertising design to product design and the talent and skills of the workers/creators/performers whose labour is essential to the whole thing.

A survey conducted by PricewaterhouseCoopers forecast that the value of the global media and entertainment industry would increase from $1.1 trillion in 2001 to $1.4 trillion by 2006, growing at an average rate of 5.5%. So the stakes are extremely high.

As one advocate for cultural diversity, Joost Smiers, has written: "It is not just the power to decide at the end of the process when the transaction is signed and the deal completed who will continue to be a client, a viewer or a listener; but power that extends to all the moments before this. It is the power to select a few artists and reject the rest; and to give those who are selected massive distribution and promotion. More and more, the decisive question thus becomes: who has access to the communication channels of the planet..."

Internet commons champion Laurence Lessig, has pointed to some of the opposing forces vying for control. Writing in *The Financial Times* (20 February 2004), he said: "The extraordinary growth in services and content on the Internet has come precisely from the neutrality of its 'end-to-end' design." In other words, the success of the Net comes from the way in which all users can be in touch with each other at any time and place, without any restriction. Lessig points to the explosion of mass creativity on the Internet and how the corporations are pressuring governments to ensure protectionism amounting to an important change. In his book, *Free Culture*, he says:

> For the first time in our tradition, the ordinary ways in which individuals create and share culture fall within the reach of the regulation of the law, which has expanded to draw within its

control a vast amount of culture and creativity that it never reached before. The technology that preserved the balance of our history – between uses of our culture that were free and uses of our culture that were only upon permission – has been undone. The consequence is that we are less and less a free culture, more and more a permission culture. This change gets justified as necessary to protect commercial creativity. And indeed, protectionism is precisely its motivation. But the protectionism that justifies the changes... is not the limited and balanced sort that has defined the law in the past. This is not a protectionism to protect artists. It is instead a protectionism to protect certain forms of business. Corporations threatened by the potential of the Internet to change the way both commercial and non-commercial culture are made and shared have united to induce lawmakers to use the law to protect them.

Thus, as in so many other ways, capitalist globalisation has reached a point where it needs to suppress the very forces that it has generated.

Compulsory freedom

Everything can become a commodity, at least during some parts of its life. While consumer culture appears universal because it is depicted as a land of freedom in which everyone *can* be a consumer, it is also felt to be universal because everyone must be a consumer: this particular freedom is compulsory.

Consumer Culture and Modernity

The music industry provides the clearest and fastest example of corporate appropriation of creativity. As music industry critic Andrew Benfield, of the Big Chill festival says, it needs

to control the whole process of cultural production, from creating content through to how that content is marketed and distributed. The growth of globalisation and the consolidation of this "culture machine" into the hands of just five firms has lead to an increasingly conservative choice of culture, highly marketed, tightly controlled and fervently policed through the mainstream media channels of TV, film and commercial radio.

Britpop music historian John Harris believes that the creative, chaotic autonomy of earlier times has been "gobbled up". The result is

> music founded in a spirit of spontaneity and self-expression ending up at the core of an ever-more standardised planet (those Pepsi ads starring Pink, Beyoncé and Britney speak volumes). Moreover, as the music industry shrinks, pop's increasing dearth of diversity is starting to impact on the UK. Each year, the odds against British acts making inroads in the US seem slimmer than ever; in music, too, there is but one superpower… how long, I wonder before Halliburton and Exxon start sponsoring festivals?

In today's world of instant digital sound reproduction, the battle between the corporations, music lovers and pirates goes on, providing a major example of how the corporate ownership of distribution and marketing channels is constantly at war with the creators of music as well as the fans and music lovers. The US Central Intelligence Agency now sends its spies to track down digital piracy around the world.

Music lovers are now swapping digital music on a massive scale, with more than two billion songs being traded on the FastTrack (a Napster clone) system every month during 2002-3. And this was *after* the passing of the Digital Millennium Copyright Act (DMCA) in 1998 to stamp out copyright abuse! (see www.anti-dmca.org)

The shut-down of music sharing programme Napster in 2000, rather than crushing this flourishing counterculture, has spawned dozens of imitators that are proving harder to stop. From the centralised music library database pioneered by Napster, the file-sharing community began a guerrilla activity, working through a de-centralised network. Napster's wild growth (40 million users in just six months) ended up with it being taken over by the Bertelsmann conglomerate, one of the very companies seeking its closure.

The latest conflict in the poacher-turned-gamekeeper wars has broken out between Real, which makes RealPlayer, the online sound and image software, and Apple, whose users have access to iTunes Music Store via their iPods. Apple has now accused RealNetwork of adopting the tactics and ethics of a hacker to break into their stash of music. The digital rights management field is full of minefields for consumers and content producers alike. In the three-cornered triangle of creator-fan-corporate ownership, the chief barrier between the musician and the fan is clearly the need for corporate profit-making.

The music industry is dominated by the big corporations who are still selling CDs and ways of listening to music at high prices, while musicians are subject to all the pressures of the industry. The mass media perpetuates the domination of an élite group of performers, while the rest of the talent struggles on the sidelines. We live in an age when teenie boppers' pester power is the last great hope for the music corporations' production-line pop which accounts for the promotion of less-than-challenging types of music.

The visual arts

Through the merger of cultural enterprises into a few big companies, what before was a separate area for visual art – painting, sculpture and photography – have been drawn into the corporate melting pot. This affects all the practising visual artists in the world – and there are a million of them in the US and Europe alone. The global art market has seen an unprecedented speculation, not only in Wall Street but throughout the world's art capitals. As one historian of the image, Richard Bolton, wrote in his critical history of photography: "This traffic in art mirrors the fervent trading of the stock exchange: investment indexes for art continue to climb; gallery owners trade artists and make deals in the style of corporate raiders." Historic photographic archiving and reproduction is dominated by two giants, Corbis and Getty. In art auctioning, Christies and Sotheby's still rule the roost, despite price-fixing scandals which led to a jail sentence and large fine for Sotheby's head Alfred Taubman in 2002. Between them they control about 90% of the world's live auction market in goods such as art and jewellery.

In this context, arts curators and gallery owners tend to become brokers who advise clients on what may be a good speculative investment. The decision-makers in this process tend to be middle class art administrators and curators who cater for the better educated and most privileged in self-perpetuating circles. In the view of many artists, the art world remains an exclusive place through an escalation of selectiveness maintained by a quasi-monopoly of operators including curators, dealers and their media friends. There is a fairly narrow group of wealthy superstar artists – a process which is intensified by the burgeoning of a lucrative contemporary art market especially in the last decade, where prices for art work can go from $5,000 to $50,000 in just a few years. We are told to consider them outstanding mainly because they have been successful, rather than for any intrinsic value their art may or may not have, much as in the other areas of the entertainment business. By definition, superstardom means that other, equally talented people, are deprived of access to audiences. The identity of mainstream art tends to be shaped by the existing élites rather than those who make art or the communities from which art springs.

As critic Nicholas Usherwood has noted (*Galleries*, July 2004) there is supposed to be "a system" whereby "the curators curate, the critics assess and, through due process, the artists we choose to represent our artistic culture emerge". But this is manifestly not the case, even more so today than it was before the grandiose Tate gallery empire, masterminded by Nicholas Serota, sprang into existence. There are many examples of outstanding artists, dead and alive, who completely disappear from view.

Spiralling prices in the world art markets mean that museums and galleries simply cannot afford to buy art to keep national collections up to date. The top British art museums – National Gallery, Tate, British Museum, National Portrait Gallery and Victoria & Albert – appear well endowed, but had their purchase allocation cut from £8m in 1982 to £1m in 2003. This is at a time when a major painting such as Raphael's *Madonna of the Pinks* can cost around £21m. In May 2004 Picasso's *Boy with a Pipe* was sold for the highest price in auction history when it fetched over £58m at Sotheby's. According to Jane Morris, editor of *Museums Journal* (*The Guardian*, 14 November 2003), museums and galleries have less money in real terms for day to day requirements, such as simple roof repairs and wardens, than they did 20 years ago.

Neither business and private sponsorship nor the much-vaunted National Lottery funding have made up the gap that constantly hits hundreds of cultural projects throughout the country, including theatre companies, cinemas and museums of all descriptions.

Funding cuts threat

In spite of the rise in council tax some areas of local authority provision are really suffering. Squeezed between the huge budgets for education and the social services, local museums and art galleries have had a raw deal, with hardly any investment beyond the occasional lottery handout…

When Labour came to power, Leicester had seven museums. One closed immediately when promised lottery cash was withdrawn. One closed in 2001, three are now proposed for mothballing – i.e. closed except for summer weekends and some school visits. One is about to close for a year for long-overdue refurbishment, and the remaining two are to close on Fridays.

… there will come a day in September when this city with such a proud museum tradition will not have a single museum open for visitors. A similar story is unfolding all around the country, for example the loss of two of our best costume museums in Nottingham and Manchester, and the proposed closure of the Daventry museum…

Robert Hartley, Leicester Museums Service
letter to *The Independent*, 2 April 2004

Meanwhile, we are educating today's and tomorrow's artists in self-marketing and a business approach is a major component of art school courses. Other areas of training such as life studies, drawing, sculpture and painting may not exist at all or be minimised. Degree shows for students who have just completed a first degree are increasingly dealer and market oriented, or towards the artist setting up her or his own business enterprise.

Our proposals

Cultural activity of all kinds is what makes and defines the human. It should not be a luxury to be enjoyed only by a privileged minority. The creative impulse is a fundamental and continual way of affirming and deepening our relationship to the world around us, both natural and social. Various kinds of artistic activity allow us to explore our own potential and faculties as living human beings in a social world. The Impressionist painter Monet, for example, once said of himself that his talent consisted of being "only an eye". "But what an eye!" was the response.

This anecdote points to the way in which artists extend and refine the ability to take in and transform the world. Making, appreciating, and participating in various art forms, as well as developing the physical abilities of the human body in sport and dance, allows humans to realise their inner potential as individuals. At the same time, these activities advance the interactions which make up society as a whole. Therefore, every form of human culture needs to be encouraged and everyone should have the opportunity to engage in it freely. The aim is to provide a framework within which all talents can flourish, rather than set out prescriptions telling artists what they should do or dictate what art is.

The leader of the Surrealist art movement, André Breton and Mexican mural painter Diego Rivera set out their aspirations in a manifesto written on the eve of World War II. In opposition to Fascism and Stalinism they called for the liberation of art from all political shackles:

> To develop intellectual creation, an anarchist regime of individual liberty should from the first be established. No authority, no dictation, not the least trace of orders from above! Only on a base of friendly co-operation, without constraint from outside, will it be possible for scholars and artists to carry out their tasks, which will be more far reaching than ever before in history.

Or, as Oscar Wilde put it even earlier: "Socialism itself will be of value simply because it will lead to Individualism." The opportunity to spend your life doing things you love doing until now has usually been the privilege of a small minority, as Wilde pointed out . "These are the poets, the philosophers, the men of science, the men of culture who have realised themselves, and in whom all Humanity gains a partial realisation." Wilde, the very antithesis of male chauvinism, was writing at a time when men dominated the arts and sciences. But his essential thought is important, because he believed that being able to "realise yourself" should not remain the privilege of the few. In his view a truly cultured and truly socialist society had to allow everyone the possibility of discovering and realising her or his own potential.

In today's world, the ability to extend the range of human faculties, for example as an athlete or other performer, is seen almost wholly as a content to be reproduced and marketed by the media corporations. Commercial sponsors desperately *need* the co-operation and attraction that they get from music celebrities and sports stars. Without such endorsement the big companies would not be able to sell their goods. *Marie Claire*, Marks and Spencer, Vodaphone, Castrol and Gillette needed David Beckham to promote their products – that is why they signed around £60 million in sponsorship deals with him between 1997 and 2004.

The labour of cultural workers is vital to the profit-making activities of the present status quo. Without their endorsement and their creative abilities as well as their physical labour, capitalist production and marketing would be in grave difficulties. Instead of artists and athletes being viewed as claimants who are dependent on precarious forms of commercial or state sponsorship, they must be guaranteed financial, material and moral resources.

Culture for all
We already have arts venues such as theatres, museums, playing fields and sports centres, libraries and community cultural

centres, colleges and educational establishments. Today, many are threatened with commercialism, closure or cuts.

Following a revolutionary change in society, all such places, public and independent, will have the resources to continue and prosper. Reorganisation will take place in consultation and by agreement with users and those who work there – students, teachers, lecturers, artists, performers, curators, administrators, technicians and local people.

Spaces will be made available for cultural activities through renovation of disused industrial, commercial properties and new purpose-built facilities. All support for independent art and cultural activity will be without state censorship or control. Where appropriate, local enterprises can co-operate and exchange goods and services with cultural centres for the purpose of mutual improvement.

Diverse cultures of all kinds will be encouraged and encouraged to celebrate and preserve the many cultural heritages and legacies. Minority ethnic communities will receive special resources to help maintain the rich variety of national, ethnic and local traditions and art forms which already make up contemporary British culture. Oral histories of communities of all kinds will be recorded and archived.

Within present society there are many organisations and ventures which demonstrate how successful self-managed and independently-owned co-operative cultural enterprises can be (even though at present they still make use of corporate sponsorship). They include the London Symphony Orchestra and the Philharmonic Orchestra. Both these orchestras are owned and run by the musicians themselves. The LSO is owned by its 100 players each of whom has one share. It recently raised more than £10 million to convert an old church in London's Islington area into an advanced music education centre to train young players. LSO musicians are concerned about the continuity of music training, because state schools have run it down.

Pioneered by painters like Bridget Riley, who set up Space Studios three decades ago, self-run and financed artists' studio and exhibition complexes show what artists can do when they take matters into their own hands. Present-day examples include the Art in Perpetuity and the Bow Arts trusts in east London. Other examples of high profile artists who are trying to break away from corporate control and establish independent, self-financing organisations run by themselves include singer-songwriter George Michael, who took on Sony in a famous legal case. In 2004 he announced that he would make future recordings available free to fans on the Internet. In 2003 singer Peter Gabriel launched a union called MUDDA (www.mudda.org), to enable musicians to sell music directly to their fans without going through corporate distribution channels. Independent film maker Michael Moore successfully challenged the monopoly of the media corporations, at first with the help of local librarians in the US, to launch his book, *Stupid White Men*, followed by his film *Fahrenheit 9/11*.

The Edinburgh international festival, for example, includes a huge fringe, a book festival, plus a jazz and blues festival. They are deluged by independent artists of all kinds. Looking through the programmes of such events shows how many outstanding and dedicated people there are who are forced to remain on the fringes and outstanding productions which never get into local cinemas or on the major television channels. The market's boast of choice amounts to the option to watch the same Hollywood films wherever you go. Thousands of actors, film makers, artists and other performers scrabble desperately for a brief chance to get into the limelight, but only a few ever achieve more than ephemeral success let alone economic or financial security.

Similarly, independent art gallery owners and state-sponsored public institutions show only a tiny fraction of the artistic production which they are offered. Every London gallery owner and critic will attest to the way in which they are besieged by talented artists looking for an opportunity to display their work to the public.

Free from pressure

Cultural activity must be made available for the whole community. It should be unrestricted in its aims and how it operates and must be seen as essential as other services and enterprises. Artistic production must be free and independent of commercial and political pressures.

Ownership, funding and control

▸ the resources of the global media companies will be owned and managed democratically by elected councils of cultural workers, technicians and users

▸ national, regional and local cultural councils with elected representatives will determine financial resources in consultation with elected Assemblies.

▸ the Internet will be self-managed by the people who create the content and those who use it with no commercial or state interference

▸ control over Internet content and other forms of distribution such as the cinema will be democratically discussed and agreed

▸ recording of sounds, images and words and publishing will controlled by the creators and users. Copyright issues to be democratically agreed by creators and users

▸ cultural workers will be financially supported by local Assemblies and publicly-funded cultural committees

▸ sporting facilities will be owned and controlled by players, sports fans and the local community.

Development

▸ minority languages, dialects, literature, arts and traditions will be supported and encouraged to prevent them being lost from society

▸ existing cultural facilities, including local and national centres, trusts, self-organised bodies such as studios, orchestras, cinemas, film clubs, arts festivals, theatres, and exhibition areas will be developed and expanded

▸ training will be provided in different areas of the arts and crafts

▸ people who have rare and unusual skills will be encouraged to train new generations

▸ sustainable architecture, design, fashion to transform public places and the lives of everyone will be encouraged

- art and culture will be brought out into the street, and the street made into art, including graffiti art (as opposed to vandalism). Public, open air, and street art including theatre, sculpture, dance, music and murals will be encouraged
- organisations like the National Trust will be supported in democratic consultation with users and their sites opened to the public free or with low admission prices
- funds will be made available for the preservation and restoration of historic monuments, listed buildings and other sites in consultation with public and professional bodies
- each community will have artists' studios. Music recording and film studios will be provided for musicians, film makers and community projects
- cultural committees will ensure maintenance of resources such as playing fields, gyms, libraries, materials and exhibition areas.

Access
- the aim will be to organise a non-corporate sponsored Olympics
- cultural centres will be opened in areas where they have been closed down or where few are available, with the help of funding from local Assemblies
- a variety of programmes and events for deprived city and rural communities will provide educational and performance facilities where none exist
- all forms of culture, entertainment and sports events will be accessible to the public including theatre, opera, art exhibitions, training for free or at very low cost to everyone
- all heritage sites, the collections of former royal palaces, stately homes, national and local sites and monuments, gardens, parks and places of natural beauty in the countryside will be opened up
- restrictions on walking in the countryside will be ended.

Cultural education
- music, visual arts and drama, plus physical education and sport will be central rather than peripheral or optional parts

of school curriculum from nursery level upwards
▸ schools, colleges and other institutions will have artists and
  sports people in residence
▸ sports facilities and training will be available for people of all
  ages, especially children.

10 Action plan for the ecological crisis

There is mounting evidence that we have reached a crucial moment in our social relationship with nature. The facts show that sustaining global capitalism is incompatible with maintaining human life. There are limits to the naked abuse of nature by capital and we have gone beyond that point. Many of the eco-systems that make up the planet's ecology, which includes humanity, have become destabilised. What some have called the "buffer" between human activities and the rest of nature has disappeared as a result of quantitative changes expressed in the rapid and uncontrolled globalisation of the productive forces.

Our relationship to nature is the cornerstone of our existence as socialised human beings. We have a given unity with nature that, while grossly distorted by capitalism, is absolute. We depend for our day-to-day existence on air, food and water and struggle to acquire those basic needs. We are also that part of nature that thinks and acts upon nature itself. In doing so, we transform the world around us and in the process change ourselves. These fundamental relationships are the basis for all human existence, its societies, great civilisations and our modern, urban life. So when nature is threatened in the way that it is now by the power and rule of globalised capitalism, we are all in danger and at risk.

Capitalism's own inner logic compels it to take from nature in an unplanned, arbitrary fashion. It does not and cannot respect nature because it regards it primarily as part of the production process, whose aim is year-on-year increase in profits. In this way, production depletes and ruins the very nature that it rests upon. Moreover, as capitalism extends its reach into areas not previously dominated by markets and production for profit – for example, the human genetic code – it deepens further our alienation, our removal from a direct relationship with the world outside of us and also with ourselves.

This alienation is not a secondary or psychological question but is a reflection in individual thought, behaviour and feelings of material social, class relations. The most significant arena in our relationship to nature is the economic process. Yet here we are deprived of any influence, let alone control. The present system is organised on a highly socialised basis, often involving workers in many different countries working in a collaborative way. But this whole process is controlled from start to finish by capital and its inherent need to expand. Nature itself produces land and raw materials. These, for the most part, are privately owned. While we are free to sell our labour power to an employer, once bought it becomes a good for use by the capitalist alone. In fact, the more the world is filled with commodities, the less we have for own use. Karl Marx discovered that "this fact simply means that the object that labour produces, its product, stands opposed to it as something alien, as a power independent of the producer". He described this process as "a loss of reality for the worker, objectification as loss of and bondage to the object, and appropriation as estrangement, as alienation". In other words, we are totally alienated from the world around us. We cannot act to safeguard nature while we are denied both the power to do so and a direct relationship with nature that is not mediated by the needs of capital.

Capitalism is a system that through its own internal logic pursues capital accumulation for its own sake. The only interest is whether commodities produced are exchanged for money because until they are, the value – including profit – they contain is not realised. As production for profit is the overriding driving force and an end in itself, it is immaterial what goods are actually produced. As it sets out to create wealth rather than meet need as its first priority, capitalism is in effect on a treadmill. Failure to accumulate sufficient capital will lead to bankruptcy and closure and the victory of competitors. The inherent drive, therefore, is towards constant expansion and transformation of the means of production. There is no standing still for capital. Even when companies turn in adequate profits, these are measured in comparison with the previous year's. When markets are saturated, capital searches for new commodities to produce and exchange. Products are built to last shorter and shorter periods, while new models are introduced in rapid succession. Scientific breakthroughs are applied as technology as soon as possible and subordinated to this goal, without a full investigation of the potential risks. These barriers are created anew and as a result, capitalism only poses the problems afresh. The only real restraints are those set by competitors in a branch of production and the periodic crises of over-production, when capitalism goes into reverse. Capital in the shape of factories and offices is then destroyed and workers made unemployed. Assessing this phenomenon as it appeared in the first part of the 19th century, Marx noted:

> For the first time, nature becomes purely an object for humankind, purely a matter of utility; ceases to be recognised as a power for itself; and the theoretical discovery of its autonomous laws appears merely as a ruse so as to subjugate it under human needs, whether as an object of consumption or as a means of production. In accord with this tendency, capital drives beyond national barriers and prejudices as much as beyond nature worship, as well as all traditional, confined, complacent, encrusted satisfactions of present needs, and reproductions of old ways of life. It is destructive towards all of this, and constantly revolutionises it, tearing down all the barriers which hem in the development of the forces of production, the expansion of needs, the all-sided development of production, and the exploitation and exchange of natural and mental forces.

Irreversible change

The period of intense globalisation over the last quarter of a century coincides with the dramatic deterioration in humanity's relationships with nature. In March 2004, the respected World Resources Institute (WRI) said that 10 years after the ratification of the United Nations Framework Convention on Climate Change (UNFCCC) the position had deteriorated. "We have not made significant progress in curbing global warming in the last decade. In fact, the latest scientific reports indicate that global warming is worsening," said Dr. Jonathan Pershing, director of WRI's climate, energy and pollution programme. He warned:

> We are quickly moving to the point where the damage will be irreversible. Unless we act now, the world will be locked in to temperatures that would cause irreparable harm. To stabilise the atmospheric concentrations of the greenhouse gases that lead to global warming, we must ultimately bring net emissions of these gases to near zero.

Climate change could drive a million of the world's species to extinction as soon as 2050, according to a report in the journal *Nature* in January 2004. A study of six world regions suggested a quarter of animals and plants living on the land could be forced into oblivion. The scientists studied six biodiversity-rich regions, representing 20% of the Earth's land area. The study used computer models to simulate how the ranges of 1,103 species – plants, mammals, birds, reptiles, frogs, butterflies and other invertebrates – are expected to move in response to changing temperatures and climate. The scientists considered three different possibilities – minimum, mid-range and maximum expected climate change, on the basis of data from the Intergovernmental Panel on Climate Change. They also assessed whether or not animals and plants would be able to move to new areas. They concluded that from 15% to 37% of all the species in the regions studied could be driven to extinction by the climate changes likely between now and 2050.

Professor Chris Thomas, of the University of Leeds, UK, said: "If the projections can be extrapolated globally, and to other groups of land animals and plants, our analyses suggest that well over a million species could be threatened with extinction." Some species will no longer have any climatically suitable habitat left, and others may be unable to migrate far enough to reach hospitable surroundings. The authors added: "Many of the most severe impacts of climate change are likely to stem from interactions between threats, factors not taken into account in our calculations, rather than from climate acting in isolation." They single out as examples habitat fragmentation and loss, and competition from new invasive species.

The danger from what we eat

Industrialised, intensive farming methods of agriculture were introduced on a large scale to increase the output of food after World War II and reduce the price of commodities. The price paid in terms of resources, soil erosion, pollution, ill health, obesity and climate change is incalculable. The position has deteriorated sharply in the last 25 years under the impact of corporate-driven globalisation. An emphasis on quantity, uniformity, and ruthless price-cutting has created an ever-greater reliance on intensive, industrialised production.

Most farmers and consumers are the source of wealth for a handful of corporations that control what is known as agribusiness – chemical manufacturers, food processors and supermarket giants. Two grain traders – Cargill and Archer Daniel Midland – control 80% of the world's grain trade; four companies (Syngenta, Dupont, Monsanto, and Aventis) account for nearly two-thirds of world pesticide sales; and in the UK, the major supermarkets now control 80% of all grocery sales. Tesco, the most ruthless and dominant firm, is now a transnational corporation, coming in as the world's sixth largest food retailer, operating in 12 countries. Tesco's profits for 2003 soared by 22% to £1.7bn, equal to half the income generated by the entire UK farming industry. The combined revenues of the world's top 30 food retailers exceeded $1,000,000 billion in 2001, according to the Institute of Grocery Distribution. The top 10 grocery retailers account for 57% of the combined revenues for the world's top 30 food retailers. On its own Wal-Mart, which owns Asda in Britain, accounted for 21%. Wal-Mart is one of America's most notorious low-paying, non-union corporations.

According to Mike Hart of the UK Small and Family Farms

Alliance, half a century ago, 50-60% of every pound spent by the consumer on food was returned to the farmer. Today in much of Europe and North America the figure is down to only 10-20%, while in the UK the share is 9%. Hart says that the increasing gap between farm gate and retail prices is in some cases down to "clear profiteering". For example, in 1991 the farm gate price of potatoes was 9p per kg and the retail price was 30p – a 21 pence difference and a 233.5% mark up. In 2000 the farm gate price was 9p per kg but the retail price was 47p per kg, the difference now being 38 pence – a huge mark up of 425%. The same applies to cauliflower's farm gate price of 24p in both 1990 and 2000 with a retail price of 73p in 1990 and 98p in 2000; an extra 25p per cauliflower and a profit increase of 35%. He told Friends of the Earth in a 2003 report:

> Both of these products require no processing other than grading and packing, both of which are done by the farmers before being put on the supermarket shelf, so clearly the increase in the farm gate to retail difference is due to supermarkets wishing to increase profit margins at the farmers' expense. This is a clear abuse of their power in the food chain and a practice which is and will cause severe damage to UK farming. British farmers have delivered the higher and higher standards demanded by supermarkets but have been rewarded for doing so by supermarkets forcing down farm gate prices to levels which cause immense hardship among farming families, to the extent that agricultural charities are now paying out record levels of support for farming families and the number claiming state benefits are at previously unseen levels. The low farm gate prices being paid to farmers by supermarkets are destroying any chance we have of a sustainable farming system in Britain. Without profitable farming the environment, landscape and rural communities suffer. It is clear that supermarkets are using their near monopoly position in the food chain to make excess profits at the expense of both farmers and consumers.

Orchards were once a key part of the traditional English landscape, but they are rapidly disappearing from our countryside. Over 60% of UK apple orchards and about 50% of pear orchards have been lost since 1970 and the decline is continuing. Apples are imported from as far away as New Zealand and China, and are produced at high volumes convenient for the supermarkets. Supermarkets shop around the globe to find the lowest prices, using communication technology to engage suppliers in a reverse auction. Transport of food over long distances, particularly by road and air freight, increases the amount of greenhouse gases produced and so contributes to global climate change. The distribution of one kilogram of apples from New Zealand sold in the UK accounts for its own weight in carbon dioxide emissions. Meanwhile, 20% of fruit and vegetables sold in supermarkets contain more than one type of pesticide residue.

In Britain, a team of agricultural economists led by Jules Pretty has calculated that the hidden cost to society of intensive farming is at least £2.3 billion each year. Significant costs arose from contamination of drinking water with pesticides, from damage to wildlife, habitats, hedgerows and drystone walls, from emissions of gases, from soil erosion and organic carbon losses, from food poisoning and from bovine spongiform encephalopathy (BSE). This figure did not include the more than £3.5 billion in government subsidies paid to farmers or health care costs from poor food choices.

Globally, farmers use 10 times more fertiliser than in 1950, and spend 17 times as much on pesticides, according to the Worldwatch Institute. While the effectiveness of these applications is diminishing, the cost to the environment is increasing. The contamination of waterways, the biodiversity decline, the spread of toxic chemicals and climate change are all results of intensive farming based on maximising output from a given area. Monoculture farms, which dominate the Midwest of the US, are heavy users of pesticides and fertilisers, since growing a single crop encourages pests while taking nutrients out of the soil. Run-offs from these farms leaks into the Mississippi and ends up in the Gulf of Mexico. The excess nutrients then help to produce algae blooms that kill life in vast areas of the ocean. These blooms, as well as coral reef destruction, are common in coastal areas on all continents.

The intensive use of pesticides, fertilisers, herbicides, antibiotics and growth agents in industrialised farming is thought to contribute to ill health in both animals and human beings. Among them are hormonally active substances which can trigger processes in the body that would not normally occur and lead to the development of disease. These chemicals are known as "endocrine disruptors".

Hormones are used to accelerate the growth rate of animals so that they can reach market earlier. Many scientists believe that the potential for hormones in food to cause metabolic and reproductive problems in humans needs further evaluation. Hormonal Growth Promotants (HGP) are in implants designed to slowly release small quantities of hormones from the ear of cattle to the tissues. Most of the beef raised in the United States today is produced with the use of hormones of some kind. The arguments for using hormones in meat production are mostly economic. With hormones, conversion of feed into meat is more efficient, thus theoretically lowering producer's costs.

Processed foods contain many artificial additives, preservatives, colourings or flavourings, and hydrogenated fats, which are directly related to increased rates of heart disease. Current UK regulations allow for 7,000 artificial additives to make food last beyond its natural sell-by date, and alter its appearance to make it more attractive to the consumer. They also allow the addition of water to increase weight. In May 2004, researchers from the University of Southampton found that additives had a "significant" impact on the behaviour of children. In tests, they discovered that the proportion of children with high levels of hyperactivity was halved when the additives were removed. The same month, the House of Commons health committee issued a stark warning about the dangers of obesity, which in England has grown by almost 400% in 25 years. The committee found among the causes was the fact that "healthy-eating messages are drowned out by the large proportion of advertising given over to highly energy-dense foods; other types of food promotion, as well as pricing also make buying unhealthy food more attractive and economical than healthy alternatives; and food labelling, a key tool to help consumers choose healthy foods, is frequently either confusing or absent".

The destruction of the soil

▸ soil erosion is responsible for about 40% of land degradation worldwide

▸ about 20% of irrigated land in the developing world has been damaged to some extent by waterlogging or salinity

▸ about 30% of livestock breeds are close to extinction. About 75% of the genetic diversity of agricultural crops has been lost since 1900

▸ an estimated 250 million people have been directly affected by desertification, and nearly 1 billion are at risk

▸ one in every five people in the developing world is chronically undernourished, a total of 777 million individuals

▸ 55% of the 12 million child deaths each year are related to malnutrition.

UN Food and Agricultural Organisation

Food safety concerns

▸ in industrialised countries, up to 30% of people suffer from food borne illnesses every year

▸ an estimated 70% of the approximately 1.5 billion annual cases of diarrhoea in the world are caused by biological contamination in foods

▸ contaminated food plays a major role in the epidemiology of cholera and other forms of epidemic diarrhoea, substantially contributing to malnutrition

▸ the incidence of food-borne diseases may be 300 to 350 times higher than the number of reported cases worldwide

▸ overuse of antibiotics has led to the appearance of resistant strains of bacteria. Factors contributing to this include overuse of antibiotics in farm animals and crops.

UN Food and Agricultural Organisation

Banana bonanza profits

Banana plantation workers are paid just a penny for every pound's worth of bananas sold in Tesco, not enough to feed their families. Tesco takes 40p. The UK importer/ripener is barely breaking even just to stay as a Tesco supplier.

If banana suppliers make a mistake in the packaging requirements or date, they have to pay Tesco £25,000 ("Emergency Product Withdrawals"). Tesco demands payments from its suppliers to cover the costs of its compliance with the Ethical Trading Initiative. According to a letter leaked to *The Grocer*, Tesco demands £69.50 per quarter per supplying site, a demand which, according to one supplier hits smaller businesses hardest since they are more likely to have a number of sites.

Information from Bananalink & *The Grocer* published by Friends of the Earth 2003

Every week Tesco makes £1m surplus from selling bananas, most of which are grown in Costa Rica, from where a GMB delegation has just returned. Bananas are the single most profitable item sold in British supermarkets and the leading stores, including Tesco, are involved in a price war that has seen the cost of a kilo of fruit plummet from £1.08 to 74p in less than two years. Because of their monopoly position, the supermarkets are able to dictate how much they pay for their produce and the net effect has been the loss of 11,000 jobs and a 40% wage cut for Costa Rican plantation workers over the same period. Working conditions on the plantations that supply Tesco are horrendous and the environmental effects of intensive banana production are disastrous. This depressing scenario is mirrored across other Latin American banana-producing countries and is a savage indictment of a global trading system dominated by corporate giants like Tesco who could not care less about the fate of the workers who enable them to declare such obscene profits.

Bert Schouwenburg, Regional organiser, GMB
The Guardian, 27 April 2004

Genetic modification dangers

Genetically-modified (GM) crops only intensify the contradictions. In the hands of agribusiness corporations, GM is a mechanism for increasing the power and control of business over food production at the expense of small farmers, organic production, consumers and the developing world. For capital, GM is a new area for profit making rather than helping to meet people's needs. As a result, risk-taking is rife while field trial results are distorted or even lied about. The fact remains that transgenic modification is certain to have unpredictable results, because of the nature of the process. Food scandals like BSE have only increased the belief that the corporations are not concerned about the long-term effects or repercussions as GM crops interact with other organisms. As a result, there is a massive opposition to agribusiness/GM throughout the world.

GM oilseed rape, maize, soya and cotton have been grown commercially in North America since 1996. They are all used in vegetable oils and animal feed, and soya is widely used in processed food. But there is evidence that all is not what the corporations claim. A study published in May 2004 revealed new evidence to show how genes from biotech crops can spread to nearby non-GM plant relatives. The data comes from research on maize engineered to produce powerful toxins in its leaves and stems. These substances, normally produced by bacteria, are lethal to insect pests that try to eat the maize plant. But an Arizona-Texas team says the way the crop is grown in some countries may lead to insects becoming resistant to the GM plant and pesticides. The research was reported in the journal *Proceedings of the National Academy of Sciences*. In the US and some other nations, Bt maize has to be grown alongside so-called "refuges" of conventional varieties – a strategy aimed at preventing insects from becoming resistant to Bt. But the new work shows that the Bt gene is finding its way into those refuge plants through pollen that is spreading tens of metres. "The refuge is supposed to be toxin-free but in fact the seeds, that is the next generation – some produce the Bt toxin," Professor Bruce Tabashnik, from the University of Arizona Department of Entomology, told the BBC. "This may increase the potential for some insects to become resistant." And this tolerance could extend to Bt sprays as well.

Richard Lewontin, the eminent American biologist and opponent of capitalism, in an article in the *New York Review of Books*, assessed the work of the US National Academy of Sciences on GM. Through its research arm, the National Research Council, it had produced an expert report to guide government regulatory policy. Lewontin noted:

> The real problem revealed in the NRC report, although it did not seem to bother the panel, is that the data on which "safety assessment" is currently based are not produced by the federal agencies themselves but are provided by the very parties who are asking for approval to distribute the new variety in the first place. Moreover, no one seems to have noticed that there is, in fact, an aspect of the process of genetic engineering that does make that process unusually likely to produce unpredictable results.
>
> All the attention has been paid to the physiological effect of the gene that has been put into the recipient, but none to the effect of where it is inserted in the recipient's genome. Genes consist of two functionally different adjacent stretches of DNA. One, the so-called structural gene, has information on the chemical composition of the protein that the cell will manufacture when it reads the gene. The other, the so-called regulatory element, is part of a complex signalling system that concerns where and when and how much protein will be produced. When DNA is inserted into the genome of a recipient by engineering methods it may pop into the recipient's DNA anywhere, including in the middle of some other gene's regulatory element. The result will be a gene whose reading is no longer under normal control.
>
> One consequence might be that the gene is never read at all, in which case it will probably be bad for the recipient and will never be part of a useful agricultural variety. But another possibility is that the cell will now produce vast amounts of a protein that ordinarily is produced in very low amount, and this high concentration could be toxic or be involved in the biochemical production of a toxin. Yet another possibility is that a toxic substance that used to be produced only in one part of a plant, not ordinarily eaten, could

now be manufactured in another part. Tomatoes are delicious, but you would be ill-advised to eat the leaves and stems because they contain toxins. It is not impossible that a genetically engineered tomato might, by bad luck, start to produce these toxins in the fruit. Thus the process of genetic engineering itself has a unique ability to produce deleterious effects and, contrary to the recommendations of the NRC report, this justifies the view that all varieties produced by recombinant DNA technology need to be specially scrutinised and tested for such effects.

For farmers, there are serious problems of economics, especially in North America where GM crops accounts for 20% of the total. GM seed can be up to 40% more expensive than non-GM varieties. There are often lower yields, despite the claims of the manufacturers. Export markets have collapsed in the face of world-wide hostility to GM. Meanwhile, the biotechnology companies are suing many farmers for infringing company patent rights, saying that they have unlicensed GM plants on their land. A US non-GM farmer whose crop was contaminated by GM was sued by Monsanto for $400,000!

Sustainable capitalism not an alternative
Given the depth and nature of the ecological crisis, nothing less than a fundamental transformation of economic and social relations will do. The nature of the crisis is global in that it affects every country. In this, it mirrors the globalisation process of the last 25 years, with its plundering of nature. The global scale of the crisis has made it even more certain that capitalism cannot deal with the issue. It has neither the capacity nor the will to undertake global action. The failure of the Kyoto Protocol demonstrates that in a conclusive way.

  But there are parties and pressure groups that believe that capitalism is capable of mending its ways, of repairing itself. This, they argue, is achievable through a mixture of regulation, localisation, limiting growth, restructuring of bodies like the World Trade Organisation, better use of technology and less consumption by people in the developed economies. All these "solutions" amount to a defence of the status quo of alienated capitalist rule and a continuation of commodity production for profit.

The Green Party in the UK argues that it is "economic globalisation" that is damaging ecosystems, because of its emphasis on free trade and the power of the markets. By deliberately using the term "economic", the Greens carefully leave capitalism as a social system out of the loop. *Green Alternatives to Globalisation*, published in 2004, says the party "aims to reconstruct the patterns of human activities and relationships so that they come to respect the natural systems on which they depend". Thus the Green Party is about *managing* nature rather than creating the conditions for establishing new relations with nature outside and beyond capitalism. In that sense, like the capitalists, the Greens see nature as a resource. Except they would treat it better.

This view of our relationship to nature is thoroughly one-sided and taken out of social context. Nature stands on one side of the equation and humanity on the other in this formulation. Their interaction is seen as inherently harmful and the inevitable conclusion is that economic activities must be restrained to "guarantee the central goal of sustainability". This is the same party, of course, that on its website advocates population control because "high rates of population growth... can have a damaging effect on sustainability".

In *Green Alternatives to Globalisation* the authors, Michael Woodin and Caroline Lucas, want to "restrain and democratise the West's power" and regret that the "enormous array of conventions, treaties and agreements by which international relations are regulated" are rarely enforced. Their starting point is that the "theory" of economic – not capitalist – globalisation is flawed and are slightly bemused that this has "provided no impediment to the spread of the process itself". They never ask themselves why because the answer lies within capitalism as a system of accumulation, which is expressed in the specific character of corporate-driven globalisation rather than globalisation in general.

Instead, for the Green Party, world leaders are supporters of corporate globalisation as a result of intense lobbying which "appears to have had a hypnotic effect". The "shameful fact" is that the same leaders have "little control" because they have handed over their powers to unaccountable bodies like the WTO. This is what they set out to remedy with a series of proposals aimed at limiting growth, localising economic production using import controls and regulating the economy to "ensure that production is driven by need rather than by profit". This is all pie in the sky, based on reducing capitalist globalisation to an idea that has had a mysterious impact on world leaders. Unfortunately for all of us, capitalism is not an idea, or a theory but a real social system whose institutions churn out ideas that inevitably reinforce the status quo. As such, those regulations that do exist can never challenge or undermine its basic mode of operations. Capitalism cannot regulate itself out of existence.

Even the authors acknowledge past failures to regulate the transnational corporations. In 1993, they point out, attempts to finalise a code of conduct on TNCs were formally killed off and the UN Centre on Transnational Corporations was closed down. A code of conduct proposed by the UN Commission on Trade and Development has been ignored. To which, we could add, the collapse of the Earth Summit in Johannesburg in 2002, where the corporations – working with supportive governments like New Labour – ensured that regulating their activities was kept off the agenda. The Green Party's agenda is essentially middle-class, against big capital for small capital, for local capital against global capital. They admire Adam Smith, the founder of modern capitalist political economy in the 18th century, whose market economics "were place-based and consists of small, locally-owned enterprises that are geared to meet the needs of the community".

Environmental groups like Friends of the Earth and Greenpeace favour a more sustainable economic system – also without changing the parameters of social ownership and control. They lobby for better regulation and control of carbon dioxide emissions, for example. These are the main contributors to global warming. Typical is the Greenpeace policy on CO_2 which appeals to the government to halve the development of new oilfields, and "start the shift to a genuinely sane energy path using renewables and energy efficiency". The government, says the pressure group, should redirect existing fossil fuel and nuclear subsidies to renewable energy technologies and energy efficiency. They remind the government that its own committee on business and the environment recommended a "transition to a low-carbon economy". The aim of all this advice is to produce a "sustainable" economy – which is one that is less harmful to nature but is otherwise unaltered. Greenpeace works with, among others, the notorious World Bank, one of the enforcers of corporate globalisation. The pressure group hopes to persuade the World Bank to adopt a more "sustainable" policy towards energy resources.

But as we have shown, capitalism continuously recreates ecological damage because its life is based on accumulation and expansion, where nature is simply a set of resources. Capital is, at the same time, all in favour of eco-friendly business practices – so long as they do not interfere with the main business of making money. Some oil corporations, for example, work closely with environmentalists to give themselves a "green image" and show concern. In essence, capitalism has incorporated the concept of sustainability unto itself. Why, even New Labour has a commission on sustainability!

BP is perhaps the best example of this. The oil corporation is now producing an annual "sustainability" report. Its first edition, published in April 2004, insists: "For us, 'sustainability' means the capacity to endure as a group by renewing assets, creating and delivering products and services that meet the evolving needs of society, attracting successive generations of employees, contributing to a flourishing environment and retaining the trust and support of customers, shareholders and communities." The report sings the praises of the corporation for the contribution it has made in the areas of community investment, human rights, education, renewable energy etc. etc. To all intents and purposes, BP is an "ethical" company, doing its best to operate in a responsible way. Lord Browne, the group chief executive, maintains that BP is driven by an "aspiration to transcend the apparent trade-off between energy-led improvements in living standards and environmental degradation. Our goal is to enable energy to be produced and consumed in ways that do no long-term damage to the planet or its people." You can't ask for more than that! Unfortunately, BP also has to acknowledge that operational greenhouse gas emissions actually rose by 1.4 million tonnes in 2003.

On the eve of the Johannesburg Earth Summit in 2002, a number of activists met in Girona, Spain, to discuss future strategy in the light of the "greenwash" of corporate globalisation. They issued a declaration and invited organisations to support it. By July, more than 80 groups around the world had signed the declaration. In it they explained that the original Earth Summit in Rio de Janeiro in 1992 was a significant victory for the corporations. "It was the first major international conference on environment and development where business successfully mobilised to engineer certain outcomes. Although governments made some positive commitments, corporations and their lobby groups succeeded in countering many demands that conflicted with the interests of business, including dismissing any notion of binding regulation of transnational corporations and substituting their own 'voluntary' agenda."

The declaration explained how organisations like the World Business Council for Sustainable Development had emerged as an international force and created a momentum which is described as "greenwash". This is basically an attempt to achieve the appearance of social and ecological good without any corresponding substance. "Through branding, corporate philanthropy, high-profile partnerships with NGOs and governments, and isolated but highly publicised 'best practice' projects, corporations are making every effort to improve their image. All in order to avoid making the necessary changes to their core business practices demanded of them by civil society. By creating a benign public image and dominating international fora, corporations have exercised a virtual veto power over many initiatives seeking to impose obligations on them or force them to comply with basic social and environmental standards."

Despite their acute analysis, the signatories to the Girona declaration ended with a tame call for "legally enforceable regulation of corporations... as a first step to asserting democratic control over the economy". This is simply not on the agenda, as the outcome at Johannesburg and the failure to implement the Kyoto Accord have demonstrated. The World Business Council for Sustainable Development (WBCSD) mentioned by the declaration is a coalition of 170 international companies drawn from 35 countries, united, says their website, "by a shared commitment to sustainable development via the three pillars of economic growth, ecological balance and social progress". These stated goals opportunistically echo the demands for sustainability made by environmental groups. As the WBCSD say: "The pursuit of sustainable development is good for business and business is good for sustainable development." In its own way, the WBCSD exposes the extremely limited nature of many of its opponents, locked in as they are to making the present system work better.

Finally, the bankruptcy of the environmental movement was perhaps best expressed by James Lovelock, the scientist and the creator of the Gaia hypothesis of the Earth as a self-regulating organism, in a shattering statement in May 2004. Implicitly acknowledging that the Earth, far from self-regulating was heading for ecological disaster, Lovelock abandoned all his beliefs and called for a rapid extension of nuclear power as an urgent remedy for global warming.

Individual efforts to halt the destruction of ecosystems range from recycling rubbish, changes in consumption patterns such as

---

Enlisting the environmentalists

Capital is more than happy to enlist the mainstream movement as a partner in the management of nature. Big environmental groups offer capital a threefold convenience: as legitimisation, reminding the world that the system works; as control over popular dissent, a kind of sponge that sucks up and contains the ecological anxiety in the general population, and as rationalisation, a useful governor to introduce some control and protect the system from is own worst tendencies, while ensuring the orderly flow of profits.

The Enemy of Nature, Joel Kovel

buying locally-produced organic produce, using public transport where possible, to small-scale production that respects nature. As gestures of goodwill towards nature it is not possible to find fault with these activities. In the end, however, they can make no impact on the most significant determinant of the crisis – a system of production where exchange values have overwhelmed use values to an unprecedented extent. In fact, they tend to become subsumed as part of the status quo. Recycling has become almost an official activity, encouraged by local councils and government. Out of that has grown an entire recycling industry.

Our proposals

The simple notion that "owning" nature is historically absurd is our starting point for proposing a way forward. However it is presented by capitalism, there is nothing "natural" or eternal in the present circumstance where external nature is deemed private property for use and exploitation in the pursuit of profit. In fact, this expropriation only dates from the late 18th century and the emergence of capitalism. We have shown how the unparalleled expansion of this type of production under corporate-driven globalisation has produced a qualitative turning point in humanity's relationship to nature. Our co-evolution with nature is threatened by a systemic ecological crisis that capitalism as a global system is incapable of tackling and can only worsen. Our destiny is to end the absurd by terminating private ownership of the forces of production, through expropriation of the expropriators. In doing so we end our alienated relationship with nature and production and thereby create the conditions for dealing with the ecological crisis. We will then be in a position to "bequeath it an improved state".

Global capital, facilitated by the revolutions in technology, has developed sufficient capacity to meet human need for the first time in human history. Far from reducing the amount of interaction between humanity and nature, we need to increase it to a higher, more scientific level than ever, developing consciously the human character of nature and the natural character of humanity.

> From the standpoint of a higher socio-economic formation, the private property of particular individuals in the earth will appear just as absurd as the private property of one man in other men. Even an entire society, a nation, or all simultaneously existing societies taken together, are not owners of the earth. They are simply its possessors, its beneficiaries, and have to bequeath it in an improved state to succeeding generations, as good heads of the household.
>
> *Capital* Vol III, Karl Marx

This is completely different to the philosophy of both the capitalists and the Greens. Both make nature and human beings into absolute opposites, ignoring the fact that human society - its agriculture, industry and cities - are now one of the biggest parts of nature. In the case of capitalist ideology, the principle is one of mastery and domination of nature and natural processes in order to produce profit. In the case of the Greens the principle is that human beings must withdraw from nature, returning to some point where their impact on it was less.

Human beings not only get from nature what they need in order to live, but they ARE nature – they are the aspect of nature that thinks, their social organism is human society. That is why our interaction with nature changes us, manifesting itself in health pandemics like Aids, malnutrition, drought, floods and even obesity.

What is required therefore is that the part of nature that has developed a scientific understanding of it, should elevate its interaction with nature to the highest possible conscious level, recognising always that nature is primary and therefore we must take great care in what we do. One of the most damaging results of alienation is that this primary relationship is hidden from most people. In the rich countries, they are driven from pillar to post for jobs, work increasing numbers of hours, are forced to eat food that makes them ill and stressed beyond belief. In the poorer countries, exploitation continues to plumb new depths.

We must ensure that we take what we need without damaging ourselves or nature. This interaction should be guided by the most advanced scientific approach, examining the complexity of our mutual relations at the deepest chemical, biological and ecological level. The Greens make human beings into defeated opponents of nature, who should withdraw from the battle and return to some mythical and harmonious past. On the contrary, we maintain that human interaction with nature IS life – productive, conscious and scientific life. Therefore our co-evolution with nature must not be minimised but maximised, made more sophisticated and more serious and careful at the same time.

Ending production based on capital accumulation will transform our ecology. We will replace the creation of exchange value with the production of useful objects, of use values. We will transform what we make, and the way in which we transform nature. Workers will co-operate internationally to plan production to the benefit of the majority. This will bring about a shift to farming for local food and a programme of infrastructure improvement to bring the basics of housing, water and power to all. Urban planning will set out to redesign and restructure the cities and end the alienation of town from country. Eliminating massive over-capacity and a refocusing of the economy to the provision of the basic necessities of life will bring improved efficiency in the use of energy and raw materials, and lessen the impact on nature.

All enterprises will have access to the best and most recent scientific and economic knowledge in order to move to life-cycle production – production planned from the extraction of raw materials to the reclamation of waste after the end of the product's life and the remanufacture of the waste products into useful components for the same, or other, productive processes. Scientific research, which is today directed towards helping capital to grow at the expense of nature, will focus instead on restoring damaged eco-systems. Economic and community planners will work with scientists and communities to produce holistic plans that meet people's needs. The resources wasted by capitalism will be redirected towards immediate large-scale investment in solar power and desalination, recycling of waste and land reclamation.

A programme for action

Production

▸ production under the control of the workforce in alliance with consumers, producing goods built to last to reduce extraction of raw materials and dependence on non-renewable energy forms

▸ an end to production for obsolescence and the artificial creation of new "needs" by advertising and marketing

▸ life-cycle production that respects eco-systems, including humanity's. All production must demonstrate eco-sustainability based on recycling and restoring principles

▸ science in the service of humanity, seeking out technological innovation, focussing on renewable energy and reuse of materials on the basis of a holistic outlook on nature and humanity

▸ immediate action on climate change. The scrapping of unnecessary transport of food and goods around the world. Implementation of new technologies to reduce carbon dioxide, nitrous oxide and methane emissions

▸ massive investment in the use of solar energy, hydrogen fuel cell propulsion systems, and biofuels to replace carbon-based energy sources

▸ investigation of the ecological case for wind and tidal power

▸ public investment in new forms of affordable public transport tailored to individual needs in both urban and rural areas. The long-term phasing out of mass private car use and a switch to car pools. An end to mass road building programmes

▸ renewal of urban settlements to make them more energy efficient, based on people having to travel short distances for work.

Agriculture

▸ social ownership of agribusiness monopolies that presently control production, distribution and retail sales of food

▸ common ownership of land
▸ an ecosystem approach to agriculture that manages soil, water, plants and animals as parts of a functional whole
▸ integrated pest and production management, preventing pest outbreaks through naturally occurring predators, parasites, pest resistant varieties and traditional cultural methods
▸ conservation agriculture, ensuring soil fertility through better nutrient cycling by micro-organisms in the soil. Low- or no-tillage and mulching to help soil structure
▸ an emphasis on crop rotation/diversification to suppress weeds and pests and reduce the necessity of synthetic applications
▸ more use of organic applications where practicable and the phasing out of pesticides
▸ integration of crops and livestock in the same farming operation, encouraging pasture and forage crops in rotation to protect soil and encourage fertility through manure
▸ an end to factory rearing of livestock
▸ moratorium on GM so that the results of technological transgenic modification can be scientifically estimated before use
▸ scientific investigation of all existing and proposed food processes to check for safety and nutritional value.

Part 3

A revolutionary change is necessary

Showing the dialectics of theory and practice

11 It's in our nature

The commonly held view of human nature is that we are fundamentally selfish. This opinion is reinforced by the tabloid press and reality TV programmes such as *Big Brother*. Meanwhile, populist philosophers such as John Gray state that we are no different from the lowest and most rapacious animals. We are not *homo sapiens*, but *homo rapiens*. Some scientists also suggest that self-centred behaviour is written in our genes.

Such points are neither historically, philosophically nor scientifically accurate. The fact is that humans must and do co-operate with others every day of their lives in order to survive and thrive. Because social relations are so complex and unpredictable they are often mystified. But without our social existence we cease to be human. Abandoned children nurtured by dogs and wolves without human contact fail to develop those qualities which define our species. They have the genetic potential to be human but cannot realise it on their own.

Our evolution and success in populating the world arose out of an interaction that began when we first hunted animals for food, clothing and shelter. We learned to make tools like spears and later domesticated animals. This began the differentiation of humans from other social groups of primates. The physiological potential for speech, interacting with the social need to communicate, led through natural selection to improved language skills. At the same time, the brain grew rapidly with an increasing ability to reflect upon, learn from experience and subsequently to predict and plan. Constantly evolving, conscious, intentional, social action is what distinguishes us from other animals.

Throughout history, our human nature – the way in which we relate to each other and to the world around us – has changed. For example, in Britain today, it is mainly the rich who hunt animals – and as a cruel sport and not for food. Most people do not believe that witches exist and ought to be burned at the stake. Even under capitalism, child labour is illegal even though it persists in many poor countries. Forms of society have included the tribal, slaveholders and slaves, landowners and serfs and predominantly today, employers and the employed.

Our existence is contradictory in itself. The *individual* can only be formed out of the *social*. The tensions which inevitably arise in this relation between the individual and the social are deepened by our alienated existence under global capitalism. Our nature is affected by a world that is more intensely socialised than ever. In South East Asia, for example, women whose role in the family was strictly defined, now work in factories for transnational corporations.

Billions of people on the planet acting in a social way make and remake their lives everyday. This is no great mystery, but the stuff of everyday life. Getting up each day and going to work, looking after children, caring for the sick, shopping, being educated, paying bills, claiming benefits, enjoying ourselves – these are just some of the activities which we think about in advance and carry out in a socially conscious way every day of our lives.

There is nothing innately bad or good about human beings. They are as capable of acting in a selfless and heroic way as perpetrating terrible crimes. This wide range of behaviour makes human nature surprising and distinct. They arise from the way we are brought up and shape ourselves and are simultaneously shaped in a wider context. The conditions of the period in which we as individuals live can either encourage or discourage particular kinds of behaviour.

Our relationship to nature is primarily through other human beings starting with our parents and our mother's body. That relation is biologically determined. But even that simple and seemingly eternal connection is being transformed, in that it can now be artificially, consciously, intentionally engineered. These and other aspects of scientific development have altered the relation of the social to the biological in new and unsettling ways. Increasingly though, in every area of our activity, we humans are acquiring the ability to choose our own future. We have within our power the ability to change things for the better. But there are some who are pessimistic.

The 'end of history'

Coming from opposite sides of the Atlantic, two well-known analysts of the modern period, Francis Fukuyama and John Gray have advanced their ideas about the future of the human. Fukuyama is best known for his "end of history" thesis and Gray for his disillusionment with the new world order that arose as the 20th century ended. These top academics are deeply hostile to the idea that there could ever be any other social order than that which exists. But they express extreme disquiet about what is happening to the human, albeit from divergent standpoints. While Fukuyama puts forward panaceas to moderate the symptoms he describes, Gray debunks any illusory hopes and dreams. They take opposite positions on the issue of human nature. But in the end, both are hostile to the idea that human beings can do anything but adapt individually and socially, to what exists.

Fukuyama's book, *The End of History and The Last Man* was a response to the break-up of the Soviet Union. The assertion that history could come to an end coalesced comfortably with the view that the Soviet Union had been a communist or socialist state. It was shorthand for a mind-set which found its political expression in Reaganite America and in Thatcher's TINA statement – There Is No Alternative. Fukuyama, an adviser to the Reagan and Bush governments, is a professor of international political economy. He argues that history has a universal direction towards the realisation of a market economic system based upon liberal democracy.

Fukuyama lumps together the ideas of Hegel and Marx, saying that they both believed the evolution of human societies was not open-ended but would terminate when human kind had achieved a form of society that satisfied its deepest and most fundamental longings. Both these German thinkers, in his view, put forward the idea that history would end. He claims that "for Hegel this was the liberal state, while for Marx it was a communist society". But, in reality, Marx never suggested that history would come to an end – in fact, he looked forward to the end of class-dominated society which he described as a kind of "unconscious pre-history" and the *beginning* of a real human history, which could be consciously shaped.

A decade after his *End of History*, Fukuyama decided that his own theory was challenged by what he describes as "a monumental period of advance in the life sciences". This realisation prompted him to write *Our Posthuman Future – Consequences of the Biotechnology Revolution*. He was now troubled by the way in which biotechnology in the wrong hands could re-shape the human for the worse. He is increasingly haunted by the ghost of the nihilist philosopher Nietzsche, who believed that human history is dominated by superhumans and the will to power – notions which later became associated with Fascist ideologies of a master race. Fukuyama is worried about forms of mass social control using pharmacology and gene-technological developments. He argues that these are already being used to iron out the diversity which characterises human individuality and temperament. In addition, he believes that the idea of a relatively fixed human nature and natural human rights go together. Lose one and you lose the other.

Today's world is measured against the dystopian visions conjured up in George Orwell's *1984* and Aldous Huxley's *Brave New World*, published in the 1930s. "Huxley," Fukuyama writes, "was right… the most significant threat posed by contemporary biotechnology is the possibility that it will alter human nature, and thereby move us into a 'posthuman' stage of history." Fukuyama shows how drugs have become instruments of social control. This aspect of mass-prescribed drugs became clear in a 1998 study which showed that significant proportions of minority ethnic children between two and four years of age were being prescribed mind-altering medication. While recognising that drugs can help people cope with mental problems, Fukuyama's comment is chillingly accurate: "Together, the two sexes are gently nudged toward that androgynous median personality, self-satisfied and socially compliant, that is the current politically correct outcome in American society."

He recognises that powerful economic interests are involved while noting that modern biotechnology could become a tool for "politically correct" ends. Fukuyama is concerned about dangers inherent in genetic engineering of various kinds, especially in relation to human beings. He points to the horrors of racist state-controlled programmes for selective breeding in the 20th century, most notoriously in Nazi Germany but also the United States, Scandinavia and Australia. His chief warning should be taken seriously. The developments in biotechnology

> will challenge dearly-held notions of human equality and the capacity for moral choice; they will give societies new techniques for controlling the behaviour of their citizens; they will change our understanding of human personality and identity; they will upend existing social hierarchies and affect the rate of intellectual, material and political progress; and they will affect the nature of global politics.

Fukuyama believes future advances in biotechnology could harm "our complex, evolved natures... and the unity and continuity of human nature, and thereby the human rights that are based on it". He is right to see this as an urgent question – having pointed already to the attempt to iron out different types of human personalities through mass drugs programmes. He proposes that countries should regulate technology politically at national and international levels. This is patent nonsense as is Fukuyama's call for regulation by the same governments who are encouraging the corporations. Regulation will not stop countries and commercial interests from carrying on with eugenics and biotechnology.

As a philosopher, like so many others, Fukuyama casts around for universals which define a permanent, unchanging human nature. This mistaken, Platonic approach, is based on the idea that we can pin down the definition of a thing by looking for some features which are essential to its existence. Unable to move out of his self-constructed mental box, Fukuyama has to resort to the mystical Factor X: "When we strip all of a person's contingent and accidental characteristics away, there remains some essential human quality underneath that is worthy of a certain minimal level of respect – call it Factor X." Moral order, he states baldly, "comes from within human nature itself and is not something that has to be imposed on human nature by culture".

Discussing the relationship between human nature and politics, he writes: "The definition of the term *human nature* I will use here is the following: human nature is the sum of the behaviour and characteristics that are typical of the human species, arising from genetic rather than environmental factors."

But defining human nature largely by genes begs the question of what formed humans as a species in the first place. As natural organisms, we make our genes through a complex process of heredity *and* interaction with our natural and social matrix, which in turn shapes our behaviour, as recent science shows.

Those like Fukuyama, socio-biologist E.O.Wilson and psychologist Stephen Pinker, who define the human predominantly through the genes, ignore this social dynamic. This leaves us with a highly passive, pre-constructed, gene-driven view of human nature, which dovetails neatly with a conservative view of governments and classes in society.

But the dogma that we are genetically programmed only to be selfish and look after No.1 is challenged by new knowledge about the functioning of evolution itself. Biologist David Sloan Wilson's research into zooplankton, the tiny organisms eaten by whales, led him to study how group selection works. The fundamental problem of social life, Wilson found, is that "selfishness beats altruism within a group. But altruistic groups trump selfish groups". His work challenged the orthodoxy of self-interest that dominated the field. In an interview with *The Guardian* (24 July 2003), he said:

> The individualistic perspective had taken a huge hold on the whole field. Explaining everything in terms of self-interest had become,

now, such a powerful metaphor that it could not be opposed. Individualism eclipsed groupism everywhere, in biology, in social sciences, and in everyday life... but now we have a sophisticated group selectionism that shows that societies can truly qualify as adaptive units in the same sense that individual organisms are adaptive units.

Humans as bad news

In 2002 John Gray, Professor of European Thought at the London School of Economics, published a collection of his thoughts under the title *Straw Dogs – Thoughts on Humans and Other Animals*. The title is based on an epigram by an ancient Chinese philosopher, Lao Tzu, who stressed the indifference of nature to all creatures emphasising that humans are not central in the world. Lao Tzu recommends his disciples to do nothing (wu wei) and to let things take their natural course. He advises rulers to keep their subjects simple and passive. For him, history is simply the story of "conflicting needs and illusions and subject to every kind of infirmity of will and judgement".

Gray prides himself on a grim form of realism, which strips away illusions we may have about our own selves and humanity. His aim is to debunk what he considers mistaken notions of liberalism, humanism and progress, to harden us up for the tough nature of the present, where the benign, providing functions of the state are being removed. He claims: "'Humanity' does not exist. There are only humans, driven by conflicting needs and illusions, and subject to every kind of infirmity of will and judgement." A former Thatcherite, Gray would seem to back the ex-prime minister's view that there is no such thing as society.

The proliferation of weapons of mass destruction is put down to "the diffusion of knowledge", rather than the conflicting interests of social classes, or national or ethnic groups. He mystifies technology and detaches it from its real physical development by human beings motivated by a desire to fulfil needs. "Technology is not something that humankind can control," he writes. "It is an event that has befallen the world, and "mass murder is a side-effect of technology". These are ludicrous, one-sided assertions. They ignore the fact that technology is also used to save lives, travel and generally improve living conditions – as well as destroying property and killing other people.

Gray imposes a jaundiced spin on every aspect of human existence under the grandiose project of putting forward a new philosophy which places human beings in their rightful position – as he sees it – at the level of a "primordial slime". Any hope of progress is yet another desperate illusion, just like science, we are told. Along with science, the idea of truth goes out the window. And along with truth, the hope of freedom. Justice is merely "an artefact of custom", words which the present Home Secretary might well endorse.

The idea that history must make sense, he says, is just a Christian prejudice. This is a typical Gray aphorism, as facile as it is easily disproved. What about pre-Christian and non-Christian historians, for example?

Gray blames all the evils of unadulterated capitalism on humans themselves as atomised objects driven by self-interest and greed over which no one has any control. He turns the crisis-ridden aspects of the present into an eternal stigma, like the mark imposed by God on Cain in the Old Testament. Because he can see no alternative to the present, he says we are all reduced to barbaric forms of behaviour.

Philosopher Daniel Dennett has answered Gray's claim that humans are just like any other animal. In an interview in the *Times Higher Educational Supplement* (28 February 2003), he said: "I've read Gray's book. It's a panicky oracle. I kept thinking 'why is he so unbalanced by what he thinks he has learnt from Darwin?' It's not romantic exceptionalism to note the differences between the human species and other species. We're very different from other animals. Yes, we have failed projects, but no other species has projects and yes, we have a lot of failed projects. But we also have a lot of projects that work."

Gray's rant against woolly humanism makes some valid points about the hypocrisy and false nature of abstractions about human rights used to cover up a multitude of sins perpetrated by corporations and governments. But his conclusions are based on a simplistic and destructive nihilism which denies any, and all achievements made by human beings. *Straw Dogs*, in the end lashes out against humanism from a hopeless, disintegrating perspective.

Science and human nature

The intense debate in philosophy and bio-ethics about these issues is driven by the possibility of human nature being altered in a more rapid and fundamental way than ever before. Two interconnected and complex systems interact in this process: our biological-genetic side and our social side – often described as nature and nurture. Who we are is the result of our individual selves making ourselves out of this raw material. Each human being, each individual creates her or himself, as Paula Allman has put it, in a process of humanisation. A futuristic leap in contemporary science is transforming our understanding of who we are and what we are and our ability to change ourselves. Genome mapping, cloning and artificial insemination, surrogate parenthood, neuropharmacology, the formation and functioning of the human brain, as well as the nature of the universe constitute an on-going scientific-technological revolution.

This dynamic is inseparable from changes in the way we live our everyday, social lives as individuals and as parts of the global workforce – from the way that people work to the widespread concern that things are at a crisis point for the planet and the life upon it. Of all these advances, control over human reproduction is amongst the mostly highly-charged issues. Few are indifferent to what happens to their inner biological selves, how their

---

No getting away from it

No political theorist, not even the completely historicist Marx, has been able to dispense with the problem of human nature: on the contrary all have found it fundamental to their construction of their world view. After all, if we want to give a normative description of society, how can we say how society ought to be organised unless we claim to know what human beings are really like?

The Dialectical Biologist, Richard Lewontin and Richard Levins

offspring are produced and who controls their reproduction. The cloning of Dolly the Sheep, for example, caused a major stir, especially when the implications of cloning for human reproduction became clearer. Germline choice technology (GCT) whereby people can genetically select features of their offspring excites controversy.

People can pay to change their bodies, and even their gender, through medical procedures, or buy babies on the Internet. Technologies such as visual mapping, DNA profiling and identity checks based on bio-metric data such as iris-pattern recognition, stimulate debates about our individual selves as well as methods of state control.

Loads of synapses

The number of human genes has been estimated to be at most about 1,000,000. The number of synapses [neuronal connections] in the adult human brain, however, is far more, some 1,000,000,000,000,000 – which is 1,000,000,000 times in excess of the basic genetic elements.

The Private Life of the Brain, Susan Greenfield

Neurologist Susan Greenfield, together with neural Darwinists such as Gerald Edelman, believes that the evolutionary approach to human consciousness – our unique ability to think rationally and to feel self-aware – is most appropriate. She describes this ability as the generation of inner resources or a higher-order consciousness. It can only grow "as the mind evolves, as cerebral inner resources are marshalled, as associations are built up within the brain in response to and retaliation to the relentless assault from objects and events in the world around us". She stresses how in evolutionary terms, we can view emotions as processes where one is highly interactive with the environment.

All these developments indicate a growing capacity to understand ourselves and to act in an increasingly conscious, collective way. This is of extreme importance in answering all those who rail against what is described as an unchanging human nature or the degeneration of the species. Just as the world of nature, organic and inorganic, operates through the interaction of predictable, law-governed processes which contain within themselves quantum and other uncertainties, so the thoughts and actions of humans as individual and social beings are also the sum of many histories. These "histories" are the result of decisions by each individual as well as chance occurrences. There are unknowns and alternative roads and actions in the life path or story of each individual as well as society.

The greatest revolution of all

We are poised for the greatest revolution of all – understanding the human brain. This will surely be a turning point in the history of the human species, for unlike those earlier revolutions in science, this one is not about the outside world, not about cosmology or biology of physics, but about ourselves, about the very organism that made those earlier revolutions possible.

Vilayanur Ramachandran, director of the Centre for Brain and Cognition at the University of California (San Diego), BBC Reith Lecture 2003

Complex histories come together and the outcome cannot be predicted in the same way as the addition of one chemical to another or the injection of fuel into an internal combustion machine. But, at the same time, human beings can and do discover the contours of tendencies, forces and developments which point to future possibilities. Based on this knowledge, we can plan what we do and act effectively.

How we understand our own role on the planet has acquired a greater importance than ever before. Humans as a species are able, both individually and collectively, to transcend blind subjection to forces they can neither understand nor control, through knowledge-driven activities, on a scale that is much greater than other animals.

Understanding history as a whole, in a co-evolutionary way is vital. Our present, class-ridden society still belongs to "pre-history", in the sense that unconscious forces, whether of blind nature or capitalist economic anarchy, predominate. The struggle against corporate domination of today's scientific and technological development poses new, important questions about our changing human nature.

Human beings as a whole cannot make history consciously, so long as they are trapped in social classes, in which the interests of one class prevail over another. Vast resources are expended fighting other human beings, rather than solving common problems. Humanity will only be able to direct and conduct its activities in a purposeful way when it overcomes domination by the restricted interests of increasing the wealth of a tiny minority. At that point we will enter the realm of real history.

12 Challenging the ideas of the status quo

Success in challenging and defeating those who hold economic and political power is conditional upon organisational skill and boldness. In addition – and crucially – it requires an outlook that distinguishes itself from traditional methods of thinking and ideas. Without this we struggle with one hand tied behind our back.

The capitalist class does not rule predominantly through the naked deployment of state force, except in the most extreme circumstances. A series of state institutions have emerged and evolved, that in one form or another reinforce and maintain the status quo of private property. Informing the work of all these power structures are systems of ideas and philosophies that together operate as conditioning agents, as the link between the rulers and the ruled.

Not only do the means of production – and what is produced – belong to a narrow group, but the output of dominant ideas and philosophies is equally in the hands of a minority. The use and manipulation of image and language have, in particular, taken on a key role in enhancing power in the period of globalisation.

Because the ideas that capitalism develops have a relative independence and life of their own, their source can prove difficult to identify. They make their appearance in the media, the education system, through marketing or in political philosophies and in the words of politicians. The dominant ideas and outlooks find their way into social consciousness in an indirect fashion. For example, liberal newspapers may oppose aspects of capitalism like excessive executive pay or aggressive marketing of GM food.

Traditional politics seem to consist of disputes about policies or ideas that give the impression that there is a real struggle going on over vital issues. Concepts like "equality", "justice" and "democracy" also have some significance for people in terms of their aspirations and possibilities for redress. The notion of freedom of expression also lends support to the claim that capitalism actually consists of a free interplay of ideas.

The overall effect is to restrict and narrow expectations, aspirations and horizons. Of course, these limits are in themselves limited in what they are capable of achieving. They may, for example, express an ideal of social harmony but as ideas in themselves they cannot succeed in abolishing objective class realities that divide society. New Labour may have announced the end of classes, for example, but they continue to exist in the real world.

Taken as a whole, however, the intended effect is to perpetuate the status quo by insisting that:

‣ the capitalist system has always existed and is the most natural thing
‣ there is no viable alternative to a society based on profit
‣ the destiny of the ruling class is to rule forever
‣ our fate is to work and be ruled
‣ revolutionary change is dangerous, brings anarchy and can never succeed.

The all-consuming ideology

Corporate globalisation has produced an all-pervasive, all-consuming ideology. A single view – that of the virtues of so-called free-market capitalism – now dominates to the virtual exclusion of all others in political and social consciousness. This ideology has incorporated into itself or obliterated what might have been considered oppositional outlooks that, while never challenging the fundamentals of the system, put forward alternative ways of doing things. Views that challenge capitalism are brushed aside by politicians, the media and academics.

Take, for example, Anthony Giddens, the leading sociologist and former director of the London School of Economics. He became the self-appointed "theoretician" of the Third Way. This is the spurious New Labour theory that declares that class interests no longer apply and that the "old"' divisions between capitalism and socialism are done with. Giddens wrote a whole book called *The Third Way*, which justifies the Blairite approach. In a defence of the status quo, he writes:

> With the demise of socialism as a theory of economic management, one of the major division lines between left and right has disappeared, at least for the foreseeable future. The Marxist left wished to overthrow capitalism and replace it with a different system. Many social democrats also believed that capitalism could and should be progressively modified so that it would lose most of its defining characteristics. No one any longer has any alternatives to capitalism – the arguments that remain concern how far, and in what ways, capitalism should be governed and regulated.

So the end of history is announced from the LSE. There is no alternative to capitalism, the worthy professor declares. The media, too, is forthright in its appeal on behalf of capitalism. And it is not just the right-wing media. The liberal *Guardian* is up there with the rest. Gordon Brown, the Chancellor, has made many speeches praising capitalist enterprise and innovation and demanding that Britain follows the American path in this respect. On 26 January 2004, with Bill Gates, the chief executive of Microsoft and other leading capitalists in attendance, Brown stressed entrepreneurship in a speech that a business chief could have given. The next day, *The Guardian* devoted an editorial to the speech and declared: "It is a fresh sign of how far the Labour party itself has changed in its attitude to wealth creation. It is not many years since the promotion of enterprise was the preserve of rightwing thinktanks. Now it is mainstream Labour party thinking. Innovation is the name of the game – for everyone."

The ideology of corporate capitalism is reinforced in countless ways during virtually all our waking lives. You could wake up to a radio bulletin announcing that New Labour is to "reform" public services through offering "more choice". This way of presenting the news accepts the use of the word "reform" – which means to make things better – in a context where this is disputed by public sector trade unionists and users of services. It also reasserts the consumerist message of "choice", which is usually applied to things like buying a new car, and incorporates it into the provision of essential services like the NHS. Having heard the news bulletin, on your way to work you might buy a newspaper that is dominated by news of what the political and business élites are saying and doing (or a paper that has no serious news in it, leaving you totally in the dark as to what is going on). You will probably walk past a billboard advising you to buy a product "because you're worth it", or ways to make your money grow, or offers of easy credit.

At work, the suffocating, alienating ideology of the status quo will more often than not ensure that hierarchy is maintained. Speaking out of turn or becoming sick will – unless you are a top executive – lead to disciplinary action and the loss of earnings. Back home, the TV will be full of uninformative life-style and consumerist programmes – punctuated by adverts that associate products with a range of emotions and desires – that reinforce the messages of individualism and consumption as the "normal" way of life. The same programmes also serve to deaden any inquiring consciousness. Or you may have been at a lecture, where the message was that there is no known, viable alternative to "democracy" or that capitalism is alright – it just needs more aggressive regulation. Perhaps you have been to school, where the curriculum is designed to prepare you for the world of work, and where the virtues of subordination and deference are driven into students. There could well have been a branch of your local bank inside the school building, with computers and books sponsored by global corporations. The bombardment is relentless, reinforcing individualism and isolation. This is how capitalist ideology is transmitted, day in, day out, 24 hours a day.

Lying is increasingly a key feature of the ideas war, as we saw over Iraq. David Miller, from Stirling University's Media

Research Institute, likened the propaganda that surrounded the 2003 invasion to the blockbuster film, *The Matrix*, where it was difficult to detect fact from fiction. Miller wrote that the attack on Iraq revealed "the yawning gulf between the political élite and the rest of us". It disclosed an increasing separation between "matrix world – where official pronouncements are treated with some seriousness, even if subject to criticism – and 'real world' where their lies are transparent and their crimes recognised. Matrix world and real world exist in a kind of parallel universe", he said, observing:

> In matrix world, Iraq had and may still have Weapons of Mass Destruction; in the real world, it did not. In matrix world, there were links between Iraq and al-Qaeda, in the real world there were not. In matrix world, Lord Hutton is a respected judge who produced an independent report [on the BBC's reporting of a government report on Iraq's WMD]; in the real world Hutton was a whitewash. In matrix world, Katherine Gun [spy station whistleblower] and Clare Short [former minister] are deeply irresponsible for breaching trust and revealing secret information; in the real world they blew the whistle on illegal and immoral official behaviour [UK spying on the UN].

He is convinced that wholesale lying and misinformation by the political élite has been learned in part from the private sector and the PR industry, "which has done so much to advance the interests of mobile global capital". Miller pointed out, however, that a growing number of people are breaking away from the lies. They have taken to the streets in large numbers while in Spain, the official explanation of the Madrid bombing was rejected by the electorate who swept the Aznar government aside. He added:

> The conclusion to draw from this is that the ideological strength of our rulers is wavering as their common sense is challenged more and more consistently from below. The more this happens, the more desperate they become and the more extreme the lies. Lies and the propaganda machinery necessary to produce them are, in other

words, built into the very fabric of neo-liberal governance.

Iraq demonstrates that we are in an especially crucial and favourable moment. Control over economic and political processes, as well as what people think, is constantly undermined and loosened by the contradictions of globalisation. Transnational corporations have spurred the development of an emerging global consciousness of opposition and resistance. The dangers of this are recognised by people like Evelyn de Rothschild, one of Britain's wealthiest men. Writing in *The Guardian* (13 July 2004), Rothschild warned that capitalism might be under threat from itself. "The collapses of businesses in the US and Europe in a cloud of alleged fraud have shaken confidence in the financial system. People who normally pay little attention to international capital flows may have the feeling that their savings and pensions are suddenly at risk." He demanded an emphasis on ethical behaviour and leadership from government and business without which, he added, "it may be difficult to restore confidence and growth".

A theory of knowledge

Underlying the systems of ideas and theories are variations on philosophies about the general laws of being and thinking that in one way or another present a fragmentary and distorted view of reality. They are used to justify, support and reinforce the existing social and class relations. These philosophical systems in general:

▸ separate processes that are actually connected to each other in reality
▸ examine reality in a static, unchanging, non-historical way
▸ base themselves on "facts" separated from their source
▸ see things as either black or white, as one thing or the other
▸ reject contradiction as problematic rather than natural
▸ regard quantitative change as something separate from qualitative change
▸ rely on subjective and impressionistic approaches to knowledge

‣ emphasise the "unknowability" of the world
‣ make sensations into a barrier to knowledge instead of the
   source.

Individual sense experience and perception are emphasised as the
foundation for all knowledge and understanding. The world is
presented as a collection of given or accepted "facts" or
empirical observations. In this way, the socio-historical origin of
the facts is ignored, which helps give them a permanence they do
not actually possess. The impression is given that knowledge is
immediately gathered and that all you have to do is focus your
senses. "Perception is reality" is a buzz phrase that you often find
flying about management and marketing seminars. In other
words, the real world is whatever our senses tell us it is.

Patently we need a philosophy that is capable of challenging
capitalist ideas and philosophies. The struggles that erupt
spontaneously against capitalism cannot by themselves lead to a
fundamental change. If they could, they would have done so by
now. Systems of thinking that predominate under capitalism are
part of *their* weaponry and are based on the preservation of
status quo. They do not in themselves prevent people from
struggling. But they do play a key role in helping the ruling class
to withstand and ultimately incorporate these conflicts while
retaining power. We need a philosophy, a theory of knowledge,
that is wholly independent of the status quo and its outlook in
order to win a living, complex, high stakes conflict.

Contemporary global capitalism is distinguished from earlier
periods by a vastly expanded area of knowledge and
information. This affects the economy, work, culture and every
aspect of daily life. It was once observed that on an average
weekday, *The New York Times* contained more information than
any contemporary of Shakespeare's would have acquired in a
lifetime. The explosive character of this process presents a
formidable challenge as to how this information/knowledge is
absorbed, processed and understood by both individuals and
corporations.

People are confronted with countless complex networks of
information, a bewildering variety of sources. Human relations

present themselves to people through bits of digitised data in plastic artefacts, which appear to have little connection with the real world of flesh and blood people. Under these conditions, there is a marked tendency to throw your hands up in the air and focus on simple things, on what you know, and what you need. Relativism, uncertainty, empiricism and scepticism predominate within systems of knowledge. These currents reinforce habits of thought which have traditionally prevailed in Anglo-Saxon societies since the 18th century.

In the last 20 years, much of philosophy has stressed what it claims is the unknowability of the world as a whole. At the same time it has focused on the subject, as an atomised individual. The postmodernist outlook combines these two components. All of these outlooks in one way or another rob us of the ability to enhance our knowledge of things from the point of view of social emancipation. They drive us towards a reliance on immediate impressions, instinct and emotions on the one side and on unstated and unproven assumptions on the other.

In a rapidly changing world, a flexible and unprejudiced theory of knowledge that grasps inter-connections and complex processes is decisive when it comes to planning for revolutionary change. A theory of knowledge defines and explains the relation between our ideas and the world which exists outside of our consciousness. Every thinking human being uses a simple theory of knowledge in order to make sense of what is going on, even if only to cross the road. Any conscious person constantly makes connections with other objects, based on their needs. From an early age, human beings, by exploring their surroundings, become conscious of this process as a social activity. Later, we use communication and language. Through all this we test out our thoughts in the real world.

Materialist dialectics – a rough guide

The relation of thought to the world around us – mind to matter – has preoccupied philosophers over the centuries. As Frederick Engels explained, in his outline of German philosophy: "Is our thought capable of knowing the real world, are we able in our ideas and concepts of the real world to form a true reflection of reality? In philosophical language this question is called the question of the identity of thought and being. The vast majority of philosophers answer this question affirmatively."

A materialist dialectical approach affirms the power of thought and knowledge to understand the world and act upon and change it. All that exists is potentially knowable. The goal is to penetrate the rapidly changing and often confusing appearance of things in order to discover and study the opposing forces, tendencies, strivings – contradictions – within objects and processes. Dialectical logic distinguishes between the form and the content of things and processes, and their dialectical interrelation.

Understanding things in this way is not an exact predictive formula or natural science but nevertheless reveals the tendencies and the dynamics of an open-ended process, how human beings make history, individually and socially. This approach can point to alternative paths of development, how ideas and thoughts become material forces and, articulated in an organisational form, lead to revolutionary change.

Our starting point is that there is a material world which exists independently of our consciousness and which is a precondition for thought. The material world consists of things, elements, parts, substances, organisms, human beings, society and thought and operates in a law-governed fashion. It has an objective *infinite* existence, whereas human beings are *relative* and *finite*. All this matter is *inter-connected* and in constant *self-movement* and change. In *transition* to new higher forms, features of the former reappear in a new way.

The infinite exists in *parts*. For example, we consist of carbon and other elements which have their origins in the beginning of time. Inter-action of the parts within themselves result in imprints, traces and reactions. Human beings in their struggle to live exist in contradiction – unity and conflict – with the world around them. There is a constant *interpenetration* between the two, as, for example, in the act of breathing and eating.

Through their activities in the material world, human beings experience *sensations*, traces and imprints which constitute the beginnings of thought. The process and practice of dialectical cognition moves from concrete living perception to abstract thought and back to the concrete and is completed by theoretically-guided practice. This philosophical approach is tested and re-tested in transformative practice. We transform the world and ourselves simultaneously.

The elements of dialectics

▸ the objectivity of consideration – not examples but the thing-in-itself

▸ the totality of the diverse relations of this thing to others

▸ the development of this thing, phenomenon, its own movement, its own life

▸ the internally contradictory tendencies and sides in this thing – all things are contradictory in themselves

▸ the thing (phenomenon etc) as the sum and unity of opposites

▸ the struggle, unfolding, of these opposites, their contradictory strivings

▸ the union of analysis and synthesis – the break-down of the separate parts and the summation of these parts

▸ the relations of each thing are not only diverse but general, universal. Each thing is connected with every other

▸ not only the unity of opposites but the transition of every determination, quality, feature, side, property into every other, into its opposite

▸ the struggle of content with form and conversely. The throwing off of the form, the transformation of the content

▸ the transition of quantity into quality and vice versa

▸ the endless process of the discovery of new sides, relations etc

▸ the endless process of the deepening of our knowledge of the thing, of phenomena, processes, from appearance to essence and from less profound to more profound essence

▸ from co-existence to causality and from one form of connection and reciprocal dependence to another, deeper, more general form

▸ the repetition at a higher stage of certain features, properties, etc, of the lower and the apparent return to the old.

From Lenin's notebooks on the study of Hegel's *Science of Logic*

Dialectical logic understands that the concepts and categories that we use are not purely thought forms. They are the result of human practice and as such are forms and an expression of the movement and content of the world itself. They contain opposing sides and tendencies. As Lenin remarked in his comments on Hegel's *Science of Logic:*

> Logic is the science not of external forms of thought, but of the laws of development... i.e., of the development of the entire concrete content of the world and of its cognition, i.e., the sum-total, the conclusion of the history of knowledge of the world.

Our context is our existence and life under a global capitalist system and our concerns about what is happening and how it might affect the future. Our senses are tuned to potential sources of new information. The world, as we have established, consists of an infinite number of processes, things, events which have their own identities. In manifesting their identities, these objects come into a mutual, necessary contradictory relationship with thinking human beings. Through its own movement in time and space, a thing and its identity assumes a new and opposite form in thought in the shape of a finite *difference* with itself. This occurs through a process that is known as *negation.*

Something is beginning to come into existence which was not there before. The thing itself comes out of itself. This is a key moment because it acknowledges that things come into being and that a new moment cannot be the same as anything that went before or be recaptured. Time and space have moved on. These moments first reveal themselves as a quantity of sensations, which are a direct connection with the world outside of us and subject to dialectical laws of movement. These sensations build up and transform themselves into a new quality. Through self-movement they are negated into what is known as a *semblance*, a fleeting moment of a much deeper process, like the foam on a wave. For example, we may hear a brief news item or read about plans to cut 100,000 jobs in the civil service. Semblance is the result of movement in the external world and as such is objective and contains – in an as yet undeveloped form –

Negation

In its ordinary meaning, the word "negate" is defined as to nullify, deny or contradict something. As developed by the 19th century objective idealist German philosopher Georg Hegel, negation has a more complex significance. It describes moments of development and change. It signifies a process by which something is cancelled out (negated) while its content and form are not lost. The way in which we reflect the world outside of thought in thought is an important example of this process. Clearly we cannot have the object physically inside our being, but we have an abstract image of it. This way of understanding movement and change is vital, because the results of the previous development are not wiped out. For example, the computer incorporates the techniques of early technologies. Capitalism contains the results of all previous human history. Ageing is an example in human life. Your changing appearance over time reflects and is the result of everything that has happened to your body.

---

essence. Essence can be viewed as the sum total of connections, relations and internal laws of a thing in its movement.

What has taken place here is the formation of a particular relation between ourselves as individuals and the universal, the world outside of us. There is an interpenetration of opposites: a passing moment of the infinite whole touches and enters the finite part. Semblance is an unresolved, unstable moment which, nevertheless, contains possibilities. An example of this is walking down a busy road and a face emerges that you think you might know. This face is different from the rest, distinguishing itself from the crowd. There is a semblance of somebody. You keep on looking – receiving more and more sensations – then at a certain point it becomes clear whether this is the person you know. Through an interconnection with something outside, the original difference – which do not forget contains the original identity – is negated once more into *appearance*. The appearance does not coincide with the essence of the thing, although it contains it. If it were the same, life would be much simpler and there would no need for science!

Contradiction

This is a philosophical category expressing the inner source of all motion and development. As Hegel says in *The Science of Logic*: "Something moves, not because it is here at one point of time and there at another, but because at one and the same point of time it is here and not here, and in this here both is and is not." He adds: "And similarly internal self-movement proper, or impulse in general… is nothing else than the fact that something is in itself and is also the deficiency or the negative of itself, in one and the same respect." Capitalism is just such a thing. Capital and labour are, objectively, opposite forces. The drive of capital is to maximise shareholder value and profits. This is achieved by depriving workers of a portion of the value that is added in production through the exercise of labour power. By their very position in class society, workers are involved in a constant struggle to minimise exploitation and to increase their share of value. These mutually exclusive interests are, however, reconciled in a relative fashion, when capital and labour are engaged simultaneously in the single production process. These relations constitute a living contradiction, which is the source of their development. As Hegel explains: "Contradiction is the root of all movement and vitality, and it is only insofar as it contains contradiction that anything moves and has impulse and activity."

Established firmly at this point is a *contradiction* between the thing and our knowledge of it. If we want to know more about the person we have just met, or the job loss announcement, we have to interact with this process or person. At this point, the knowledge we already have begins to be synthesised with the developing process of the new. To grapple with the essence of the process that gave rise to appearance, means referring back to the source of the original sensation, at another moment in time. Thus, we discover new sides and aspects, to enrich our knowledge, to make it multi-dimensional, not one-sided, grapple with it in its movement. This is what using concepts in a dialectical way means.

An example – analysing political change

Take the fall in turn-out at the general election of 2001 as our subject matter. We have to look at the different aspects, assemble the data, compare the results with previous elections over time, what kind of people did not vote, their age and so on. A dialectical approach enables us to go much further, however. We take this part – the election result – and synthesise it with our previous analysis. The very dialectical nature of the thing we are investigating drives our understanding. For example, we know that the thing under investigation has a contradictory life in and of itself. Unlike superficial, bourgeois thinkers, we see parliamentary democracy, for example, as a phenomenon that has an historical trajectory. It came into existence at a certain time under specific conditions. These have changed with the evolution of capitalism. The parliamentary system is not a permanent feature of history and is in transition. The concept of parliamentary democracy contains elements of a new, opposite, more developed democracy. On this basis, we can make an assessment of the nature of the qualitative change that is manifested in a slump in turn-out, tracing its connections to the driving force of globalisation.

In more philosophical detail, this is what has taken place. We continue to analyse the parts, the features, the properties, moments of this process. These are brought into thought through negation because, as we have said, they cannot be the same as the object itself. These are abstract reflections of the living movement outside. The abstraction gains richness and becomes more concrete in this practice of cognition. This abstract image is the appearance in subjective thought of the objective content. That objective content is an absolute within the relative of our existing knowledge.

What we have done is to recreate in thought an objectively existing "whole". In this case, it is a totality of inter-connected processes and things connected to the fact of the election result. In this new whole, all the parts, features and properties we knew from before, continue to exist in a new relation to other parts. For example, more people can be said in an objective sense to be rejecting the legitimacy of the political order. The whole is, most importantly, not simply the sum of its parts but has an objective existence and logic of its own, which then drives the part as a law-governed process. For example, the capitalist system is made

---

Laws of motion

A dialectical approach begins from general principles about the operation of nature, society and thought. The relationship between things operates according to laws of motion. These exist independently of thought and are discovered by human activity and reflected in thought. In inorganic nature, many things can be predicted with absolute accuracy. In society, the outcomes are less certain because they are the result of human action, based on conscious decisions and practice which alter reality. This is made even more complex by the fact that these "decisions" are parts of a social whole, with each part having an effect on other parts. Nevertheless, because we are part of nature, our social existence develops in a law-governed fashion which can be expressed in concepts. In the *Dialectical Biologist,* Lewontin and Levins explain

> The first principle of a dialectical view then, is that a whole is a relation of heterogeneous parts that have no prior existence *as parts*. The second principle, which flows from the first, is that, in general, the properties of parts have no prior alienated existence but are acquired by being parts of a particular whole… A third dialectical principle, then, is that the interpenetration of parts and wholes is a consequence of the interchangeability of subject and object, of cause and effect… Because elements recreate each other by interacting and are recreated by wholes of which they are parts, change is a characteristic of all systems and all aspects of all systems. That is a fourth dialectical principle.

Our objective is to discover the course of development within things themselves. In deepening our knowledge of things, processes, phenomena we go from appearance to more profound understanding as we discover the unity and connection, the reciprocal dependence of the world. As we discover more and more connections within and between things, identical, enduring qualities reveal themselves as essential relations. It is in these relations that dialectical laws are given a concrete expression.

up of parts like corporations, finance centres, national governments, international bodies, political and cultural traditions and other phenomena. These inter-connected parts are drawn into a global logic that has its own dynamic. For example, it has a globalising tendency which penetrates and drives the parts, and can be revealed as the actual source of the fall in turn-out mentioned above.

This globalisation process is therefore a cause of new *effects*, both economically, socially, politically and culturally. There is a reciprocal process whereby the effects themselves turn into new *causes*. All this is built up in thought through dialectical logical concepts to the point of *actuality*. This is the closest we get to the real world in thought and is the highest point of essence. We have established an objective truth, which is itself relative in time and space. From here the necessary impulse is to the external world in the form of transforming practice. We are anticipating what we have to do. This will be based on the possibilities that appear at this point. These take the form of *abstract notions*. We are back in the world of practice. This philosophical approach is realised, tested and re-tested in transforming practice and the analysis of practice in the light of theory.

The value of cognising things in this way is that changes in the world outside of us are allowed their own life within our thoughts. The temptation in subjective idealist thought is to paste an image derived from previous experience on to the world rather than to grapple with the fact that there are changes going on. A non-dialectical approach turns away from the source of sensation and relies simply on the past to interpret what after all at this point is only an image. In other words, we must avoid a rush to making a judgement about the significance of this moment.

Viewing the dialectical life of all phenomena and the internal relations within things enables us to study changes in history from the standpoint of today. By analysing a particular part or feature of capitalism, we are able to reach conclusions about its specific history in relation to the whole of the social system. This approach brings us closer to the crises, possibilities and real movement of forces which in their inter-relationship constitute history and indicate possibilities for the future.

Science and dialectics

Quantum mechanics demonstrates in a powerful way how contradiction is an inherent property of matter. In other words, a thing can be two mutually contradictory things at the same time. At a "macro" level, change may appear smooth and continuous, as in the flow of light from a source like the sun. But at a micro-level, on the scale of atoms and molecules physical processes are discontinuous and occur in quantum leaps. Particles of light, "photons", are outstanding examples of this. A quantum entity, the photon, may behave as a wave or a particle, depending on the circumstances. In terms of scientific observation and measurement, wave and particle properties are mutually exclusive opposites. This is known as "wave-particle duality". This duality demonstrates the unity and conflict of opposites. Left alone, photons maintain the characteristics of both wave and particle. But when they interact with other matter – a metal surface or a prism of glass – they take on the characteristics *either* of a particle *or* a wave. Included in this wave-particle duality is the transformation of opposites, as well: an electron ejected as a particle from a heated metal surface may be diffracted by a crystal, showing its wave nature in the process.

The relation between the whole and the part is shown by the development of the human brain. We are all born with some 100 billion neurons – brain cells, backed up by ten times as many support cells, which exist within the whole of our brain. The relations between these cells is determined by the unique experience of each individual, as the activity of the child in a particular environment, surrounded by specific human relations shapes its brain, particularly over the first two years of life. The whole life of the individual influences and shapes the parts, in particular in the brain.

One fundamental property of matter-in-motion in nature is the negation of the negation. The tree in the forest grows leaves during the spring, leaves that are living, breathing organs responsible for powering the whole tree. In the autumn, as the tree begins to shut down for the winter, the leaves fall to the ground – the first negation of living matter to dead. But the dead leaves are themselves food for new living organisms – fungi, plants and, eventually, new trees – taking part in the second negation, the negation of the negation, to be incorporated once more into living matter.

* * *

The significance of postmodernism

Postmodernism can be shown to provide a consolation to those who consider themselves critical of aspects of contemporary capitalism, but who also lack the belief and confidence that it is possible to transform reality for the better.

The key exponents of postmodernism are the French philosophers Michel Foucault, Jacques Derrida, Gilles Deleuze, Jean-Francois Lyotard and Jean Baudrillard. All but Baudrillard arose from the French philosophical school called post-structuralism of the early 1960s. The crisis within post-war Stalinism resulted in a philosophical vacuum which began to be filled by the post-structuralists. By the early 1980s Lyotard, Derrida and Foucault became popular and were seen as the prophets of a challenge to all existing ideologies and world views. In literary theory, architecture, the visual arts and media studies, postmodern ideas and theories became a major theme in university courses and the theory underpinning modern marketing practice.

The rise of the information economy and a world market based upon increasingly sophisticated forms of specialisation and fragmented markets seemed to vindicate postmodernist emphasis on plurality, difference and the blurring of the difference between image and reality. The global economy of the 1980s and 1990s and the demise of the Soviet Union reinforced the popularity of postmodernism's modest philosophical stance. For some it was a viable ideological alternative to the universalist themes of the Enlightenment, whether of the Marxist variety or the pure bourgeois narratives. Hence postmodernism became popular as a kind of theorisation of the development of the global economy, and also a critique of this globalisation in non-totalising and particular terms. Its rejection of "ideologies" and "overarching theories" fitted in well with a world where the old certainties of the cold war came tumbling down and society headed into a new period of history.

The durable attraction of postmodernism can be explained by its ironic attitude to the world, which is reminiscent of the practical impotence of Hegel's beautiful soul. The German philosopher outlined how the beautiful soul and the unhappy consciousness are often generated when people feel that they have little capacity to change the world, but instead can only comment about the world in an ironic and possibly sceptical manner. Postmodernism can be shown to provide a consolation to those who consider themselves critical of aspects of contemporary capitalism, but who also lack the belief and confidence that it is possible to transform reality for the better. It thus acts as an oppositional ideology at the level of popular consciousness for those who believe that something is wrong, and yet are also sceptical and pessimistic about the possiblity of a better historical alternative. It functions as a trend that lacks a vision of the future, and instead accommodates to what exists in the present in the form of its ironic stance.

The "left" school of postmodernism, personified by Derrida, Deleuze and Foucault often makes strong criticisms of capitalism, but they are limited by a sceptical approach to the possibility of truth and an irrationalism that doubts the very validity of philosophy and social theory. Overwhelmed by the totalising drive of global capital, it tends to deny the fundamental contradiction between social being and social consciousness and thereby the possibility of revolutionary transformation. Hence, postmodernism can be generally characterised as a petty-bourgeois ideology that vacillates between capitalism and socialism because of its resigned scepticism about knowing the world and the possibility of altering it for the better.

Do we live in a postmodern world?

American literary critic Fredric Jameson has characterised postmodernist theory and views as the logic of contemporary capitalism. The emphasis on diversity, plurality, fragmentation, irony, and even the cynicism of postmodern type ideologues is certainly an expression of profound historical processes, and has become indispensable to the imperatives of capital accumulation. So within the spheres of culture, architecture, economics and political ideology, postmodernism characterises what is required in order to maintain and expand modern capitalism. But it would be wrong to describe contemporary global capitalism as a "postmodernist world" because this would turn the relationship between social being and consciousness on its head. For the market state economies are still objectively and materially defined by the alienated and exploitative character of the capital-labour relation. In this context, a number of postmodernist ideas can be incorporated into the logic of capital accumulation, such as plurality and irony. But these ideas do not in themselves constitute or explain the essential historical logic of capitalism or in its essential being.

Given the complex and often contradictory origins of what became postmodernism, it would be simplistic simply to dismiss it as a right-wing trend that makes no important criticisms of the status quo, despite its blanket rejection of Enlightenment ideas. On the contrary, the founders of postmodernism – the French post-structuralists referred to above and their Romantic predecessors – outline significant criticisms of the historical limitations of capitalism. Deleuze and Foucault, despite their formal rejection of Marxist historical materialism and disdain of Hegel, are still capable of making formidable criticisms of its social limitations. In the centre is Derrida, who generally avoids any type of direct political comment, but who was motivated to defend his own conception of the legacy of Marx, even if he did not connect Marx to any integral revolutionary commitments. The right-wing trend is expressed by ex-Marxist Lyotard, whose The Postmodern Condition published in 1979, was a vision of post-industrial societies dominated by information technologies. With Baudrillard the irrational, deeply reactionary side of postmodernism comes to the fore. He claimed that the first Gulf War did not take place since all we can know is fictitious images and we are incapable of differentiating between the real and its simulacrum.

* * *

Is globalisation just a policy?

*There are many campaign groups, trade unions and political
organisations who maintain that capitalist globalisation is
essentially a series of policies that corporations and states can
and will adjust if they come under sufficient pressure.*

If globalisation is just a *policy*, then there is no need to change
the nature of the capitalist system of production. We simply have
to persuade bodies like the World Trade Organisation (WTO)
and governments to see sense and help the poor.

Tony Woodley, leader of the Transport and General Workers
Union, has called on the New Labour government to support
industry in Britain as an incentive for employers to keep
production at home rather than export it to cheaper-labour areas
of the world, which is known as off-shoring. The number of
manufacturing jobs in Britain has fallen by 750,000 since 1997,
with the majority going abroad.

The World Development Movement is a major campaigning
group that claims it tackles the underlying causes of poverty. The
WDM's website says; "We lobby decision makers to change the
policies that keep people poor. We research and promote positive
alternatives. We work alongside people in the developing world
who are standing up to injustice. The world has the wealth and
means to end poverty. Yet nearly half of the world's population
live on less than £1.40 a day. And over 11 million children will
die from poverty-related illness this year alone. *Policies* of
governments and companies are keeping people poor. *Policies*
that ensure global trade benefits the rich, not the poor. The three
richest men in the world are wealthier than the 48 poorest
countries combined. *Policies* that give increasing power to
multinational companies. For every £1 of aid going into poor
countries, multinationals take 66p of profits out." [emphasis
added] Among WDM's campaign successes, the website says, is
the decision in 1999 by the International Monetary Fund to link
debt relief to poverty reduction.

The Socialist Workers Party (SWP) are presently the most influential Left group in Britain, and what they say and do is considered by significant numbers of people as an expression of Marxism. But the SWP too sees corporate-driven globalisation as a policy question first and foremost.

The Marxist outlook maintains that the material world is the primary basis for understanding the role of human practice and consciousness. Thus human activity depends on its relationship with nature in order to meet material needs. Specific social relations become the historical basis for realising these needs. Consequently, the material and social being of humanity is the objective ground for understanding the subjective role of consciousness.

Capitalist globalisation is not an ephemeral and transitory phenomena that stems from thoughts and ideas, or the particular policies of specific capitalists and politicians. Instead, globalisation represents the present structural development, or social being of the system within the imperialist stage of world capitalism. The essential economic content of globalisation is today expressed by the competitive and contradictory domination of transnational capital. This is the result of the transformation of national monopoly and finance capital.

Alex Callinicos is the main proponent of the SWP on questions of globalisation and imperialism.

But in his *Anti-Capitalist Manifesto*, he makes no analytical mention of the importance of transnational capital. Instead, his approach is based upon an idealist emphasis on the importance of what occurs at the level of the political superstructure – what is said and done by politicians and bureaucrats.

Thus for him, globalisation becomes a policy and ideology. His book labels such policies "Washington Consensus", or the "neo-liberal" agenda. These terms, which are taken directly from bourgeois social science, embrace trade liberalisation, competitive exchange rates, privatisation deregulation, and fiscal discipline. They formed the ideological dogma of the Reagan and Thatcher administrations and have since become orthodox economic outlooks.

For Callinicos, "neo-liberalism" has represented a "conscious strategy" carried out by the American administration, the US Treasury, IMF and World Bank. He tends to suggest that globalisation is exaggerated as an economic development, and that it does not represent an irreversible tendency towards greater economic integration. Globalisation is considered as tenuous and something that could break down. In his view, it is a "contingent" and "reversible process".

Callinicos argues that the anti-capitalist movement has posed a challenge to the "neo-liberal" agenda. The 1999 Seattle demonstration against the WTO in particular represented a new level of anti-capitalist militancy. This shows, he claims, that it is possible to challenge, modify and even change the present agenda of world capitalism. He maintains: "If the neo-liberal hegemony began with the opening of the Berlin Wall on November 9th 1989, then it lasted barely ten years, to the first great demonstration in Seattle on 30th November 1999. The Washington Consensus continues to provide the framework for policy-making in virtually every state, but it is now intensely contested." This view represents a naive and misleading optimism that plays up the success of the anti-capitalist movement and correspondingly downplays the resources of capital. This is done in order to reinforce the illusion that all that is necessary to overthrow the current agenda is the adoption of new policies, via pressure on pro-capitalist governments.

It is undoubtedly important to show the historical importance of struggles against global capital's policies, such as the Zapatistas' rebellion in Mexico against the NAFTA treaty, and protests in Nigeria against the role of the transnational corporations (TNCs), campaigns against Third World debt, strikes in France against privatisation, mass upheaval in Argentina, plus the ongoing momentum of international anti-capitalist demonstrations. Callinicos, however, not only gives these movements a transforming quality they do not actually possess. He goes further and equates the emergence of the anti-capitalist movement with a development of ideas which challenge the domination of capitalist ideology. For example, he argues that the movement represents the ascendancy of a new intellectual paradigm. He says: "And so the great debate over capitalism has resumed, two hundred years after it began in the aftermath of the Great French Revolution. Postmodernism is now history... Nevertheless, the debate has moved on, less because of some decisive theoretical refutation of postmodernism... than because the world-wide rebellion against capitalist globalisation has changed the intellectual agenda."

In other words, he sees the consciousness of the need to challenge capitalism as a system arising spontaneously out of struggles and practical activity on this or that issue. Callinicos maintains that the "logic" of the anti-capitalist movement can resolve strategic questions because capital is ultimately not a structure. It is rather an expression of a policy that can be challenged and even overcome by the application of enough mass pressure.

He contends that any ambiguities within the anti-capitalist movement about understanding and defining globalisation can be resolved simply by self-definition. The *Anti-Capitalist Manifesto* considers globalisation as a formal shell and a dispensable outer layer, while the policies are considered as the inner content and essential to the operation of capital. But this is a subjective illusion, in that the structural content of globalisation is based upon the domination of the transnational corporations (TNCs). This idealist inversion between form and content is expressed by the SWP's reformist programme that is a substitute for a revolutionary approach.

Formally, Callinicos is for the traditional Marxist goals of social ownership, workers' control, self-management and socialist planning to replace the anarchic domination of a market economy. But this is the aim of a long-term and "ultimate" strategic programme. The immediate aim is to challenge the policy aims of capital in order to create the conditions for its transcendence in the future.

He eclectically accepts that a transformation of form leaves the content essentially unchanged and admits that changing the policy of contemporary capitalism means that we are still a "long way" from socialist planning. However, he tentatively "overcomes" this problem by saying that what matters, what is immediate, concrete and practical, is to come up with a programme that is essentially a left-wing but nevertheless reformist alternative within the limits of capitalism. Revealingly he writes:

> Socialist planning... is both a feasible and a desirable alternative to capitalism. But we are a long way from it. Indeed, the neo-liberal policies of the Washington Consensus are driving us in the opposite direction, towards a world where everything becomes... a commodity to be bought and sold for profit. A movement that is seeking to reverse this process must therefore organise mass struggles to demand measures that would both offer immediate remedies and begin to introduce a different social logic.

The strategic question that obviously arises is: how is it possible to prevent the logic of capital from integrating these reformist demands into itself? There is no objectively valid strategic answer to this problem. Instead he can only outline the moral/ethical criteria of the programme of the new "left" reformist government. This includes abolition of Third World debt; introduction of a tax of international currency transactions; restoration of capital controls; introduction of a universal basic income; reduction of the working week; defence of public services and renationalisation of privatised industries; progressive taxation to finance public services and redistribute wealth and income; abolition of immigration controls and extension of citizenship rights; a programme to forestall environmental catastrophe; dissolution of the military-industrial complex and a defence of civil liberties.

He outlines the main aspects of his strategic approach, which is to put mass pressure on nation states in order to create the conditions for implementing these anti-capitalist demands. He writes:

> First, the demands listed above are generally placed on states acting singly or in concert. This reflects the fact that, whatever the effects of globalisation, states are still the most effective mechanisms in the world as currently constituted for mobilising resources to achieve collectively agreed goals... But, states, because they are at least

partially dependent on securing the consent of their subjects, are vulnerable to political pressure from below.

Mass movements can therefore extract reforms from them. It is, however, crucial to understand that any such concessions will be won, not through negotiations with ostensibly sympathetic governments, but through mass struggles. The reforms outlined above go against the logic of capital. They can only be won by a movement that maintains its political independence and has the power, thanks to the central role played within it by the organised working class, to wrest concessions from the system.

This stance shows the political significance of Callinicos's view of globalisation as a collection of policies rather than a phenomenon with a cohesive structural content. The importance of globalisation is considered as secondary in relation to the continuing significance of nation states. If nation states are the essential political content this means that a national reformist political strategy retains its validity, despite globalisation.

His conception contains nothing on the importance of overcoming the TNCs as a strategic aim of labour. Indeed, Callinicos has essentially replaced the class struggle of capital and labour with that of political struggle between the nation state and the people. This formulation suggests that the nation state can be pressured and transformed into meeting the objectives of the mass struggles of the people. The objectives of the working class are effectively dissolved into the mass abstract democracy of the people.

This also means that revolution, as the expression of the victory of labour over capital, can be downgraded into a distant and secondary issue. The result of this opportunism is to create an objective divide between reforms and revolution. That is why the SWP's anti-imperialism in practice results in support for and organising of pressure group politics. Their aim is to try and change the policies of the capitalist nation state rather than striving to overthrow this state. This is the reality behind the radical rhetoric.

13 The case for a revolutionary party

Globalisation has created a vastly more unequal, intensely commercialised, ecologically damaged and altogether a more dangerous world. At the same time, the conditions for building a new democratic society based on co-operation and collective efforts are also present. *A World to Win* has attempted to demonstrate that no serious change is possible outside of a struggle for political and economic power. The strategic objective, therefore, is the ousting of the moneyed élites and their political backers as the precondition for creating a just society.

The stakes are high for the future of humanity. Increasing numbers are aware of this and want do something about it. How in practice do we achieve this transformation? It will not happen without leadership and organisation committed to this task. Social revolution is a high form of conscious practice requiring knowledge, training and skills to take and hold on to power. We are not describing a coup, nor the actions of a few dedicated people. A social revolution has to involve millions of people who want to transform society with a definite purpose in mind. There is an inescapable fact in all this – a political organisation is needed to carry it through.

Parties and power
Political parties in the sense that we understand them today first came into existence in the 19th century throughout the capitalist world. They followed the extension of the franchise, which

began in Britain with the Reform Act in 1832, although the working class was excluded from the ballot box until after 1867. These political reforms marked the start of a period which has become known as parliamentary or representative democracy. This has been based on voting to send to parliament people who stand for election under the label of a political party. The Tory Party and the Liberal Party were the two major parties of that period. These developments in Britain were also associated with the consolidation of the political triumph of the manufacturing bourgeoisie and their middle class supporters over the landed aristocracy. Both the Liberals and the Tories represented different tendencies and groups within the ruling classes.

These democratic changes were accompanied by turbulent periods of mass struggle, including the rise of the great Chartist movement in the late 1830s and 1840s and, much later, the Suffragette campaign for women's votes. The right to vote, as well as the right to form a political party, were clearly an advance on the extremely restricted, corrupt, clique system that existed before modern parliamentary politics.

Today, as we have shown in other parts of the book, these historic gains are undermined in a variety of ways, a process that is intimately connected with the intensity of globalisation. A stark expression of this is the fact that the traditional parliamentary parties in Britain all stand for more or less the same thing. New Labour, meanwhile, has become the governing party in place of the Tories, because it expresses most closely the interests of corporate and financial capital. The reduction of representation to that of only the ruling classes effectively disenfranchises large sections of the population. These recent changes have contributed to a large-scale disillusionment with politics and traditional parties.

We are convinced, however, that it is not the *notion* of a political party that is wrong and outdated, but *existing* parties and state structures. Politics is part of what it means to be human. We need to debate, be represented and have a say, not simply individually but collectively too. We should set out to *extend* democracy so that it takes on new meaning for the majority, going beyond the increasingly empty shell of existing parliamentary politics. A new type of party is needed to create the conditions for this change to take place.

The capitalist class in Britain took shape within the womb of feudal society. It began to accumulate capital through trade and finance in a way that challenged the economic and political framework of feudalism. Rival ideologies arose on the basis of the new wealth that questioned the myths, religion and hierarchies of absolute monarchy. When the two forces could no longer co-exist, a revolutionary conflict burst into the open in the form of the English Civil War. The Parliamentary side under Oliver Cromwell organised the New Model Army for the purpose of overthrowing the Crown. It was both a military machine and an arena for political debate and struggle. The power of the absolute monarchy was broken, leading to the dominance of parliamentary rule and the start of the economic freedoms capital demanded.

While the nascent capitalist class of the 17th century built economic wealth and with it a distinct ideological and philosophical outlook *within* the existing feudal system, this advantage is unavailable to those who need to make a social revolution in the 21st century. As a result, we are obliged to construct a virtual future in the present in the shape of a revolutionary political party.

Conditions for social revolution can mature but cannot succeed without leadership, strategy and tactics. These require prior preparation and cannot grow spontaneously. An understanding of the need to take political power and actually doing it, do not and cannot arise intuitively out of people's experiences. This is primarily because of the powerful, limiting and restrictive role that capitalist ideology and its guiding philosophy plays within social consciousness.

The ruling classes are not complacent about political power. They know that running and controlling the system requires conscious leadership and they take nothing for granted. They have long experience of doing this and are aware that a rapidly changing world requires frequent adjustments, including the generation of new ideologies. Thus they work at political leadership and invest a lot of effort in it. The leadership qualities displayed by Thatcher and Blair in forcing through change in often difficult conditions are examples of this. Anything that even implicitly threatens the capitalist is treated very seriously. A factory take-over, a major industrial action such as the miners' strike, or a series of mass demonstrations provoke a variety of responses, including provocations, arrests, racism, nationalism and force. Under these conditions, the actions of individuals or even large groups of individuals cannot by themselves lead to the change we seek.

What a revolutionary party is

A revolutionary party is an organisation created out of the historic need to bring about the transition from capitalism to a society formed on the basis of common ownership and democratic control. Its aim is to organise and lead this change. The revolutionary party is a membership organisation that people freely join and has a structure and a constitution. It is the place where the theory, strategy, training and practice of social revolution are generated.

The role of the party

A revolutionary party has a series of roles to carry out in the areas of training, democratic discussion, political intervention as well as to act as a rallying point and focus for the struggle for power itself. Its tasks include to:

Training and development

- ‣ encourage and help all members to become leaders
- ‣ train members in the philosophy of contradiction and change, materialist dialectics
- ‣ facilitate and support self-development of members
- ‣ bring out the different capacities, talents, abilities and potential of members.

Democratic discussion

- ‣ provide a space where all revolutionary currents and tendencies can participate
- ‣ be an arena for members to debate and discuss policies,

practice and strategies in a democratic way
▸ reflect in discussions the diversity of interests of workers
▸ organise maximum participation in democratic decision-making processes.

Political intervention
▸ establish a relationship of trust and confidence between the party and those in struggle against capitalist policies
▸ support and encourage spontaneous actions while bringing out the essential political issues they contain
▸ decide on tactics such as whether to contest parliamentary elections as a platform
▸ advocate political action for the practical transformation of capital-labour relations
▸ learn from history and from day-to-day struggles while assessing the party's interventions.

A rallying point
▸ be a symbolic entity
▸ show and lead by example.

Struggle for power
▸ give the mass of the people a sense and understanding of their own potential power
▸ ensure that the issue of political power is at the heart of its work
▸ organise the struggle for power.

How a party functions
A revolutionary organisation, by its very nature, is concerned with leading change, both within and outside the organisation. Therefore it has constantly to learn from what is happening around it and involve the entire membership in making the changes that are needed. This requires self-motivation and self-organisation based on the commitment and enthusiasm which can only come from a shared aim.

Strong connections, interconnections and democratic involvement at all levels are necessary. The areas for involvement

> **Blasting through inertia**
>
> Only leadership can blast through the many sources of corporate inertia. Only leadership can motivate the actions needed to alter behaviour in any significant way. Only leadership can get change to stick by anchoring it in the very culture of an organisation."
>
> "Real leaders take action because they have confidence that the forces unleashed can be directed to achieve important ends."
>
> "In an organisation with 100 employees, at least two dozen must go far beyond the call of duty to produce a significant change. In a firm with 100,000 employees, the same might be required of 15,000 or more."
>
> "New decision-making processes are needed because no one individual has the information needed to make all major decisions or the time or credibility needed to convince lots of people to implement the decisions.
>
> *Leading Change*, John P. Kotter

include training, education, research, developing policies, communications, monitoring progress and holding the leadership to account.

A revolutionary party has to be designed to:

▸ ensure accountability of leaders and members
▸ make transparent the internal decision-making process
▸ facilitate continuous development and training of leaders and members
▸ avoid bureaucratic inertia and complacency
▸ involve members in developing policy
▸ ensure that minority interests and differences of view have an equal voice
▸ study and learn from failures and mistakes
▸ combat subjectivism and egoism
▸ intervene in struggles external to itself
▸ learn from and build alliances with movements in other countries.

A dialectical systems thinking approach emphasises

interrelationships and processes. Things are seen in movement, in relation to a whole, the big picture. So, for example, party structures should function horizontally and vertically within a given process. Reciprocal relationships between the elected leadership, departments, units of membership and members will be the norm.

Globalised capitalism, in the course of its development, has produced new methods and technologies which provide better conditions for revolutionary organisations. Workers in general are better educated and are familiar with communications methods such as email, the Internet, video-conferencing, mobile phones with email and visual links, personal computers and so on. These techniques allow mass involvement more quickly through transfer of complex documents, visual materials including video and music, as well as simple and urgent

---

Connection and creativity

When people connect to each other and to powerful ideas, creativity and action are ensured. Barriers to the flow of information and new ideas are lowered as people forge links with others. Work also flows more smoothly, because people learn how what they do fits into the larger whole, and how to access needed resources. When people connect to each other, they become known to each other. They stop being stereotypes, roles, functions and members of that hated 'other'. They become human beings with their own real-life issues and concerns. People who are doing their best to get the job done. People with unique talents to share."

"Meeting today's challenges cannot be done by any one person single-handedly. We need a community of people who willingly provide their talents and insights to address increasingly complex issues. Community is important because one person no longer has the answer. Answers reside in all of us. When we create community, we move beyond a group of people who may have personal connections with each other to developing a group of connected people who have both the will and willingness to work together to accomplish a goal that has meaning for them.

Terms of Engagement, Richard H. Axelrod

Developing new policies – an example

A member is in discussion with a transport campaign group and comes to the conclusion that the party's policy on the issue needs developing. She tells the group that she will start the process of renewing the party's transport policy. An internal email to the party's relevant policy section makes the preliminary case for an amended policy. This is posted on the policy bulletin board with an invitation to support the proposal. Sufficient support triggers the launch of the actual policy change process. The policy section, with the agreement of the member, suggests the areas that need updating. This is communicated to the other policy bodies of the party and to the basic membership units of the organisation for discussion. These units have the responsibility of involving the local members in the discussion. They will also talk to external bodies and individuals to deepen their understanding of the issue. A draft policy is put together by the policy section out of all the communications it has received from members and branches for further consultation. Consultation on the proposal is widened to include the campaigning transport group. When a final draft is reached, an e-conference is called to approve the new policy, which is then published on the party's website.

messages, news and information.

For example, all decisions and minutes of discussions can be communicated to the relevant bodies soon after they take place. Involving membership in this way can help to encourage openness and a shared awareness, commitment as well as shared responsibilities. Making maximum use of communications technology will help create an organisation in which challenging views through open debate and improving ways of doing things is the norm.

The advantages of collective, participatory leadership over old-style, hierarchical structures has, paradoxically, been recognised by top management gurus who advise capitalist firms. Because of the combined rapid pace of change and its global nature, corporations have been compelled to identify the training of leadership as a top priority. A key function of this leadership is to involve their workforces in decision-making processes. These gurus have written detailed explanations of why this should happen and how it should take place. They emphasise the significance for the life and future of an organisation of having leaders who are in continuous training and retraining. What they call for is a "learning organisation". These experts demonstrate a concept of leadership which goes far beyond the narrow group of senior managers to embrace workers at all levels of the firm. The underlying approach is that all staff are capable of changing and involving themselves at high levels. Working in this way, they have discovered, can vastly improve performance.

Naturally, this egalitarian, democratic, non-hierarchical, participatory, collective, committed, team-working approach is equally designed not to challenge the fundamental issue of ownership and control of the corporation which exists solely for the purpose of enhancing shareholder profit. This is a kind of collective working combined with private ownership. Nevertheless, these advances in organisational techniques, combined with revolutionary ICT, are important for a 21st century concept of a revolutionary party. By emphasising the group rather than the élite, a revolutionary organisation becomes a more powerful unit. Democratic structuring and functioning in turn will become the basis of the authority of elected bodies of leaders. Equally, it underlies the principle that decisions arrived at democratically are everyone's property and carry with them an obligation to carry them out, regardless of whether you are in the minority or the majority.

If all members and leaders work in this way, their collective efforts can help to ward off the inherent tendencies in any organisation to conservatism and bureaucracy. A scientific approach enables us to identify seats of resistance to change, bring out the opposites, understand the change possibilities, identify issues and the sources of complacency and inertia. Operating in this more advanced way will allow us to tackle difficulties and problems that have dogged revolutionary movements in the past.

* * *

The real origins of Stalinism

*Some suggest that a revolutionary party of the type we have
described, if it were to come to power, must lead to the type of
dictatorship that arose in the Soviet Union.*

The real difficulty with this view is that it presumes an
inevitability about history that simply does not exist. There are
alternative paths that history can follow that are decided by the
interplay of objective and subjective factors, by real human
beings in struggle under circumstances not of their choosing.
There was nothing pre-ordained about what happened in the
Soviet Union.

The history of the Bolshevik Party both before and after the
1917 revolution is one of constant discussion and struggle over
fundamental questions. Both left and right wings of the party
participated in long and often sharp disputes over political
perspective which engaged the best minds of the period. The
decision to lead a revolution, the terms of the treaty with
Germany that took Russia out of World War I, the shift towards
a market economy in 1921, increased self-management and
democratic life were all forged out of intense, openly-waged
inner-party debates. Even at the height of the post-revolution
political crisis, seats were reserved on the leading committees for
factions like the Workers Opposition.

During the most traumatic period of the early 1920s, there was
an amazing flourishing of culture, science and the arts. This
creative period had a profound influence throughout the world.
All these events are well documented, especially since the
glasnost period under Gorbachev where much of hidden history
came to light.

After the revolution, the Bolshevik Party was extremely small
and in no position to impose dictatorship. For a period it worked
with other parties in the government, but this arrangement broke
down and Lenin's party was left in charge of the state on its own.
The circumstances in which they found themselves began to exert

intolerable pressures. These were to prove more decisive than the nature of the party itself. Russia in 1917 was an extremely backward country and the largely illiterate peasants made up 80% of the total population. There was no history of democratic life in the country and the state had always played a directing role in people's lives. From the early days, workers' self-management and democratic control proved difficult to establish. The political leadership under Lenin found itself having to encourage these processes from the top, from positions of power. This contradiction brought them into ever closer relationship with the state bureaucracy, which like all administrative bodies was inward looking and conservative.

The internationalist wing of the Bolshevik Party hoped that the extension of revolution to countries like Germany would provide the resources to overcome Russia's economic and political difficulties. When the German revolution of 1923 failed, the perspective of international revolution was put to one side and, with the death of Lenin a year later, the bureaucracy began to exert a greater and greater grip on the party. Trotsky led the growing resistance to this degeneration, forming the Left Opposition which included many of the leaders of the revolution. The Opposition fought for internationalism, the planned development of industry and rejected the Stalinist policy of building "socialism in one country". But a combination of internal and external social and political conditions counted against the Opposition and they were eventually defeated.

After a bitter internal struggle that lasted for most of the 1920s, Stalin finally seized political control of the party – as the spokesman for the bureaucracy. Trotsky was expelled from the party and exiled in 1929. The political leadership eventually merged with and was swallowed up by the state apparatus and by the mid-1930s an authoritarian dictatorship exerted an iron grip over the country. The old leaders of the revolution were among the first targets of the dictatorship. So, far from creating the conditions for authoritarian rule, the party was its victim. Trotsky analysed the degeneration of the Soviet Union in his classic work, *The Revolution Betrayed*, which called for a political revolution to overthrow the Stalinist bureaucracy and restore democracy. Gorbachev ended the rule of the Stalinist bureaucracy and tried to introduce economic and democratic change while preserving non-capitalist, state-owned property as the basis for development. He wanted to build on the tremendous sacrifices that the Soviet people had made in constructing a modern society in spite of the crimes of Stalinism. His political revolution broke the power of the old regime but the collapse that accompanied the changes proved too difficult to control and the Soviet Union disintegrated.

This break-up is described by the media and even in school books as the "end of communism", rather than the overthrow of Stalinism. Presenting complex events in such a simplistic fashion reinforces the message that anything but capitalism is bad for your health and is doomed to failure. But even a cursory examination of history shows that the Soviet Union never reached socialism, let alone communism.

The real issues of this history, therefore, are not solely to do with the nature of the party but the whole set of conditions that existed in Russia in 1917. Were a socialist revolution to succeed in Britain or one of the other advanced capitalist states, it would inherit much more favourable circumstances, especially the long struggle for democratic and basic rights. These are outlined elsewhere in the book and would certainly present outstanding opportunities to advance swiftly and democratically to a socialist society.

14 De-alienation, regime change and power

A World to Win has shown that you cannot reform or regulate global capitalism. Moreover, a merging of economic with political power has transformed the way the capitalist state functions. The state no longer attempts to solve the serious problems humanity faces and increasingly directly expresses corporate interests and objectives. People are more alienated than ever as a result of the globalisation process and this gives rise to often unbearable tensions within individuals and society as a whole. The state's role in protecting its citizens against outside threat has turned into its opposite through the "war on terror". This has made ordinary citizens targets and potential victims of both oppression and terrorist attacks.

The state remains the lynchpin of the social system of capitalism, holding it all together. It provides the essential ideological, political, social, legal, educational and military frameworks without which society in general and capitalism in particular cannot function. Therefore, the state – who controls it, the way it is organised and in whose interests – is our main political focus. As the present state is capitalist in its nature and functions, it follows that it cannot serve a society with entirely different foundations or be used to create such a society. Without new forms of state power, it is inconceivable that we could reorganise the economy along collective, self-management lines, put an end to war and act on the ecological crisis. Without a comprehensive regime change we cannot breathe new life into democratic achievements and make the right to vote mean something again.

We have argued that the major problems facing humanity are caused ultimately by the alienation of people's labour and natural resources from them by existing social relations. These relations are founded on private ownership of the means of producing goods and services for profit. The exploitation of human labour in this way is the barrier to progress that we must sweep aside. This is the road to de-alienation. For this to happen, the domination of capital that is expressed through the corporations and the state powers which act for them must be ended.

Human beings, under the present system have taken things as far as they can, so progress now depends on a transfer of power from minority ownership to mass democratic ownership. The challenge is to take power from the minority. That means taking control and then *remaking* (see Chapter 8 for our proposals) the state while encouraging and supporting the democratising of ownership and control of workplaces. One without the other will not succeed.

A Gallup International poll unveiled in November 2002, at the World Economic Forum in Davos, showed a massive swing towards distrust of corporations, governments, politicians and democratic institutions. The poll, commissioned by global business leaders, interviewed 15,000 people in 15 countries and found that 48% expressed "little or no trust" in global companies. Some 52% expressed similar scepticism about "large national businesses".

The poll concluded: "Trust has been eroded far beyond the corporate sector. Two-thirds of those surveyed were of the opinion that their country was not 'governed by the will of the people'. Additional opinion polls coupled with declining voter turnout – particularly among the young – point to an increasing disenchantment with politicians and political institutions. The current breakdown of trust also reflects an uncertainty about contemporary values."

These and many other surveys reveal that most people feel that they have little or no control over the forces that really determine what happens on the planet. They know that more than ever before the mass of people are not represented politically by the existing forms of democracy. As the poll added: "There is also declining trust that the world is going in the right direction. Today, a majority of citizens across the 15 countries do not agree with the direction in which the world is moving. This disagreement is up significantly in half the countries surveyed, compared to a year ago. The research delivers further evidence of citizen distrust in the democratic process: fully two-thirds of those surveyed world-wide disagree that their country is 'governed by the will of the people'."

But while they may feel powerless about the direction in which the world is led by corporations and governments, people have no choice but to confront the problems which they face at all levels, from the strictly personal to the public and political. They may be indifferent to the hollow words of politicians but they join all kinds of clubs and non-profit organisations in large numbers. They try to overcome their powerlessness by finding other ways of doing things that are not based simply on personal gain and interest. They participate in mass marathons and sports events. They contribute generously to charities and fundraising for the less advantaged. They resist their employers when they encroach on hard-won conditions and intensify the work process.

Despite all attempts by governments to force people to accept dependence on the market for crucial services like health, education and pensions, the overwhelming majority still believe that there should be public provision according to need. They see right through the spin about "choice" and "modernisation".

The British Social Attitudes survey 2003 reported that "increasing material affluence and a changing occupational structure have had *less* impact than we might have expected", adding: "Support for better public services such as health and education is as high now as it ever has been. The public continues to believe that access to publicly funded health care should be based on need rather than income... grants not loans... Although income inequality may have grown, there is no evidence that it is tolerated to any greater extent now than was the case twenty years ago. Equally we have also uncovered little evidence to suggest that growing material affluence has reduced class differences in social attitudes and values… The result is a society where social class still seems to make a difference to the attitudes and values of its citizens."

People globally are trying to overcome the forces that are oppressing them in a variety of ways, as they decide that governments do not represent them at all. The mass demonstrations in February 2003 against the invasion of Iraq were the high point of people "voting with their feet" as tens of millions took to the streets around the world. It was a watershed moment in the attempt to force governments to listen to those they are supposed to represent.

Undeterred by their governments' attempts to justify the "war against terror", in Britain and elsewhere, people have expressed opposition to the occupation of Iraq on a scale never seen before in history. Mass demonstrations are an attempt to have a political voice denied by the traditional institutions of parliamentary democracy. And they confounded the cynics who believe that people will only ever go on the streets in defence of direct self-interest. The demonstrations proved that people are prepared to act if they see a possibility of their actions making a real difference – in other words, to stop governments. It was no accident that numbers dwindled dramatically after British and American forces marched in, and it seemed impossible to alter this course of events.

What is not so plain is that ordinary people *do* have the power to change these circumstances. At present those in charge have the power and we have very little or none at all. If two million could not change Blair's mind, then sheer pressure of numbers on the street poses the question: how can people determine the course of history in accordance with their aspirations?

Within that question lies the problem itself. Is it actually a question of *changing the minds* of those in power as those who engage in protests of various kinds believe? Can the existing political structures be modified and moulded to fit the needs and will of the majority? Or do we have to get to grips with deeper problems? What is it that makes us think we cannot change things and achieve democratic control over the planet's resources and the way they are used? In what ways are people prevented from having control over their lives? What is it that separates people from power? These are the questions revolutionary organisations must answer in a concrete way if they are to win the support of the majority to take and remould state power.

Within globalised capitalism itself changes have gone on which can facilitate the transfer of power. Production has had to adopt an increasingly socialised form, drawing in workers in different countries organised to work co-operatively. All the key decisions are taken by salaried employees. Millions have therefore experienced potential power in their workplace – except that it remains out of reach while the reality remains private control of their labour. Nevertheless, we can glimpse a future organised rationally and quite differently from today's world of ruthless competition and work until you drop. The revolution in technology has also opened up dramatic possibilities for addressing human needs and solving problems. This technology is equally the product of human labour. A revolution in communications means that states and governments cannot lie their way through life without being found out very quickly. We can also keep in touch and organise mass movements in new ways, using mobile phones, e-mail and messaging which the state finds increasingly difficult to control.

Finally, globalisation has resulted in a broadening out of the working class to include the vast majority in society. Despite de-industrialisation, there are more than 26 million people who work for an employer in Britain, while another 3.8 million are self-employed. The once privileged middle class is largely a thing of the past because no job is safe in the global market economy and exploitation is intense. A MORI poll in 2002 revealed that two-thirds of British adults considered themselves to be working class.

On the other side economic power is concentrated into fewer and fewer hands. We indeed are many and they are few. This new working class is the only revolutionary force in society capable of transforming society in a progressive way because in its very being it is in direct opposition to corporate wealth and power.

The working class's future interests lie in realising its potential power by converting the forces of production into socially-owned and controlled resources for common use.

History shows that in extraordinary times people are capable of being altruistic, if they see the coming together of their own interests with those of others and can act as a class and a unified social force. People do this when they are able to, when the social environment allows them to and when there is a perspective for success. Indeed, inspired by the idea of collective endeavour, people can act in ways that defy all predictions and stereotypes. The history of Britain reveals the power of class and community traditions, defiance and contempt for the state. These continue in less dramatic ways in the everyday sacrifices of people, including those who care for the vulnerable and those who frequently put their lives on the line such as firefighters.

No one is suggesting that struggling for power is not a complex task. It requires theoretical and practical preparation and uncompromising leadership that has its sights firmly on the main prize. History is full of examples of revolutionary change, from Britain in the 17th century, France and America in the 18th century, Russia and China in the first part of the 20th century, the revolutions for colonial liberation and more recently the largely peaceful overthrow of Stalinist dictatorships.

A mass transfer of power is not the same as a coup carried out by a tiny minority within the state. Challenged by a mass upheaval with a determined leadership, the control exercised by the ruling class will weaken and fracture. Mass movements in themselves do not lead to violence, as the anti-war protests of 2003 showed. If the ruling élite is overwhelmed it will be unable to strike back.

The conditions for revolutionary change are emerging day by day as the contradictions of life under global capitalism pile up and reach breaking point. In Britain, the history of past struggles and sacrifices, achievements, victories and defeats, are with us. We can and will walk in the footsteps of the Peasants Revolt, the struggle of the Levellers during the English Revolution, the Chartists who fought for the vote and built a national convention outside parliament. The 1880s saw the formation of mass trade unions, followed by the sacrifices of the Suffragettes to achieve votes for women. The building of the Labour Party, the General Strike of 1926, the sacrifice of ordinary people in two imperialist world wars, the building of the welfare state, the bitter struggles against Thatcherism and de-industrialisation, and now against the market state and its foreign wars for global corporate interests all go to make up an inspiring history which will serve us well as we set out to overturn the old order.

A revolutionary change is obviously fraught with difficulties, dangers and uncertainties. But we already live in uncertain times, where state violence is used to impose so-called free market economies as in Iraq. The one guarantee is that leaving things as they are will spell disaster for the planet. You have the opportunity to make a difference, to contribute to a new chapter in human history. You should take it and make it. In 1848, in their stirring *Communist Manifesto,* Karl Marx and Frederick Engels penned two famous sentences that still have real significance for today: *"The proletarians have nothing to lose but their chains. They have a world to win."*

Let's make it happen

Now that you have read the book, the challenge is to put the ideas into practice. You have the opportunity to take part in shaping the future in these ways:

▶ **Come to *A World to Win* events.** We are organising local discussions and debates as well as a conference. These aim at taking forward the proposals set out in the book. For details go to www.aworldtowin.net or write to *A World to Win*, PO Box 942 London SW1V 2AR
▶ **Contribute to the discussion.** Send your comments, ideas and alternatives to us and we will publish them on our bulletin board to keep the debate going
▶ **Spread the word.** Set up discussions about the book with your friends and work colleagues, at your trade union branch, book club or with your fellow students at school or university. Let us know and we'll send a speaker
▶ **Promote the book.** Help push sales of *A World to Win* by getting it into public libraries, on to school and university reading lists. Let your friends know about it and publicise the book on e-lists. You could always write a short review for a website or magazine.
▶ **Tell us about events.** If you know about any events, demonstrations or festivals to sell the book at, let us know.

www.aworldtowin.net
info@aworldtowin.net
PO Box 942 London SW1V 2AR

Visit the Movement for a Socialist Future website @

www.socialistfuture.org.uk

A forum for debate plus a wide-ranging resource and archive for alternative politics, campaigns, art and culture, economics, philosophy and ideas. Feedback, articles, photographs and images for publication are welcome. You can find news, articles and images about the Movement for a Socialist Future, our manifesto, FAQs, how to join, publications, links and back issues of *Socialist Future Review*. The 21st Century Art section has reviews, listings, articles and a contemporary art gallery with featured artists.

Also by Corinna Lotz and Paul Feldman

Gerry Healy:
A revolutionary life

"At a time when political memories are growing increasingly short, it is good that the effort has been made to record the life of Gerry Healy, a revolutionary Marxist who had a massive impact on the working class socialist movement, in Britain and internationally."
Ken Livingstone

This 380-page book is divided into two parts, which cover the whole of Gerry Healy's life. The first part is a personal account of the last four and a half years of his life. Part two outlines Healy's work in the revolutionary movement from his arrival in England in 1928 up until 1985. There is also a fold-out section with the projection of the path of cognition, developed by Healy as a teaching aid.

ISBN: 0 9523454 0 4
Lupus Books £13.50

References

Foreword

Homelessness and poverty in America. National Law Centre on Homelessness and Poverty www.nlchp.org

Internment lesson plan is under attack. Thomas Alex Tizon, *Los Angeles Times* 12 September 2004 http://pqasb.pqarchiver.com/latimes

A Theory of Global Capitalism: Production, Class, and State in a Transnational World. William Robinson, The Johns Hopkins University Press 2004

Time to consider Iraq withdrawal. *Financial Times* Editorial Comment 10 September 2004 www.commondreams.org/views04/0911-26.htm

The Sorrows of Empire: Militarism, secrecy and the end of the Republic. Chalmers Johnson, New York, Henry Holt 2003

Preventative war: a failed doctrine. *The New York Times* 12 September 2004 www.truthout.org/docs_04/091304Y.shtml

Tide? Or Ivory Snow? Arundhati Roy, Public Power in the Age of Empire 2004 www.democracynow.org/static/Arundhati_Trans.shtml

Chapter 1   Alien nation

One World Ready or Not. William Greider, Penguin 1997

Alien Nation www.scifi.com/aliennation

Grundrisse: Foundations of the Critique of Political Economy. Karl Marx, Penguin Books 1973

Health and Safety Executive www.hse.gov.uk/stress/index.htm

British Social Attitudes 20th report. National Centre for Social Research, Sage Publications 2003

Changing Britain, Changing Lives. Ferri, Bynner and Wadsworth, IoE 2003

Disability claims, Department of Work and Pensions www.dwp.gov.uk

Social Trends 34. Office for National Statistics 2004 www.ons.gov.uk

Bully OnLine www.bullyonline.org/stress/suicide.htm

British Crime Survey of 2002/3. Home Office www.homeoffice.gov.uk

The environment: where's the risk, and where are children safe? World Health
  Organisation, June 2004. www.who.int

Left Out, Left Behind. Policy Exchange 2003 www.policyexchange.org.uk

Hidden Harm. Home Office 2003. www.homeoffice.gov.uk

The Money Programme. BBC 25 February 2004. www.news.bbc.co.uk

Stress is the No.1 pain. Evening Standard, 14 August 2003

Impact of restructuring, job insecurity and job satisfaction in hospital nurses.
  Esther R. Greenglass1, Ronald J. Burke and Lisa Fiksenbaum

Stress News January 2002 Vol.14 No.1

British Medical Journal. February 23 2004 www.bmj.bmjjournals.com

Hazards report March 2004 www.hazards.org/privacy

Occupation and Environmental Medicine Journal, Vol 61, pp 254-261, 2004

Equal Opportunities Commission report quoted in TUC Report, *Women and
  pensions*. www.tuc.org.uk/pensions/tuc-7755-f0.cfm

New guideline to standardise care for people who self-harm. National Institute
  for Clinical Excellence 2004 www.nice.org.uk

In too deep – CAB clients' experience of debt. National Association of Citizens
  Advice Bureaux 2003 www.nacab.org.uk

Alliance for a Caring Economy www.future500.org

Danziger's Britain – A journey to the edge. Nick Danziger, Flamingo 1996

Homeland. Nick Ryan, Mainstream 2003

Chapter 2   The global corporate web

Communist Manifesto. Karl Marx and Frederick Engels, Oxford Paperbacks
  1998

Capital, Vol III. Karl Marx, Lawrence and Wishart 1962

Globalisation – Capitalism and its Alternatives. Leslie Sklair, Oxford University
  Press 2002

When Corporations Rule the World. David Korten, Berrett-Koehler 2001

The Transnational Capitalist Class. Leslie Sklair, Blackwell 2001

A fairer globalisation: creating opportunities for all. International Labour
  Organisation 2004 www.ilo.org

*Making the links: a peoples' guide to the World Trade Organisation and the Free
  Trade Area of the Americas*. Maude Barlow and Tony Clarke, The Council of

Canadians and the Polaris Institute www.polarisinstitute.org

Globalisation and the Nation-state. Article by Jan Annaert, Edward Elgar 2000

Global Transformations, David Held et al, Polity Press 1999

The Enigma of Globalisation. Robert Went, Routledge 2002

Trade and Development Reports 2002, 2003. United Nations Conference on Trade and Development

United Nations Conference on Trade & Development www.unctad.org

Eliminating world poverty: making globalisation work for the poor. Department for International Development 2000

Triennial central bank survey of foreign exchange and derivatives market activity. Bank for International Settlements 2003 www.bis.org

The scorecard on globalisation. The Centre for Economic Policy Research 2001 www.cepr.net

Oligopoly, Inc. Concentration in corporate power. Etc Group 2003 www.etcgroup.org

Share ownership in 2003. Office for National Statistics www.ons.org

Human Development Report 2003. United Nations Development Programme www.undp.org

World Development Report 2001-2, 2002-3. World Bank www.worldbank.org

Water grab. Polaris Institute 2003 www.polarisinstitute.org

Out of service. Special report on Gats. World Development Movement 2002 www.wdm.org.uk

Structural adjustment: the policy roots of economic crisis, poverty and inequality. The Structural Adjustment Participatory Review International Network (SAPRIN) 2004. www.saprin.org

Globalisation and education, Glenn Rikowski, a paper prepared for the House of Lords Select Committee on Economic Affairs Inquiry into the Global Economy, 22nd January 2002 www.attac.org.uk/attac/document/rikowski-globalisation-education.pdf?documentID=123

Alliance for a corporate free UN letter to Kofi Anan www.ibfan.org/english/pdfs/kananjan02.pdf

Greenwash + 10. The UN's global compact, corporate accountability and the Johannesburg "Earth Summit". Corporate Watch 2002 www.corpwatch.org

Trading away our rights: women working in global supply chains. Oxfam 2004 www.oxfam.org.uk

Imperialism – The highest stage of capitalism in *Selected Works* Vol 1, V.I.Lenin, Progress Publishers Moscow 1977

Chapter 3   From welfare state to market state

Open Society: Reforming Global Capitalism. George Soros, Public Affairs, 2000

The State. Vladimir Lenin, Progress Publishers Moscow 1973

The State and Revolution. Lenin, *Selected Works* Vol 2, Progress Publishers Moscow 1977

Contribution to the Critique of Political Economy, Karl Marx, Progress Publishers Moscow 1977

The Making of the English Working Class. E.P. Thompson, Penguin 1978

Radical and revolting. Revolutions Per Minute 2004

Labour and Politics, 1900-1906. Frank Bealey & Henry Pelling, Macmillan 1958

Parliamentary Socialism. Ralph Miliband, Merlin Press 1961

Governing as New Labour. edited by S. Ludlam and M. J. Smith , Palgrave Macmillan 2003

Submission to Treasury review on child poverty. TUC December 2003

The Age of Consent. George Monbiot, Flamingo 2003

The Shield of Achilles. Philip Bobbitt, Penguin 2002

Globalisation and the Nation-state. Philip Cerny, Edward Elgar 2000

The Last Prime Minister. Graham Allen MP, Imprint Academic 2003

The Future of the Capitalist State. Bob Jessop, Polity 2003

MediaLens www.medialens.org

Global Transformations. David Held, Polity 1999

The Handbook of Globalisation. Jonathan Michie (Editor), Edward Elgar 2003

Manufacturing now: delivering the manufacturing strategy. TUC, July 2004. www.tuc.org.uk

The state and the contradictions of the knowledge-driven economy. Bob Jessop, www.comp.lancs.ac.uk/sociology/papers/jessop-state-and-contradictions.pdf

British Social Attitudes: the 18th Report. National Centre for Social Research, Sage 2001

Parliament and Revolution. Ramsay MacDonald, A Lane 1972

What Does the Ruling Class do when it Rules? Goran Therborn, Verso 1978

The Point of Departure. Robin Cook, Simon & Schuster 2003

Chapter 4   All consuming culture

Global Transformations. David Held et al, Polity Press 1999

Reclaiming the Commons. David Bollier (www.bostonreview.net). Based on *Silent Theft: The Private Plunder of Our Common Wealth.* Routledge 2002

UN Human Development Report 2001 www.hdr.undp.org/reports/global

The Big Picture: Understanding Media through Political Economy. McChesney and Foster, Monthly Review Press 2003

The Problem of the Media, US Communication Politics in the 21st Century. Robert McChesney, Monthly Review Press 2004

www.itfacts.biz

Arts Under Pressure. Joost Smiers, Zed Books 2003

Inquiry into the British Film Industry. Select Parliamentary Committee on Culture, Media and Sport 2003

Summary of Communication Act. www.rogerdarlington.co.uk/CommsAct.html

Handbook of New Media, Social shaping and Consequences of ICTS. Lievrouw and Livingstone, Sage 2002

Hubs, nodes and bypassed places. Matthew A Zook, www.zooknic.com

Fewer moguls, bigger empires – Congress wrestles with media ownership. San Francisco Chronicle, 12 February 2004

Privatising Culture: Corporate art intervention since the 1980s. Chin-Tao Wu, Verso 2002

The McDonaldisation of Society. George Ritzer, Sage Publications (US) 2004

The 13th edition of the Deloitte annual review of football finance. www.deloitte.com

Chapter 5   Simply not natural

Marx's Ecology. John Bellamy Foster, Monthly Review Press 1999

Greenpeace UK www.greenpeace.org.uk

Paper Tiger, Hidden Dragons. Friends of the Earth 2001 www.foe.co.uk

GM Watch www.gmwatch.org

Biotech Century. Jeremy Rifkin, Phoenix 1999

Investing in the future: harnessing private capital flows for environmentally sustainable development. Worldwatch Institute 1998, www.worldwatch.org

State of the carbon market 2003. World Bank 2003

Climate change and human health – risks and responses. World Health Organisation, December 2003 www.who.org

Not on the Label. Felicity Lawrence, Penguin 2004

Terminator technology – five years later. ETC Group, www.etcgroup.org

Climate Change 2001: the Third Assessment Report. Intergovernmental Panel on Climate Change, www.ipc.ch

Journal of Climate, the American Meteorological Society. www.kiwi.atmos.colostate.edu/JofC/JofC.html

Climate change and Southern Africa 1996. Report by the Climatic Research
   Unit, University of East Anglia
   www.cru.uea.ac.uk/~mikeh/research/cc_safr.htm
*The management of obesity and overweight: An analysis of reviews of diet,
   physical activity and behavioural approaches.* Health Development Agency
   2003 www.HDA.nhs.uk
Genetically modified foods & health: a second interim statement. British
   Medical Association March 2004 www.bma.org.uk
*Genetically modified plants for food use and human health – an update. Royal
   Society* 2002 www.royalsoc.ac.uk/gmplants/
What's wrong with supermarkets? Corporate Watch 2004
   www.corporatewatch.org.uk

Chapter 6   Tying science to business

Investing in innovation – a strategy for science, engineering and technology.
   Office of Science and Technology 2002 www.ost.gov.uk/policy/invest-
   innov.htm
Delivering the commercialisation of public sector science. National Audit Office
   2002 www.nao.org.uk
Degrees of capture. Corporate Watch and the New Economics Foundation
   2004 www.corporatewatch.org
The Captive State. George Monbiot, Macmillan 2000
Corporations invent people to rubbish their opponents on the Internet. George
   Monbiot, Transnational Corporations Observatory May 2002
   www.transnationale.org
The Dialectical Biologist. Richard Lewontin and Richard Levins, Harvard
   University Press 1987
Scientists for Global Responsibility www.sgr.org.uk
Science, Agriculture and Research – a compromised participation? William
   Buhler, Earthscan 2002

Chapter 7   Transforming the economy

Capital, Vol I. Karl Marx, Penguin Books 1976
The Independent Review. 25 May 2004
Survey on China. Financial Times 22-26 September 2003
*Major Trends in East Asia: What are their implications for regional co-
   operation and growth?* World Bank Policy Research Working Paper 3084,
   June 2003 http://econ.world-bank.org

International Herald Tribune, 26 March 2004

Financial Times, 22-26 September 2003

A fair globalisation: creating opportunities for all. ILO report 2004
www.ilo.org

A rough guide to the UK farming crisis. Corporate Watch May 2004
www.corporatewatch.org.uk

Growth Fetish. Clive Hamilton, Pluto Press 2004

Leadership and the New Science, Discovering Order in a Chaotic World.
Margaret J Wheatley, Berrett-Koehler, 1999

The Success of Open Source. Steven Weber, Harvard University Press 2004

Scientific American, May 2004

Cosmic Evolution: The Rise of Complexity in Nature. Eric J. Chaisson,
Harvard University Press 2001

Shareholding in Britain 2003. National Statistics www.ons.gov.uk

International Institute for Sustainable Development
www.iisd.org/measure/compendium

Redefining progress indicators www.redefiningprogress.org

Chapter 8   Reconstructing the state

The State and Revolution. V.I. Lenin, Progress Publishers Moscow 1975

Just Law. Helena Kennedy, Chatto & Windus 2004

Insatiable appetite. American Civil Liberties Union, 2002 www.aclu.org

Plan of Attack – the road to war. Bob Woodwood, Simon & Schuster 2004

The Black Act. E. P. Thompson, Penguin 1977

The Empty Throne – Democracy and the rule of law in transition. Sophie van
Bijsterveld, Lemma 2002

George Soros on Globalisation. Public Affairs 2002

Globalisation: the dangers and the answers. David Held, OpenDemocracy 2004
www.opendemocracy.net

The Age of Consent, A manifesto for a new world order, George Monbiot,
Flamingo 2003 www.fireandwater.com

The annual crime figures for England and Wales. Home Office, July 2004
www.homeoffice.gov.uk

The Concept of Socialist Law. Christina Sypnowich, Clarendon 1990

Legal Action Group, www.lag.org.uk

The Origin of the Family, Private Property and the State. Frederick Engels,
www.marxists.org

Home Office Department Report 2004. www.homeoffice.gov.uk

An introduction to the DTI. www.dti.gov.uk

Critique of the Gotha Programme. Karl Marx, www.marxists.org

Briefing from the Prison Reform Trust 2004. www.prisonreformtrust.org.uk

Letter from Fredrick Engels to Conrad Schmidt in Berlin 1890.
www.marxists.org

Hungry and homeless. Refugee Council report on destitute asylum seekers.
April 2004 www.refugeecouncil.org.uk

*Destitution by design – withdrawal of support from in-country asylum
applicants.* Mayor of London, February 2004 www.london.gov.uk

*Forbidden Relations? The UK's discourse of human rights and the struggle for
social justice 2002.* Professor Bill Bowring's Inaugural lecture, 2002
www.londonmet.ac.uk/research-units/hrsj/lecture.cfm

Rethinking crime and punishment. www.rethinking.org.uk 2004

Decriminalising criminology. John Muncie, Papers from the British Society of
Criminology Conference, Liverpool, July 1999
www.britsoccrim.org/journal.htm

The self-policing society. Charles Leadbetter, Demos 1996 www.demos.co.uk

Education and the future

*Revolutionary Social Transformation: Democratic hopes, political possibilities
and critical education.* Paula Allman, Bergin & Garvey 1999

*Critical Education Against Global Capitalism: Karl Marx and Revolutionary
Critical Education.* Paula Allman, Bergin & Garvey 2001

*There is an alternative: in Business, Business, Business: New Labour's
Education Policy.* Caroline Benn and Clyde Chitty, Tufnell Press 1999

Pedagogy of Freedom. Paulo Freire, Rowman and Littlefield 1998

*What do people need to know, and how do they need to come to know it, in
order to be free?.* Rich Gibson 2003 www.pipeline.com/%7Ergibson/free.htm

*Can communities of resistance and transformation be born in the social process
of school?* Rich Gibson, *Teacher Education Quarterly*
www.rohan.sdsu.edu/%7Ergibson/CCTERG.htm

Tailism and the Dialectic, In defence of history and class consciousness. Georg
Lukacs, Verso 2000

Theses on Feuerbach. Karl Marx, (1845), Addendum in K. Marx & F. Engels,
The German Ideology, Progress Publishers Moscow 1968

*On General Education, Speech to the General Council meeting of the
International Workingmen's Association.* Karl Marx, (1869), Marx and
Engels Collected Works, Vol 21 Lawrence & Wishart

Che Guevara, Paulo Freire, and the Pedagogy of Revolution. Peter McLaren, Rowman & Littlefield 2000

The business takeover of schools. Glenn Rikowski, Mediactive: Ideas Knowledge Culture, Issue 1, 2003

Once Bitten, Twice Shy. Richard Shepherd, 1993 unpublished manuscript, Norwich, England

Chapter 9   Culture for all

Capitalism, Computers and the Class War on Your Desktop. Bob Hughes, November 2003 www.dustormagic.net

Who watches the watchmen: Internet content rating systems, and privatised censorship. Cyber-Rights & Cyber-Liberties (UK) November 1997 www.cyber-rights.org/watchmen.htm.

Google Watch. www.google-watch.org/bigbro.html

Consumer Culture and Modernity. Don Slater, Polity Press 1997

Entertainment & media global overview 2003-2007 www.pcwglobal.com

Arts under Pressure: Promoting cultural diversity in the age of globalisation. Joost Smiers, Zed books 2003

Free Culture. Laurence Lessig, Penguin Books 2004

The Big Chill. www.bigchill.net

John Harris www.johnharris.me.uk

Contest of meaning: critical histories of photography. Richard Bolton, MIT 1992

Towards a free revolutionary art. Signed in 1938 by André Breton, Diego Rivera in collaboration with Leon Trotsky, New Park Publications 1975

The Soul of Man under Socialism. Oscar Wilde, Oriole Chapbooks

Brand it like Beckham. Andy Milligan, Cyan 2004

Chapter 10   Action plan for the ecological crisis

The Enemy of Nature. Joel Kovel, Zed Books 2002

Economic and Philosophical Manuscripts of 1844. Karl Marx, Progress Publishers Moscow 1977

Marx's Ecology: Materialism and nature. John Bellamy-Foster, Monthly Review Press 2000

Grundrisse, Foundations of the critique of political economy. Karl Marx, Penguin Classics 1993

WRI warns of worsening warming. World Resources Institute, March 2004 www.wri.org

Extinction risk from climate change. Nature, 8 January 2004
    www.nature.com/nature

State of the World 2002. Worldwatch Institute www.worldwatch.org

Oligopoly, Inc. Concentration in corporate power. ETC group 2003
    www.etcgroup.org

Get real about food and farming. Friends of the Earth, 2001 www.foe.co.uk

An assessment of the total external costs of UK agriculture. J.N. Pretty et al.
    Agriculture Systems 65 2000

Study on food additives and the behaviour of young children. University of
    Southampton May 2004 www.soton.ac.uk

Select Committee on health, 3rd report, May 2004
    www.parliament.uk/parliamentary_committees/health_committee.cfm

*Contamination of refuges by Bacillus thuringiensis toxin genes from transgenic
    maize*. Proceedings of the National Academy of Sciences, May 10, 2004
    www.pnas.org

The politics of science. Richard Lewontin, *New York Review of Books* May
    2002

Green alternatives to globalisation. Michael Woodin and Caroline Lucas, Pluto
    Press 2004

The Green Party, www.greenparty.org.uk

Greenpeace UK, www.greenpeace.org.uk

Defining our path: sustainability report 2003. BP April 2004 www.bp.com

Girona Declaration, March 2002 www.corporateeurope.org/un/gironadecl.html

World Business Council for Sustainable Development www.wbcsd.ch

Nuclear power is the only green solution. James Lovelock, *The Independent*, 24
    May 2004

Chapter 11   It's in our nature

"The bourgeois relations of production are the last antagonistic form of the
    social process of production – antagonistic not in the sense of individual
    antagonisms, but of one arising from the social conditions of life of the
    individuals; at the same time the productive forces developing in the womb
    of bourgeois society create the material conditions for the solution of that
    antagonism. This social formation brings, therefore, the prehistory of society
    to a close." Preface of *A Contribution to the Critique of Political Economy*.
    Karl Marx, www.marxists.org

The End of History and the Last Man. Francis Fukuyama, Penguin 1992

Our Posthuman Future. Francis Fukuyama, Profile Books London 2002

"The essence of human nature in general can be revealed only through a quite concrete study of the 'ensemble of social relations', through a concrete analysis of those laws which govern the birth and development of human society as a whole and of each human individual." *The Abstract and Concrete in Marx's Capital*. E.V. Ilyenkov, Progress Publishers Moscow 1982

Straw Dogs – Thoughts on Humans and Other Animals. John Gray, Granta Books 2002

The making and meaning of humanisation. Paula Allman. A paper presented at the Marxism and education: renewing dialogues seminar, October 2002, Institute of Education, University of London

The Private Life of the Brain. Susan Greenfield, Penguin 2000

Genetic Engineering, Dream or Nightmare. Mae-Wan Ho, Gateway 1998 See also: *Human Nature and History, A Response to Sociobiology*. Kenneth Block, Columbia University Press NY 1980

The Dialectical Biologist. Levin and Lewontin, Harvard University Press 1985

The Emerging Mind. Vilaynur S. Ramachandran, BBC Reith Lecture 2003 www.bbc.co.uk

Chapter 12   Challenging the ideas of the status quo

Dialectic: The pulse of freedom. Roy Bhaskar, Verso 1993

The Third Way: The Renewal of Social Democracy. Anthony Giddens, Polity Press 1998

Caught in The Matrix. David Miller, Scoop April 2004 www.scoop.co.nz/mason

Ludwig Feuerbach and the End of Classical German Philosophy. Frederick Engels, 1886 www.marxists.org

Philosophical Notebooks. Vladimir Lenin, *Collected Works* Vol 38, Lawrence & Wishart 1976

Materialist Dialectics and the Political Revolution. Gerry Healy, Marxist Publishing Cooperative 1990

Science of Logic. George Hegel, Routledge 2002

The Dialectical Biologist. Richard Lewontin and Richard Levins, Harvard University Press 1987

The significance of postmodernism

Spectres of Marx. Jacques Derrida, Routledge 1994

The Condition of Post-Modernity. David Harvey, Blackwell 1989

Post-Modernism, Or the Cultural Logic of Late Capitalism. Frederick Jameson, Verso 1991

German Philosophy 1760-1860. Terry Pinkard, Cambridge University Press 2002

Modernity as a Philosophical Problem. Robert B Pippin, Blackwell 1991

Hegel and the Phenomenology of the Spirit. Robert Stern, Routledge 2002

Uncritical Theory: Postmodernism, Intellectuals and the Gulf War. Christopher Norris, Lawrence and Wishart 1992

Chapter 13   The case for a revolutionary party

What is to be Done? V.I. Lenin, *Selected Works* Vol 1, Progress Moscow 1977

Terms of Engagement, Richard H. Axelrod, Berrett-Koehler Publishers Inc 2000

Leading Change, John P. Kotter, Harvard Business School Press 1996

The real origins of Stalinism

Revolution Betrayed: what is the Soviet Union and where is it going? Leon Trotsky, New Park Publications 1973

Index